PROFILES OF BLACK GEORGIA BAPTISTS

Two hundred and six years of Black Georgia
Baptist History, one hundred years of National
Baptist History as told by:

Clarence M. Wagner

Privately Published
P.O. Box 2283
Gainesville, Georgia 30501

Bennett Brothers Printing Company
2930 Flowers Road, South
Atlanta, Georgia 30341

i

DEDICATED TO MY MOTHER

Mrs. Dovie Whiteside Peavy

October 15, 1900 - October 15, 1972

PREFACE

This book comes out of a need for the traverse of Black Baptists in America to be heralded, their bestowments displayed and their history recapitulated, for present and future registers.

It is further wrought out of the necessity for a consolidated, concise reference of activities of the General Missionary Baptist Convention of Georgia, Inc., churches, associations and personalities; the National Baptist Convention, U.S.A., Inc., affiliated Conventions, Associations, Churches, philosophy and personalities.

Many documents, pictures and oral statements make up this volume. It is intended to produce graphic and enhancing reading.

Black Baptist lineage is traced from the first recorded fruit bearing convert, who entered the ministry. To one of his converts with a quest for the same Spiritual zeal, who founded, pastored and built the First Black Baptist Church, to its soaring growth into Conventions and Missions, worldwide. The three National Conventions population alone exceeds twelve million.

To conquer the unknown beyond, we must know from where we have trod and those who preceded us. This book will acquaint us with the patriarchs of our denomination and destinies they sought.

ACKNOWLEDGEMENTS

A work of this nature can be done only with the help and cooperation of a lot of people.

My deep appreciation for their contributions are hereby expressed. To my wife, Mrs. Bettye J. Wagner, our two children, Clarence and Dionne, for their unselfish understanding to allow me the time. Our church family, First Baptist Church of Gainesville, Georgia, for their patience and encouragement. The larger Baptist family of the General Missionary Baptist Convention of Georgia and President Cameron M. Alexander for expressing the need for such a writing.

The many others for their direct contributions. Mrs. Deborah Mack, for typing the manuscript. Mrs. C.M. Pearson and Rev. H.M. Alexander for their oral history. Rev. Clyde Hill, Rev. J.S. Wright, Rev. Calhoun Sims, Rev. John Parkman, Rev. O.B. Yates, Mrs. Mildred Benton, Mrs. Black, Rev. R.L. Freeman, Mr. Andrew J. Lewis, II, all of whom helped in a significant way in providing portions of the historic documents.

Table of Contents

Chapter 1
BUILDING ONTO THE LEGACY

Black Baptist lineage can be traced to a Virginia born slave, named George Liele, exposed to the Gospel exhortations of Matthew Moore, a rural Baptist preacher in 1774, in Burke County, Georgia. George professed belief in Jesus Christ, was baptized, and accepted the call to preach the Christian Gospel.

This pioneer Black Baptist Preacher sowed the seeds of his witness well. Good seed was sown into generative soils, and bounteous harvests reaped.

Two hundred and six years later, in America there are three Black Baptist Conventions of national scope and one covering a region. They are the National Baptist Convention, U.S.A., Inc., 6.6 million members, organized in 1880; Lott Carey Convention heavily concentrated in Virginia and North Carolina, an approximate membership of five hundred thousand, organized in 1899; National Baptist Convention of America, Inc., 3.3 million members, organized in 1915; and Progressive National Baptist Convention, Inc., approximately 1.2 million members, organized in 1961.

Roughly 11.6 million blacks in America today are Baptist. Many are spiritual descendants of that one slave converted in 1774.

The only one of the national groups to have churches, associations, state or regional conventions, covering all the fifty states, Bahama Islands and Africa, is the National Baptist Convention, U.S.A., Inc., the mother body. Dr. Joseph Harrison Jackson, Pastor of the Olivet Institutional Baptist Church, Chicago, Illinois, has been the Venerable leader since September 1953. Serving as eminent secretary from the same date has been Dr. Theodore Judson Jemison, from a patriotic convention family.

These four bodies have been deprived of their justifiable recognition in the mainstream of our nation's ecclesiastical visibility. So much has been done by all of them from the grass-roots of the local churches locations to the national arena toward molding the fibers of this land, not only for people of color, but all backgrounds and colors. Their total contribution has been unselfish, colorless, unbiased and ecumenical. So many achievements have gone unheralded, unrecognized and probably unappreciated. Their purpose was not for praise, but out of commitment, responsibility and the existing needs. Gratitude expressed for toil, is stimulating for the doer, regardless of the motive.

The National Baptist Convention, U.S.A., Inc. is the largest and most powerful Black organization in the world, economically, resourcefully and numerically. During the height of the civil rights struggle in the early sixties, Dr. Jackson advised its constituents not to rely solely upon marching, picketing, chanting and protest. But admonished, to go, "from Protest to Production". This organization and many of its members accepted that challenge and helped to break the back of segregation, knock the walls down, and open doors by utilizing their talents and abilities as producers.

1

Many persons, organizations, black and white, local, national and international have coined that phrase. Both the oratory and philosophy of, "from Protest to Production" have been adopted, without any recognition given to the original literary rhetorician who conceived the idea.

Twice a year for most, but at least once for all, her delegates converge upon the major cities of the nation by the thousands. All modes of travel are employed, air, auto, rail, bus, and possibly pedestrian. No less than three days are spent in hotels, from the most luxurious, to the most economical. Expensive and inexpensive cuisine is consumed. Those delegates from the length and breadth of this nation are not beggars or paupers, but Redeemed Celebrants. Their purpose is not to destroy, but to fulfill, uphold and uplift the name of their Crucified and Risen Savior.

Through the genius of President Jackson, the National Baptist Convention, U.S.A., Inc. is being accorded all gratuities and benefits by the cities as any other large convening group. This did not come voluntarily on the part of the cities. But by negotiating on the part of this administrator. State Conventions which carry similar clout on their level have followed this example and are doing likewise, especially the state of Georgia.

Integration has many appreciable assets, but accompanying it, there have been many threatening horrors. Among which have been financial dilemas experienced by the National Association for the Advancement of Colored People and exclusive Black educational institutions. Much financial support was given to the fledgling N.A.A.C.P. in the midnight of its financial distress by the National Baptist Convention, U.S.A., Inc. and its related churches, associations, conventions and members.

Meharry Medical College, Nashville, Tennessee received forty thousand dollars; Morehouse School of Religion, Atlanta, Georgia, five thousand dollars. Florida Memorial College, Miami, Florida; Selma University, Selma, Alabama; Arkansas Baptist College, Little Rock, Arkansas; all have been financially stimulated. Most recently, financially disabled Bishop College of Dallas, Texas, a Baptist School that for more than a century has been the training ground for many of this nation's leading pulpiteers and other prepared people, was given one hundred and fifty thousand dollars in January 1980, to be appropriated over three years at fifty thousand dollars per annum.

These are but a few of many feats that have been done by Joseph Harrison Jackson, President of the National Baptist Convention, U.S.A., Inc., who picked up the mantle of this organization twenty-seven years ago and continued in the same vain of his accomplished predecessors.

All of whom engaged in building onto the legacy passed to them by our Black Baptist Father, George Liele; of which was anchored by the first successful Black Baptist Pastor, Andrew Bryan; concretized by the first Black Baptist warrior and pastoral pacesetter, Andrew Marshall; extended by his many accomplished successors.

GEORGE LIELE
FATHER OF BLACK BAPTIST IN AMERICA, JAMAICA AND AFRICA

Roger Williams is believed to have organized the first Baptist Church in America in Providence, Rhode Island, with eleven other persons sometime prior to March, 1639. Like all other new movements, much suffering and persecution occurred. Its opposition, cultivated, fertilized and watered the soils for this denomination's widespread growth.

Baptist churches began dotting the upper and middle colonies of Massachusetts, Pennsylvania, and Delaware before the end of the Seventeenth Century. By the first of the Eighteenth Century, began moving into the upper southern colonies, Virginia and North Carolina. Toward the last quarter of the century, churches were organized in South Carolina and the eastern border of Georgia.

George Liele (or Lisle) was born around 1750 in Virginia. His master, Mr. Henry Sharp moved to Burke County, Georgia a few

years before the Revolutionary War. Under the preaching of Rev. Matthew Moore, Pastor of a Baptist Church in the proximity of his master's plantation, George was converted, and felt called of God to preach the Gospel of Jesus Christ.

Through the kindness of his master, a deacon of a Baptist church, Liele was emancipated, in order that his unusual ministerial gifts might be used freely. He traveled up and down the Savannah River, preaching to the slaves wherever friendly plantation owners would permit on both sides of the river, Georgia and South Carolina.

There was a church in South Carolina across the river from Augusta, known as Silver Bluff Church, whose black membership now exceeded the white. George Liele frequently visited this congregation and preached. Mr. Jonathan Bryan, Esq., owner of the Brampton Plantation near Savannah, encouraged his visits to preach to his slaves. The white church in Burke County of which he was a member, utilized his services as well, along with other white churches. Most of the white churches had black members, in many cases the black membership was larger than the white.

The unrest and uncertainty of the Revolutionary War brought intimidation and suffering for all the citizens, but for the Black Christian pioneers theirs was pressed down and running over. Liele and many of his Christian compatriots were unable to travel as freely during that time and concentrated in Savannah. Although there is no record of a church being established by them per se; their missionary and evangelistic efforts seemed to have

3

been very fruitful during this period.

From 1779 to 1782 the British occupied Savannah. It seems as though Liele expressed sympathy toward them. Mr. Sharp died during this time and his heirs attempted to re-enslave him for this or because of their love for gold. Liele borrowed seven hundred dollars to prevent himself, wife and four children from being placed back into slavery. His church activities became very limited in America from then on.

Colonel Kirkland, a British officer, was leaving Savannah for Jamaica in 1783. George Liele became his indentured servant and sailed with him. While waiting in the Savannah harbor in July 1783 for the weather to clear up so they could sail, George Liele returned to Savannah up the river and preached somewhere around the Yamacraw section, a heavily populated black area. Four people were converted to Christ and baptized by him, Andrew Bryan, his wife Hannah, Kate Hogg and Hagar Simpson, all slaves. Thus ending his Christian Ministry in America.

Arriving in Kingston, Jamaica, Colonel Kirkland requested him to be employed by the Governor of Jamaica, General Campbell. Working hard and saving his money in 1784 received his manumission. This freedom allowed him to begin his ministerial work there. With four other black men, who had migrated there, he founded the first black Baptist church on the island. George Liele was a powerful preacher. His church grew rapidly and soon much opposition came from the Established Church of England. Frequently their services were interrupted with cruel persecution, being invoked upon him. He and other companions were once imprisoned and charged with preaching "sedition", a capital offense under their law. All were tried for their lives, one was hanged and George Liele barely escaped. Other great sufferings followed, but he was allowed to continue his work.

This congregation grew to a membership of around five hundred and began spreading to other areas of the city and into the rural, with deacons and elders assistance. He was also engaged in raising money to erect a church edifice. Steven A. Cook, who was a member of the Jamaica Assembly secured money in England for the church and other influential people helped in the fund raising.

In 1842, fifty or more missionaries were sent by Liele from Jamaica to work in Africa. Making him the first Black preacher of record to become engaged in missionary work.

George Liele, a black slave, is the first recorded licensed and ordained Black Baptist Preacher-Missionary in America. The initiator of foreign missions among Black Baptist in the world.

Our Black Baptist heritage stems from the seeds planted by him in the soils of difficulty in America, Jamaica and Africa. Those seeds were incubated by the love of Jesus Christ, germinated by the power of the Holy Spirit and protected by the infallibility of God's Holy Word.

"The sower went out to sow his seed; and as he sowed, some fell beside the road; and it was trampled under foot, and the birds of the

4

air ate it up. And other seed fell on rocky soil, and as it grew up, it withered away, because it had no moisture. And other seed fell among the thorns; and the thorns grew up with it, and choked it out. And other seed fell into good soil, and grew up, and produced a crop a hundred times as great". Luke 8:5-8a.

His heirs of the following pages and others unmentioned and unaccounted for, have been no less faithless or faithful, their hands likewise have been on the plow.

Bibliography: **Lifted From The Minutes,** W.W. Weatherspool, 1979; **The First Colored Baptist Church in North American,** J.M. Sims, 1888.

Chapter 2
ANDREW BRYAN
FIRST PASTOR-BUILDER-DEVELOPER OF
THE FIRST COLORED BAPTIST CHURCH
SAVANNAH, GEORGIA
JANUARY 20, 1788

Andrew was born on a plantation near Goose Creek, South Carolina about twenty miles from Charleston, sometime around 1716. It is thought, from his features, he was of unmixed African decent. He wore a smooth, smiling face, brilliant eyes, pearly white teeth. Medium height and build, upon a determinately erect body. His characteristics were of African aristocracy, a most eloquent and deliberate speaker.

As mentioned in the previous chapter, he was converted to Christ under the preaching of George Liele in July 1783, and baptized by him prior to his departure to Jamaica.

Approximately two years later, in 1785, he was called to preach.

He like Andrew the disciple for whom, possible he was named, "first found his brother", Sampson and led him to Christian belief. Others were persuaded to follow Christ, by him.

After baptizing forty-five converts in one day in the Savannah River about three miles southwest of Savannah on the Brampton Plantation, he was joined by Abraham Marshall (white), Pastor of Kiokee Baptist Church of Columbia County, Georgia, Moderator of the Georgia Baptist Association, and Jessie Peters Golphin (Black), a member of the Silver Bluff Baptist Church, South Carolina, on January 20, 1788. They organized these newly baptized believers into a Baptist Church. Ordained Bryan into the Gospel Ministry making him pastor of this church, with full authority to administer the ordinances of the church.

Sampson Bryan, Andrew's brother, became his first deacon. Pastor, deacon and members were all slaves and would be permitted on Sundays to attend church. This church grew rapidly provoking envy from the other churches (white) of other denominations of the community.

Pastor Bryan, Deacon Andrew Bryan and about fifty members were beaten, thrown in jail with blood streaming from their backs, and their meeting house confiscated around 1789 or 1790. Mr. Jonathan Bryan, Andrew's master, interceded for these who were being persecuted like their first century predecessors. This excruciation was prompted out of wickedness and prejudice.

They were examined by the Justices of the Inferior Court of Chatham County, Georgia, Henry Osborne, James Habersham and David Montaque, who found them innocent and released them.

For some time, their meeting was held on Mr. Jonathan Bryan's, Brampton Plantation, in the barn. Their scathers were displeased with this and continued following them. They were known to eavesdrop around Andrew Bryan's home. One day as he prayed, one of the merciless beaters was listening to him outside his home and heard him praying for him. This loving and forgiving Spirit, penetrated his calloused heart to such a degree, he was unwilling to remain silent, and told it abroad. An unusual amount of sympathy and support was enlisted for Andrew Bryan and his followers. They were then granted permission by Chief Justice Henry Osborne to continue their worship anytime between sunrise and sunset.

June 1, 1790 is the purchase date of the first property bought by Andrew Bryan, Lot No. 12, North Oglethorpe Ward. "This lot was conveyed in 1789 by Jacob C. Waldhaver to Thomas Gibbons, on June 1, 1790 to "Free Andrew", - H 168,170." A rough wooden building was erected here. Andrew earned his freedom either that year or the year before. The remainder of his life was devoted to full time Christian Ministry.

Lot No. 7, Middle of Oglethorpe Ward, land description, ninety-five feet front, one hundred and thirty-two feet deep, was purchased September 4, 1793, from Matthew and Catherine Mott for one hundred and fifty dollars, by Andrew Bryan. The present structure stands on this parcel, the longest known continuously owned property by Blacks in America.

A family residence, forty-two by forty-nine, for Pastor Bryan was erected on the east end of the lot in 1794. The church or "meeting house" as called by members, was completed in 1795. It was necessary for the majority of the membership to secure permission from their owners to attend services. They were granted certificates to present to the patrols.

Andrew Bryan is reported to have been a strict doctrinarian, requiring proof of marriage before baptism.

The church joined the Georgia Baptist Association in 1790, with Abraham Marshall, Moderator. In 1795, Marshall was dismissed from his position. The Colored Baptist Church, as it was known then, withdrew along with twenty-two others, and formed another association. The church membership was reported to be three hundred and eighty-one at that time.

In 1789, Bryan was preaching in Newington, Effingham County, Georgia about eighteen miles from Savannah. Major Pollhill (white) and his wife were converted and baptized by Rev. Alexander Scott. From these converts, a White Baptist Church was organized, becoming the oldest White Baptist Church in Southeast Georgia.

Sampson Bryan died January 23, 1799, at fifty-three years of age. This is the first recorded death of a Black Baptist deacon.

Dr. Henry Tucker organized the Savannah Baptist Church, in

1800 with twelve members, nine women and three men. He organized the Second Colored Baptist Church of Savannah in 1802, with Henry Cunningham (Black) becoming the pastor. In the same year these three pastors, Bryan, Tucker and Cunningham organized the Savannah River Baptist Association. Bryan's church was now known as the First Colored Baptist Church and had a membership of four hundred and seventy-six. In 1803, Ogeechee Colored Baptist was organized.

When eighty years old, he looked very distinguished, was said to have dressed like a London Bishop and rode in a luxurious horse drawn chariot. Wisdom exuded from his lips through conversation.

His nephew, who was named for him, Andrew Marshall, was called to preach, licensed and ordained by Pastor Cunningham of the Second Colored Baptist Church. After closely observing his spiritual growth and ministerial development, during his waning years began to use him to assist him. During this time, he frequently mentioned to the church his desire for Marshall to succeed him at death.

On October 6, 1812, at around ninety-six years of age, Andrew Bryan died. His death and funeral united black and white. Never before in the state's history had a black man's death had such an impact upon a city, neighboring community and plantations. They turned out to honor the earthly departure of this stalwart servant of God.

Reverend Henry Kollock, D.D., Pastor of the Independent Presbyterian Church and Rev. Johnson, Pastor of Savannah Baptist Church, preached the sermons from Andrew Bryan's pulpit that celebrated his Home going. More than five thousand people were in attendance. Many of them followed the body to the grave where other addresses were made, by Thomas Williams, Esq. and Rev. Henry Cunningham, who also committed the mortal remains of Andrew Bryan to its final resting place.

Death brought an end to the physical life of one who fought such a courageous battle against such odds. His influence remained alive, it could not be stopped by death nor contained in the grave. Time has not erased his indelible memory, nor the rains washed it into the sea of forgetfulness, neither the winds blown it into oblivion. The sun has refused to fade its impression. So long as one of color is baptized, Andrew Bryan will live. So long as the full Gospel of Jesus Christ is preached in the Black tradition, Andrew Bryan will live. So long as the mind's eye of imagination is employed, Andrew Bryan will live. So long as Black Baptist Churches are organized, built and pastored, Andrew Bryan must live. He was not our Savior, but is our Patriarch.

He was survived by his wife and daughter, whose freedom he had also purchased, the amount is unknown. His estate at death was valued at more than three thousand dollars, a tremendous amount for that day.

God called him, as he had called Abraham, centuries before, "Now the Lord said to Abraham, Go forth from your country, and from your relatives and from your brother's house, To the land which I will show you; And I will make you a great nation, and I will bless you, and the one who curses you I will curse. And in you all the families of the earth will be blessed". Genesis 12:1-3.

FIRST COLORED BAPTIST CHURCH
SAVANNAH, GEORGIA
1812 - 1832

Never having been leaderless before, the church was at a loss. For some reason Andrew Marshall had disqualified himself, maybe because of his flourishing drayage business. Rev. Evans Grate, a former deacon of the church, had been dismissed in 1802 and was part of the organization of Second Colored Baptist Church, had been called to preach, licensed and ordained by his church. He also was a helper of Pastor Bryan during his declining years and supplied the church as pastor for more than two years.

Early in 1815, a Sunday was set aside for prayer for God to direct them in their choice of a shepherd. They prayed from their dawn service to noon, at which time proceeded with the business at hand. The were torn between two positions, Grate had been faithful, but they remembered Bryan's choice was Marshall. Finally they voted, with Andrew Marshall receiving the largest number of votes. Evans Grate being a good Christian was unaffected. He, the church and Marshall remained good friends.

Churches of South Carolina decided to withdraw from the association in 1818 to form an association with the churches of their state. The Georgia churches met November 7, 1818 in the Sunbury community, in Liberty County, Georgia at the Sunbury Baptist Church, pastored by Rev. Charles O. Screnon (white). Representatives from the following churches were present: First Colored Baptist Church, Savannah Baptist Church (white), Second Colored Baptist Church, Great Ogeechee Baptist Church (black membership), and Sunbury Baptist Church (mixed membership). First Colored Baptist had a membership of one thousand, seven hundred and twelve at that time, when in 1810, the total black church membership in Savannah among three churches was one thousand and five hundred. Second Colored membership was five hundred and thirty-eight, with Ogeechee's being four hundred and sixty.

Marshall's crisis of 1819-1820 (see chapter three), and its pleasing outcome possibly gave him a sensitivity for Andrew Bryan, Sampson Bryan and the other members misery of 1789. He led the church in bricking Bryan's grave with the following inscription in 1821:

"Sacred to the memory of Andrew Bryan, Pastor of the First Colored Baptist Church in Savannah. God was pleased to lay his honor near his heart, and so impressed the worth of weight of souls upon his, mind, that he was constrained to preach the gospel to a dying world, particularly to the sable sons of Africa. Though he

9

labored under many disadvantages, yet, taught in the schools of Christ, he was able to bring new and old out of the treasury, and he has done more good among the poor slaves than all the learned doctors in America. He was imprisoned for the gospel and without ceremony was severly whipped, but while under the lash, he told his persecutors, he rejoiced not only to be whipped, but he was willing to suffer death for the cause of Christ. He continued to preach the gospel until October 6, 1812. He was supposed to be ninety-six years of age. His remains were interred with peculiar respect. An address was delivered by Revs. Mr. Johnson, Dr. Kollock, Thomas Williams, and Henry Cunningham. He was an honor to human nature, an ornament to religion and a friend to mankind. His memory is still precious in the mind of the living."

> "Afflicted long he bore the rod,
> With Calm submission to his maker God.
> His mind was tranquil and serene,
> No terror in his looks was seen.
> A Saviors smite dispelled the gloom.
> And soothed his passage to the tomb."

> "I heard a voice from heaven saying
> Unto me, write, from henceforth blessed
> are the dead who die in the Lord: even
> so saith the spirit, for they rest from
> their labors."

"This stone is erected by the First Colored Church as a token of love for their most faithful pastor, A.D. 1821."

The membership continued to grow according to the Sunbury Association minutes, 1823 - one thousand, eight hundred and forty-eight. 1824 - one thousand, nine hundred and twelve. 1825 - one thousand, eight hundred and eighty-six. 1826 - two thousand, one hundred and forty-one, this was the year the Sabbath school was organized by Lowell Mason, Superintendent of the Independent Presbyterian Church of the city. 1827 - two thousand, two hundred and seventy-five. By 1831 it was two thousand, seven hundred and ninety-five.

Actual reasons are unknown, but in 1823, the Sunbury Association began listing all churches with exclusive black memberships as African, rather than colored. This church is known until 1832 as First African, from then until 1865 as Third African by the Association. Black members had no voice in the association unless called upon to answer a question or make a statement, therefore no protest could be levied.

THIRD AFRICAN BAPTIST CHURCH
SAVANNAH, GEORGIA
1832 - 1837

Shaken by an ecclesiastical holocaust (details in chapter three). This rock has been swayed, by the gates of hell, now pastorless, and only a remnant of members remained. Deacon Adam Johnson, a good man by any evaluation, had been misled, misguided, misinfluenced and used as a tool, by a doctrinal disguise. When in reality it was a subtle one stroke attempt to destroy the power forever of the black pastor, the black Baptist Church and eternally hog tie all blacks in America.

Feeling that calling a pastor would settle the dust of their confusion, Rev. Thomas Anderson, a member of Second African Baptist Church, was called. Pastor Anderson, Deacons Adam Johnson and J. Sampson were delegates to the Sunbury Association. They reported a membership this year of three hundred and ninety-eight and were received into the Association as the Third African Baptist Church, although they were occupying the building built on the original site in 1795 on Lot No. 7, Middle of Oglethorpe Ward, purchased in September 1793.

Association's minutes reveal why they were received as the Third African Baptist Church, rather than as First African Baptist Church.

> Application was made by the Third African Church to become a member of this association. Granted by unanimous vote.

> "Resolved, That this association approves of the conduct of S. Whitfield, J. Clay and others, who separated from the First African Baptist Church and recommends them to full fellowship with all churches."

> "Resolved, That this association express its disapprobation of the conduct of such member or members as attempted to invalidate, one or more of its resolutions."[1]

> "Resolved, That it be considered respectful and safe for any church differing as to the expediency or propriety of any resolutions of this association that they submit their views at the next annual meeting, and defer until such time operations on subjects."[2]

Third African Baptist Church is only mentioned in the association minutes of 1834 as being "engaged in its duties with diligence and Christian zeal".[3]

Thomas Anderson resigned as pastor in 1835 and was succeeded by Rev. Stephen McQueen. He and Brother Sampson Whitfield were delegates to the Association. They reported ten baptized, eight

---

[1]Sunbury Baptist Association minutes, 1833, paragraphs 25, 26 and 27.
[2]Sunbury Baptist Association minutes, 1833, paragraph 28.
[3]Sunbury Baptist Association minutes, 1834.

received by letter for the year with a total membership of two hundred and twenty-four. In 1836, Rev. McQueen, Brothers Sampson Whitfield and John Harris were delegates, a total of ten had been baptized, six received by letter, with a total membership of one hundred and eighty-three. In 1837 Rev. McQueen and July Ward were the delegates, six had been baptized, membership was now one hundred and eighty-nine. During this Association the five year battle between Third African Baptist and First African Baptist was settled with an association committee being the arbitrator. (For details, see chapter three.)

The administration of the Sunday School organized in 1826 by the Presbyterians was terminated and assumed by the church.

1838 -1865

McQueen remained as pastor until 1840. Rev. John B. Devoux succeeded him in serving from 1842 to 1844. His successor was Isaac Roberts from 1846 to 1849, who was followed by Brister Lawton from 1850 to 1851, then Garrison Frazier from 1852 to 1859.

Ulysses Houston, a former choir member, deacon of the church, licensed and ordained by the church was called to pastor in 1861. Its membership was not more than two hundred at the time. He labored tenaciously with this group throughout the turbulence of the Civil War, keeping them together and nourishing them spiritually.

FIRST BRYAN BAPTIST CHURCH
1865 -

Freedom was granted, the shackles of slavery were removed. They were also free to choose a name for their church, although they were rightfully the First Baptist Church in Savannah, twelve years older than, First Baptist (white), forty-four years older than

First African Baptist. They were not willing to relinquish their firstness or their identity. Andrew Bryan was their founder. They occupied the grounds purchased by him and worshipped in the building erected by him. They were Bryan's church, Bryan's church was the first, Baptist Church, black or white. The proper name would be First Bryan Baptist Church. In 1866 they were chartered by the State of Georgia. The church was one of the founding bodies of the Zion Missionary Baptist Association, July 14, 1865 in Hilton Head Island, South Carolina. Pastor Houston served two terms in the Georgia State Legislature, 1867 - 1871.

The decision to build the present structure was crystalized in 1873 and was completed in 1878. An invitation was extended to the Missionary Baptist Convention of Georgia to meet with them in 1888 to hold the Baptist Centennial with them on the original grounds. Emanuel King Love was pastor of First African Baptist Church, Vice-President of the convention and had presented the idea of such a celebration in 1884. The convention chose to meet at First African for the observance and decided over against the sentiment of the majority that First African Baptist Church, Franklin Square in Savannah was the oldest church. (See chapter six for details.)

After twenty-seven years of service as pastor, Ulysses Houston died in 1888 and was succeeded by:

1888 - 1909	Rev. Gilbert W. Griffin
1909 - 1922	Rev. Daniel Wright
1923 - 1935	Rev. L.M. Glenn
1936 - 1943	Rev. L.M. Terrill
1943 - 1949	Rev. M.E. Holsey
1949 - 1965	Rev. R.M. Williams
1965 - 1973	Rev. E.R. Jennings
1974 -	Rev. A.D. Sims

The "Mother Church" has been an integral part of convention affairs since the founding of the Missionary Baptist Convention of Georgia, and the Foreign Missions Convention in its beginning. As a matter of fact, Pastor Houston was a delegate to the Consolidated Missionary Baptist Convention of the United States in Alexandria, Virginia in 1864. Five times to entertain the State Convention, 1896, Rev. Gilbert W. Griffin, Pastor; 1910, Rev. Daniel Wright, Pastor; 1920, Rev. Daniel Wright, Pastor; 1946, Rev. N.E. Holsey, Pastor; 1977, Rev. Arthur D. Sims, Pastor.

First Bryan is affiliated with the Berean Baptist Association, General Missionary Baptist Convention of Georgia, Inc., and National Baptist Convention, U.S.A., Inc.

Bibliography: **The First Colored Baptist Church in North America,** J.H. Simms, 1888; **Lifted from the Minutes,** W.W. Weatherspool, 1979; Records of the General Missionary Baptist Convention of Georgia, Inc.

Chapter 3
FIRST AFRICAN BAPTIST CHURCH
LOT NO. 7
SAVANNAH, GEORGIA
1815 - 1832

Andrew Cox Marshall was born in South Carolina, around 1755. His mother was pure African and father was an Englishman. As a gesture of gratitude, his master Governor Houston of Colonial days, granted his freedom at death because, Andrew had saved his life sometime before. The Executors of the estate failed to grant freedom.

Later, Andrew escaped and while at large Judge Clay bought him, to become his coachman. This enabled him to travel many

times to the north, frequently seeing General Washington. When the General became President and visited Savannah, Andrew was appointed his body servant.

Around the age of fifty, he was converted to Christ under the preaching of a white minister, whose text was, "But now they have no cloak for their sins". John 15:22. He united with the Second Colored Baptist Church of Savannah and was baptized by Pastor Henry Cunningham.

His uncle, Andrew Bryan, needed an assistant pastor of the First Colored Baptist Church in Savannah and he was chosen for that position in 1806.

After conversion, Mr. Richard Richardson, business partner of his master, Mr. Robert Bolton, advanced him two hundred dollars, and with what he had already saved, allowed him to purchase his freedom. Soon thereafter, purchased his wife's freedom, four children, father-in-law and his stepfather's.

For two years after Andrew Bryan died in 1812, First Colored Baptist Church was without a pastor. In 1815, after much prayer and Divine guidance, Andrew C. Marshall was called. He was a successful businessman, engaged in the drayage business, and was well liked by the white businessmen of the city.

Unlike his predecessor, he was not involved in the Savannah River Baptist Association, composed of churches in Georgia and South Carolina. His noninvolvement could have been because of business involvement or disinterest. However, the church was always represented by at least two deacons, until the churches in South Carolina withdrew to organize their own association.

Thus the churches in Georgia organized the Sunbury Association in 1818. First Colored Baptist Church, Second Colored Baptist Church and Ogeechee Colored Baptist Church, along with Savannah Baptist Church (white) and others of Chatham and

14

adjoining counties comprised the founding churches. Although the church was represented, Pastor Marshall is not listed.

Unable to write at all, but slight reading ability, his main source of reading material was the Bible and Dills Commentary. He became a proponent of antinominism, a doctrine which adhered the law is not a rule over the life of believers under the gospel dispensation. This triggered many successive problems.

First, his popularity began to wain among his denominational and ecclesiastical peers between 1818 and 1821. This could have been because of his failure or unwillingness to fellowship with them. Or because of his material success.

Further complications were added when he undertook to build a two story brick home, in 1819 to 1821. This was unheard of for blacks of that day, igniting more confusion. He further agitated it by purchasing bricks from slaves who did not have tickets that granted them permission to buy and sell. A requirement of them by law.

Although this practice was generally done by whites to have encouraged it in the first place. Because of the limited number of blacks who were in a position to do so. It was a penalty for him. This material was reported to have been stolen from a Mr. McAlpen, who pressed charges.

Taken to court, and found guilty of charges, Andrew Marshall was sentenced to be whipped in public. The intent of this was to be demeaning to this man of material accomplishments, a preacher of the gospel, pastor of the oldest and largest Baptist church in the city, irrespective of color.

Mr. Richard Richardson, who had befriended him earlier by lending money so he could acquire his manumission, appeared in court to intercede on his behalf. Having gotten the support and sympathy of several other influential white citizens. Accompanied him to the place of execution and instructed the constable, that his skin should not be scratched, nor blood drawn. He stood by his side to see to it being carried out, thus only a similarity of whipping took place.

With this portrait of Andrew Marshall, we can better understand the things which later occurred that led to a controversy, that even the balm of time has not healed. Nor shall the scars ever be removed.

There is a need to understand the importance of associational relationships. All Black preachers, whether slave or free, were required by law to have the approval of a white minister, association, synod or presbytery. Which ever was the recognized group of his denomination. In the case of Baptist, it was the association. The associational ministers approved of the yearly licensing, that was granted by the city and county. If they became disenchanted about the ministers performance because of doctrinal or other reasons they could be canceled. This did not seem to affect Andrew Marshall, he was still unidentified with the association.

Probably for identity reasons in the session of 1823, the Sunbury Association began designating the churches with exclusive black memberships as African, rather than colored.

Every year in the association, it reported an increase in membership, reaching a high in 1831 of two thousand, seven hundred and ninety-five.

Dr. Alexander Campbell, founder of the Disciples of Christ Church, visited Savannah in 1832. Andrew Marshall invited him to preach his new doctrine at First African. This infuriated all orthodox Baptists of the city and many members of the church, including Deacon Adam Johnson, a leading and influential member.

Further aggravation took place after the message, when Pastor Marshall heaved flameable fuel upon already burning embers, by saying after given time for further study of the doctrine, there is a possibility of his subscribing to it.

Such turbulence resulted in the membership over the following Sundays, city police were called in to quell the disturbances. One time, members were whipped by the city marshall. A hopeless unmendable division developed. Their problems became a topic of gossip throughout the city.

A split over misunderstanding, outside interference, agitation and a deacon who fails to understand his limitations and respect the pastor's bounds.

Andrew Marshall was too free to be enslaved by the opinions of his time, very subtly rebelling and setting a pace for all his Black pastor successors. By not allowing deacons, association or members to dictate to his pastoral decisions, doctrinally or otherwise, or pulpit guest. His courageousness must be admired and emulated.

Oral tradition reports his motto was, "Get wisdom, get knowledge, but with all thy getting, get understanding". Prevented from formal education, he sought every opportunity for information. After having a chance to examine the Campbellite doctrine, he continued in his Baptist persuasion. Unfortunately, he was misinterpreted, and unjustly ridiculed, because of his hunger for knowledge.

**FIRST AFRICAN BAPTIST CHURCH
FRANKLIN SQUARE
SAVANNAH, GEORGIA
1832**

A departure from the original site was the only solution to peace. The wounds were that severe and death was evitable. All who believed in the pastor and were willing to support him, would have an opportunity to show their stance. Andrew Marshall withdrew from the original site, lot no. 7 Middle of Oglethorpe Ward, the grounds purchased by Andrew Bryan, and the building erected by him. It is estimated that sixteen hundred members followed, Pastor Marshall.

Many others, because of the uncertainty of who was right, joined the other two exclusive Black Baptist Churches, Second and Ogeechee African Baptist. This experience stymied others spiritually and they floundered. Less than two hundred members remained, to follow Deacon Adam Johnson.

The Savannah Baptist Church (white) had just completed a new structure in Chipewa Square in 1832. They had moved from the facility erected in 1800 in Franklin Square. Influential white friends interceded for Andrew Marshall, enabling him to purchase that building, of which was far more commodious than the one he had been forced to leave.

On November 10, 1832, the Sunbury Association met at Walthourville, Liberty County, Georgia. First African was not represented. But a committee had been appointed, and reported on said day.

The committee to whom was referred the consideration of the difficulty existing in the First African Baptist Church, Savannah, made their report.

Your committee, after a serious consideration of the painful and difficult task assigned them, would present to your body the following resolutions, as a result of their consideration:

"Resolved, That we approve highly of the recommendation of the council of minister's that was called, That A. Marshall be silenced; and we concur in the opinion that he be silenced indefinitely."

"Resolved, That the First African Church, as a member of this association, on account of its corrupt state, be considered as dissolved; and that measures be adopted to constitute a new church as a branch of the White Baptist Church."

"Resolved, That we advise our coloured brethren in the country, now members of African churches in Savannah, to take letters of dismission and either unite themselves with neighboring churches of our faith and order to be constituted into separate churches."

"The committee recommend the public expression of this body extending their entire approbation of Christian deportment of the Second African Church."

"Resolved, That a copy of the above resolutions be transmitted to the Mayor of the City of Savannah."

Signed,
Samuel S. Law,
Moderator

Oliver Stevens,
Clerk [1]

There is no evidence of this resolution ever being enforced, other than the silencing of Andrew Marshall from preaching. The intent is worthy of analyzing.

Obviously, Andrew Marshall was powerful, economically, spiritually and civicly. He did much for his people then, the impact of his life is still being felt, and must be recognized as a civil rights warrior of the Nineteenth Century. The public beating of the past decade was designed to break him. That intent was foiled.

Now the intent is to utterly destroy him and the effectiveness of the Black Church. First they wanted to stop him from preaching, a measure to stymie his following and ultimately break the back bone of the church. Unfortunately for them and fortunately for Marshall, that had been tried throughout the Bible. But the

---

[1]Minutes of the Sunbury Association, held at Walthourville, Georgia, November 9, 10, and 11, 1832.

18

patriarchs resorted to prayer. Paul was arrested in Philippi for preaching, and thrown in jail. He started singing and praying, the inmates, jailer, his family and townspeople were converted. John was sentenced to the lonely Island of Patmos, for preaching. One Sunday morning he had a song and prayer service, got heavens attention, was escorted to heaven on a personal tour and stood before the throne of God. Daniel was thrown into the lions den for praying, revolutionized the lions den and made it a haven of rest. A child of God cannot be stopped when he is on assignment for God.

Marshall was silenced from preaching. The new building attracted throngs of people, who came to join him in **prayer**. His congregation grew, outreach spread and like Job, had more after the storm than before. Caution was used, a friendly white person was always present.

Suppose, First African would have been dissolved, because of corruptness as alledged and became a branch of the White Baptist Church. Eventually all of the Black churches that predated 1863 would have been victims of the same prey. We would not have had any churches of our own after Emancipation, or Associations, Conventions, schools, businesses. Probably there would not have been an Emancipation in 1863.

While the resolution appeared to be stacked against Marshall and First African, its final intent was to close up all the African Baptist churches, by advising all the coloured brethren in the country who were members of churches in Savannah to unite with neighboring churches of the faith. God has always kept watch over His own, at all times. But, His watchfulness can be seen so graphically at times of vulnerability and helplessness. Thankfully, He made sure that resolution was never invoked. The total effect it would have had on them, and generations unformed cannot be realized or expressed. To say the least, it would have been devastating.

The continued invasion of this battle can be seen in 1833,

"Resolved, That this association having undoubted testimony of Andrew Marshall holding the sentiment avowed by Alexander Campbell, now declares him and all his followers to have thrown themselves out of the fellowship of the churches of this association, and it recommends all of its faith and order to separate them, according to the advise of the Savannah Baptist Church". [2]

They had not forgotten their previous position in the last session regarding fellowship with First African, was dissolved by the association. A footnote in the minutes said a committee was appointed to transmit the resolution to the State Legislature and Mayor of Savannah, with an explanation.

Now being very coy, Andrew Marshall sends representatives from First African in 1834 to enroll in the association.

---

[2] Minutes of Sunbury Association, 1833, paragraph 29.

Application was made by the First African Church in Savannah for membership but difficulties beyond the control of the association being presented, with the consent of the representatives of said church, a committee was appointed consisting of J.S. Law, A. Harmon, O. Harmon, T. Mell, W.W. Wash and H. Furman, who should request the assistance of Rev. C.B. Jones, and who should act for the association in the adjustment of these difficulties. [3]

Given a year to report,

The committee appointed by the preceding Association to settle differences existing between the African Churches in Savannah, report the following as the conditions upon which an amicable adjustment might be affected. That the First African Church act aside from her pastor, thereby dissolving her illegal and disorderly connection with him; that she renouce the unscriptural doctrines taught by Andrew Marshall; that she satisfy the Second African Church in relation to her excommunicated members; that she return to the Association in the faith and order of the churches which compose that body.[4]

Very clearly can be seen the intent to subdue Andrew Marshall. To cause further division among the Black Christians and rebellion within his church family. But they had been trained and knew the shepherd's voice,..."the doorkeeper opens, and the sheep hear his voice, and he calls his own sheep by name, and leads them out. When he puts forth all his own, he goes before them, and the sheep follow him because they know his voice". John 10:3,4. How many times since, have the Pharoahs, Uzziahs, Ahabs, Herods and Pilates tried to turn members against Black pastors, by calling them heretics, radicals and questioning their doctrines. This is another meaningful contribution, Andrew Marshall made.

First African is on the conscious of the association. Pastor Marshall and members plan further strategy to break their back bone, since they have them wobbling and know where their artillery is stored.

The committee appointed at the last session of this association for the adjustment of the difficulties in the First African Church in Savannah, being called upon, presented their report, which being read, was accepted.[5]

A committee from the First African Church presented a letter addressed to the association by one of its trustees, and also a petition for restoration to the fellowship of this body.[6]

---

[3] Minutes of Sunbury Association, 1834, page 1, paragraph 16.
[4] Minutes of Sunbury Association, 1835
[5] Minutes of Sunbury Association, 1836, page 4, paragraph 12.
[6] Minutes of Sunbury Association, 1836, page 4, paragraph 13.

The letter was read, and examined by a committee. They returned to the body with a recommendation,

The letter and petition being, read, on motion, a committee, consisting of Brethren J.S. Law, J. McDonald, and A. Harmon, was appointed, to report upon the petition.[7]

The committee appointed to examine the letter from the First African Church thus reports: that they truly admire the spirit in which the petition of that Church to your body was dictated, and would affectionately advise them to accede to the terms of reconciliation stated in the report of your late committee, as the only terms upon which reconciliation can be made in the present state of things. We would also recommend that the clerk furnish the delegates of said church a copy of this report.[8]

The truce has not been signed, but the battle has been won. The enemies are rapidly retreating.

Sheep cannot be separated from the shepherd. He has protected, fed, nursed, nourished, comforted, consoled and cared for them now for twenty-one years. They have not forgotten all he has done for them. Neither are they ingrates. Pastor Marshall has been the general of the warfare, the fight has not been his alone, but their's and all other blacks who refuse to be intimidated.

Another letter from First African to the Association,

A letter was presented from the First African Church, requesting to be readmitted a member stating that the difficulties heretofore existing were removed.[9]

A negotiating committee had met at the Savannah Baptist Church (white) in attempt to unite the two opposing forces, First African Baptist Church and the Sunbury Baptist Association together. They proceeded with their report,

Your committee after laborious service are now able to report that they have reason to believe the long existing difficulties between the several African Churches are brought to a close; each has expressed itself satisfied, and all has been done by the First African Church in accordance with the resolutions and recommendations of the Association; and Andrew Marshall, having made full renunciation of holding the peculiar sentiments of Alexander Campbell, with which he has been charged, there seems to be no difficulty in his holding full fellowship in the church to which he belongs.[10]

First African was then admitted into the Sunbury Baptist Association and Andrew Marshall could again preach.

Much credit must be given to Rev. J.S. Law, Pastor of Savannah

---

[7]Minutes of Sunbury Association, 1836, page 4, paragraph 14.
[8]Minutes of Sunbury Association, 1836, page 5, paragraph 20.
[9]Minutes of Sunbury Association, 1837, page 6, paragraph 13.
[10]Minutes of Sunbury Association, 1837.

Baptist Church (white) for this victory as well. He became pastor of the church in the midst of the bickering between the association and Marshall. A very warm friendship was developed between him and all the black pastors, including Marshall.

J.S. Law had arranged a meeting in his church for Adam Johnson and Andrew Marshall to reach a reconciliation. There were three sets of witnesses, representing the three involved groups. Rev. J.S. Law, Chairman of the Committee of Sunbury Association, J. McDonald, Abraham Harmon. The church group that remained at Lot No. 7, Oglethorpe Ward, called Third Baptist by the Association, Rev. F.R. Sweet, Pastor, Deacons Adam Johnson, Jack Simpson, and Adam Sheftall, First African Baptist Church, Rev. Andrew Marshall, Pastor, Deacons Benjamin King, Robert McNish and Samuel Cope.

Adam Johnson spoke first, stating his charge against Dr. Marshall, following Mr. Alexander's proclamation of erroneous doctrines from the pulpit of their church which created a division among the membership, that Pastor Marshall condoned such doctrines by himself preaching them from the same pulpit. He nor the church harbored any personal ill feelings for Rev. Mashall, who was an outstanding personality and had done so much good among his people. There was no desire on their part to impede his progress. The entire matter could be settled, with a confession by Rev. Marshall.

Next, Andrew Marshall stood before the council. He stated, "what brother Adam and the other brothers have said about this matter was true only with this difference, - that he did not say from his pulpit that he agreed with Mr. Alexander, but that being favorably impressed from hearing him expound, when he had examined the doctrines himself, if he found them true according to Mr. Campbell's views of them, then he should join him; but upon a more thorough examination of the Scriptures, he saw no reason to change his faith in the doctrines he now held by his Baptist brethren".

After this statement, Adam Johnson arose, stating that he and brothers present from his church, whom the church had entrusted the settlement of this long menacing matter was now settled. Johnson and Marshall then approached each other and extended hands for fellowship and peace.

During this same period, Andrew Marshall was engaged in a legal battle to acquire lot no. 7, Oglethorpe Ward, Savannah, Georgia. His legal claim was, being heir of Andrew Bryan, the property where the church stood, he had left from belonged to him. The best legal council in Chatham County was secured to fight this case. He was not as victorious in this fight. The Court ruled in favor of the trustees, Moses Cleland, Josiah Penfield, Edward Coppee.

With this evidence it is clear to determine the age of First African Baptist Church, Franklin Square, Savannah, Georgia. The name, First African was given by the association as was the name, Third African given the remnant that remained on the original site.

Although they were members of the association, they had no voice in the proceedings, unless called upon. Neither group had any choice in the selection of those names, although the larger number followed Marshall, they left the place of the original church. Only one church was founded January 20, 1788, and elected Andrew Bryan as pastor.

Her claim of being the Birthplace of Baptist in the U.S.A. is historically weak, because she left her birthplace and was transplanted in new soil in 1832. The group that has continuously occupied Lot No. 7, Middle of Oglethorpe Ward since September 4, 1793 is the oldest uninterrupted Black Baptist Church in America, now known as First Bryan Baptist Church, a name chosen by them.

Andrew C. Marshall served without any other problems until his death in 1856. A total of forty-one years in the pastorate, seventeen at the mother church before the split and twenty-four at the fourth oldest Baptist Church in Savannah, First African Baptist Church.

His successors have been:

1857 - 1877 William J. Campbell
1878 - 1884 George Gibbons
1885 - 1900 Emanuel King Love
1901 - 1907 James Wesley Carr
1909 - 1913 Willis J. Jones
1915 - 1923 Thomas Jefferson Goodall
1923 - 1928 Edgar Garfield Thomas
J. Alfred Wilson
Ralph Mark Gilbert
Curtis Jackson
William Franklin Stokes, III
1974 - 1980 Lawrence McKinney

The Cornerstone of the present edifice was laid October 13, 1873 under the pastorate of William J. Campbell

Five times this church has hosted the General Missionary Baptist Convention of Georgia, Inc., 1882, George Gibbons, Pastor; 1888, Emanuel King Love, Pastor; "The Baptist Centennial" was held there, 1916, James Wesley Carr, Pastor; 1932, J. Alfred Wilson, Pastor; 1966, William Franklin Stokes, Pastor.

Two times hosted the National Baptist Convention, 1892 under the pastorate of E.K. Love and 1916 under the pastorate of Thomas Jefferson Goodall.

First African is affiliated with the Berean Baptist Association, General Missionary Baptist Convention of Georgia, Inc., and National Baptist Convention, U.S.A., Inc.

Bibliography: **The First Colored Baptist Church in North America,** J.M. Simms, 1888. (J.M. Simms was a member of First African from baptism by Andrew Marshall, the first Sunday of April 1841, until 1865.) Minutes of Sunbury Baptist Association; Minutes and records of General Missionary Baptist Convention of Georgia, Inc.; Minutes of National Baptist Convention, U.S.A., Inc.

Chapter 4

CHURCHES
1793 - 1869

Other known churches organized during this period, whose history was not available are the Pleasant Hill Baptist Church, Roswell, Georgia, dated in the late 1850's; Shady Grove Baptist Church, Columbus, Georgia, dated in the early 1860's; First African Baptist Church, Thomasville, Georgia; Jerusalem Baptist Church, Groveland, Georgia, both dated in the mid 1860's.

There are four origins of all of these churches listed. Some were organized by black preachers and members won to Christ through their persuasion. Others were organized by white missionaries or pastors of white churches who guided them in selecting a black pastor. Another group resulted from blacks joining the church of their master or mistress, with the black membership eventually outgrowing the white membership, but a white minister was obtained. The fourth group was born during and after the Civil War, when slaves were unwanted in the white church, since there were no longer legal ties between them and their masters. The churches felt they at least owed them to organize a church rather than completely abandon them. Little did they realize what power was being placed in their hands and what confidence they were manifesting in them.

These church histories reveal so very much about the social, educational, religious, economic and fraternal life of our people for the past one hundred and ninety-two years. Through them, we see the population shift from the extreme southeastern region of the state, up the Savannah River on the eastern boundry. Then move throughout the state.

Our churches represent the grass-roots of our total society. It cannot be said too frequently, nor must we be ashamed to say it, everything accomplished in America by Blacks, must be attributed to the Black church and Black pastor. The church played a key role in our being liberated from the manacles of slavery and second class citizenship. The black church gave birth to our schools, newspapers, financial institutions, political influence and the civil rights movement.

Their vitality must not be underestimated in the total culture of the American society. The churches listed in this chapter are representative of their sisters of the state and nation. They have grown from crude beginnings to strong spiritual hightowers, who watched over the Spiritual, moral and civic welfare of the total municipality. Neither were their warnings only for its parish, race or era, but for all people of all times.

SPRINGFIELD BAPTIST CHURCH
AUGUSTA, GEORGIA
1793

Most credible historians of the Black Baptist Church give 1793 as the year Augusta's Springfield Baptist Church was organized, except the author of the **History Book** of the said church, who gives 1787 as the beginning date.

This rendition of history presents many conflicts. According to that author, Silver Bluff Baptist Church of South Carolina is suppose to be the parent church and the histories of the two churches are closely interwoven. With Springfield gradually emerging as an all Black Baptist Church. Therefore alleging Springfield of being the oldest "Negro Baptist Church in the United States". She validates this with Silver Bluff Baptist Church being closed two years (1862 - 1863).

Discrepancies with this historic position are first invalidated by Silver Bluff's history, that in 1793, Rev. Jessie Peters and George Liele returned to Augusta and organized the Springfield Baptist Church. It is further disproved by J.M. Simms in his book, **The First Colored Baptist Church in America, 1888;** Emanuel

25

King Love, **History of First African Baptist Church,** 1888; and Edgar Garfield Thomas, **First African Baptist Church of North America,** 1923 and the position taken by the Centennial Celebration of the Negro Baptist of Georgia held in Savannah, Georgia, June 6 - 18, 1888, at the First African Baptist Church. All of whose historic posture is the oldest existing Black Baptist Church in the world was organized January 20, 1788, by Jessie Golphin and Abraham Marshall. With Andrew Bryan becoming the first pastor.

Silver Bluff and Springfield Baptist Church histories present further historic controversy in their claim of George Liele being one of the organizers. Again most credible historians have George Liele enroute to Jamaica when Andrew Bryan was won to Christ and baptized by him in 1783. As he was delayed by a storm, while waiting on board ship at the mouth of the Savannah River at Tybee. He went back to Savannah preaching somewhere around the Savannah River. Bryan and three others heard him, accepted Christ, were baptized, thus ending his Christian ministry in America.

Liele is credited with being the first Black Baptist preacher in North America. History gives him no credit for organizing any churches in America. His ecclesiastical organization is in Jamaica where he sailed as personal servant of a British Army officer, because of fear of loosing his life or freedom. This same fear coupled with intimidations from the British and American War caused Rev. David George, Rev. Jessie Peters Golphin and Rev. George Bryant all of Silver Bluff to be driven into exile.

Because of the need of sanction by a white preacher of an association, synod or presbytery. In this case association, the other minister who participated in the organization was probably Rev. Abraham Marshall, who pastored Kiokee Baptist Church of Columbia County, Georgia, the oldest Baptist church in the state. He was most influential during that time and seemed to have been a friend of Black Christians.

When Springfield was organized, there was only one other church of another denomination in Augusta. She is the "Mother Baptist Church" in that city. Predating First Baptist Church (white), which was not organized until 1818.

Rev. Jessie Peters Golphin served as pastor until 1818, to be succeeeded by Rev. Ceasar McCradley. In 1819, Rev. Jacob Walker was ordained and called as third pastor, remaining until his death in July, 1846.

Under Rev. Walker's pastorate there grew a need for another Black Baptist church in the southeastern section of the city. Slaveowners of the section were displeased about the distance their slaves had to travel to church. Out of this need the Independent Baptist Church was organized April 26, 1840, by the pastor, members and deacons of the Springfield Baptist Church. Rev. Samuel Bell became the first pastor. The name Independent was later changed to Thankful.

On August 29, 1847, Rev. Kelly Lowe was ordained and called as fourth pastor. Two men, who later served as presidents of the Missionary Baptist State Convention and one who served as president of the General Baptist State Convention, were baptized by him, called to preach under his pastorate and ordained by him, Rev. J.C. Bryan, 1882 - 1883; Rev. W.J. White, 1894 - 1895; Rev. George H. Dwelle, Corresponding Secretary, 1870 - 1884, President 1893 - 1901. The Church Sunday School was also organized during this period.

His life's assignment ended, Janury 3, 1861. Rev. Henry Watts was called to pastor in 1862. Under his leadership the building was completed in 1873. Many significant Christian organizations were born in this church as well as Ebenezer Baptist Association, 1866; August Baptist College (Morehouse College), 1867; Harmony Baptist Church.

After his passing October 30, 1877, Rev. Gilford Arrington was called, being the youngest pastor ever at that time. Before his death at age thirty-seven, on October 28, 1881, the Union Baptist Church was organized. Rev. Williams succeeded him, serving only a few months before resigning in 1882. His successor, Dr. G.E. Eagles served from 1883 to 1885, after succombing to illness and death.

One of the famous sons who had gained recognition as a denominational officer, and pastor in southwest Georgia, Rev. George H. Dwelle was called in December 1885. His is remembered for constructing the present edifice. After twenty-six years of service, he resigned in December, 1911 and preached his farewell sermon, the fourth Sunday in April, 1912.

A colorful list of distinguished ministers have rendered commendable service from that date to present:

Rev. James Madison Nabrit, A.M.; D.D.; May 1912 - May 1921
Rev. W.P. Sanders, January 1923 - April 2, 1931
Rev. William Henry Perry, A.B.; B.T.H.; October 31, 1931 -
    December 1935
Rev. J.H. Sanders, December 1935 - December 26, 1944
Rev. C.K. Steele, 1945 - February 1950
Rev. E.J. Dyson, Jr., June 1951 - 1954
Rev. Robert C. Blossom, January 13, 1955 - August 1956
Rev. Raymond H. Smith, June 1957 - 1959
Rev. M.E. Braxton, November 1959 - February 1971
Rev. E.T. Martin, October 1971 -

Thanks to Springfield, there has been a light shining in the darkness in east Georgia since the last of the Eighteenth Century. This light has been in the hands of black sons and daughters brought to this land against their will. But found their purpose and refused to curse the darkness - they were lighted by His light and gladly let theirs shine. They were the first in that section to fly the Baptist banner.

Her affiliations are Walker Baptist Association, General Missionary Baptist Convention of Georgia, Inc., and National Baptist Convention, U.S.A., Inc.

Bibliography: **History Book** of Springfield Baptist Church; History of Silver Bluff Baptist Church, Silver Bluff, South Carolina; History of Thankful Baptist Church, Augusta, Georgia, and records of General Missionary Baptist Convention of Georgia, Inc.

FIRST BAPTIST CHURCH
LAGRANGE, GEORGIA
1828

This historic west central Georgia church was organized in 1828, and had a list of outstanding pulpiteers to shepherd her, Dr. C.T. Walker, Dr. Sandy F. Ray and Dr. Phale Hale. Other respectable pastors were Rev. William Henry Perry, Rev. R.L. Hill, Rev. Neal, Rev. Jackson, and Rev. John Giles.

In the past, this Christian family was affiliated with the Western Union Baptist Association, General Missionary Baptist Convention of Georgia, Inc. and National Baptist Convention, U.S.A., Inc.

Bibliography: 110th Church Anniversary Program celebrated in 1938, and oral testimonies.

FIRST BAPTIST CHURCH
MACON, GEORGIA
1835

In 1835, there were two hundred and eighty-three slave and free black members of the First Baptist Church (white) in Macon, Georgia, and one hundred and ninety-nine white members. The blacks were privileged to have their own services, conducted by black licensed ministers.

Prior to 1860, there is no record of her pastors. The licensed preachers probably served under the direction of the pastor of the parent church. On October 5, 1860, Rev. Robert Cunningham (white) offered to serve for one hundred and fifty dollars annually. He served until 1866.

Their first ordained Black pastor was Rev. Milton Tilinghast, serving from 1866 to 1867. His successors were:

       1867 - 1869 Rev. Milus Wilburne
       1869 - 1871 Rev. William Plant
       1871 - 1873 Rev. Lewis Pope
       1878 - 1886 Rev. Henry Williams
       1887 - 1895 Rev. T.M. Robinson

Rev. Robinson laid the cornerstone for the present structure and the basement. Following his death, a dispute arose over the selection of a pastor. On November 2, 1896, the church was closed by court action. A group withdrew over a division on selecting a pastor and organized the Tremount Temple Baptist Church.

On December 27, 1896, a call was extended to Rev. William Gilbert Johnson of Augusta, Georgia, a profound pulpiteer, administrator and organizer. The keys to unlock the physical doors were turned over to him, as well as the spiritual keys. Immediately he united this disgruntled Christian family and by November 21, 1897, the sanctuary was completed and opened for worship. By 1903, the building was paid for in excess of sixty thousand dollars.

More than five hundred souls were added to the church during Rev. Johnson's first revival. He organized the Baptist Young People's Union, and First Baptist became the first black church in the region to install a pipe organ. During his eighteen year pastorate, before death on November 13, 1914, the church membership reached nineteen hundred.

William Gilbert Johnson was succeeded by:

       1916 - 1917 Rev. T.L. Balloo
       1919 - 1925 Rev. S.E. Piercy
       1926 - 1927 Rev. G.L. Harris
       1928 - 1932 Rev. E.G. Thomas
       1933 - 1936 Rev. Sandy F. Ray
       1936 - Rev. Roland Smith
       1936 - 1940 Rev. F.N. Marshburn

Robert Earl Penn, a native West Virginian, recent graduate of Clarke College and a student at Gammon Theological Seminary was called to pastor the church in 1940. During his brief tenure before resigning to enter the United States Army Chaplaincy in 1941, he paid off the church indebtedness of two thousand dollars. He was succeeded by:

1945 - 1947 Rev. H.J. Sherard
1948 - 1953 Rev. A.F. Taylor

Rev. Charles W. Ward, a scholarly leader, served from 1954 to 1959. He is accredited with baptizing two hundred and four candidates, organizing the Youth Fellowship, Calendar Club, Junior Ushers, Annual Vacation Bible School, and installing a new roof on the church, a new heating system, new lights and rewiring the church.

With his departure to assume the pastorate of another church, the call was extended to Rev. Van J. Malone, a native Mississippian, who was pastoring in Memphis, Tennessee. From his assumption of the helm in 1960 to 1965, more than one hundred and seventy-six members were baptized. He organized the Boy Scouts, Cub Scouts, and Progressive Club. The first unit was renovated, electric organ installed, church sanctuary carpeted and choir stand built.

This congregation was again faced with the selection of a pastor. Rev. Marshell Stinson was called in 1965 remaining until 1970. His successor was Rev. Julius Ceasar Hope, a flamboyant preacher, evangelist, Civil Rights fighter, who led the church in building and paying for the pastorium, and the purchase of a tract of land for relocation. His tenure ended when he resigned in 1978 to accept the directorship of the Church Works Committee of the N.A.A.C.P. in New York City. First Baptist's present pastor is Rev. John P. Harris, who was called from his pastorate in South Carolina.

First Baptist has provided a state president for the General State Baptist Convention of Georgia, in W.G. Johnson and a president of the Sunday School and Baptist Training Union Congress of the General Missionary Baptist Convention of Georgia, in Julius Ceasar Hope. She has hosted the annual session of the Convention eight times, 1880, 1892, 1902, 1909, 1921, 1927, 1938, 1961, the Midwinter Board Meeting numerous times and the State Congress or its predecessors on occasions. In 1882, she hosted the Foreign Mission Convention, predecessor of the National Baptist Convention.

Her affiliations are Middle Georgia Orthodox Association, General Missionary Baptist Convention of Georgia, Inc. and National Baptist Convention, U.S.A., Inc.

Bibliography: Church history.

30

FIRST BAPTIST CHURCH
GAINESVILLE, GEORGIA
1838

Little is known of the First Baptist Church, Hall County, Georgia activities from 1838 to 1877, because of the absence of written records. When the oral records were given, they either went unrecorded or were lost. Therefore, there are thirty-nine silent years.

When the present sanctuary was constructed in 1923, the cornerstone was laid with the following inscription:

FIRST BAPTIST CHURCH
ORG. APPROX. 85 YRS. AGO
REBUILT 1923
REV. W.M. DORSEY, PASTOR
REV. A. HARRIS, ASST. PASTOR
BUILDING COMMITTEE
W.K. BUTLER, CHR.
JACOB HOWELL - W.F. SIMS
FRANK BELL - PERRY WILLIAMS
D.S. LOWE - GEORGE COUCH
L.G. GREENLEE - J.W. THOMPSON
TREAS.

Sometime around 1877, Rev. Jack Nichols, a life long resident of Hall County, became the Pastor. He had been a slave, owned by the Thompsons.

His conversion and call to the ministry naturally pre-dated his call to this church as pastor. He was not a member of the First Baptist Church (white). Nor do the rolls of the Wahoo Baptist Church (white), located in the community where he was born, reared and interred in February 1903, carry his name.

Jack was probably a son of this church and proudly the members called him as pastor. His enviable record over the next twenty-six years did not disappoint them. More than four hundred members were baptized, and a new church building constructed probably around 1901 on the corner of High and Pine Streets.

His influence was sought community wide. Considered one of the leading lights among Black Baptists in Northeast Georgia, being politically astute, influential in County and State Politics of the Democratic Party, and highly respected among the whites of his community.

Successor to Jack Nichols was Rev. Sisson, 1903-1906. Rev. William Dorsey was called in 1906. In the same year he led the church in affiliating with the Northwestern Baptist Association. Ground was purchased on Myrtle Street to erect a new sanctuary, in 1923. The church family moved into its new spiritual home. Rev. Dorsey's pastorate concluded in 1929. It is under his pastorate the first record is seen of the church affiliation with the General Missionary Baptist Convention of Georgia, Inc. His successor was Rev. L.B. Moon. His pastorate terminated in 1936, and was succeeded by:

1936 - 1939 Rev. Jackson
1939 - 1942 Rev. Smouts
1942 - 1945 Rev. C.L. Daughterty

Rev. A.G. Walker was called in 1945. He is credited with renovating the church, brick veneering the sanctuary, building the fellowship hall, kitchen, basement and restrooms. After departing in 1948, Rev. Richard Bizzell followed him in 1949, initiating respectful administrative procedures. His tenure ended in 1950 and was followed by Rev. W.H. Huff, who remained until 1960. Rev. M.R. Dinkins was called in 1960. He led in building the educational wing and departmentalized the Sunday School. After resigning in 1964, Rev. Calvin Williams, a native of Hall County, was called from a pastorate in Rome, Georgia. The nine room parsonage, costing forty thousand dollars, was built in 1965. A new sixty-three passenger Bluebird Ford bus was purchased in 1969. He resigned in 1972 and was succeeded by Rev. G. David Horton in 1972. Rev. Horton's contributions were equipping church office, replacing public address system, organizing nine mission circles, central treasure, incorporating the church and many additions were received. He resigned in 1976 to accept another church.

Rev. Clarence M. Wagner was called in April, 1977. During his pastorate, central heating and air conditioning installed, church and parsonage completely renovated, weekly radio broadcast, many additions received, church united and spiritually revived, other improvements, organizations and accomplishments too numerous to mention.

For the first time in the one hundred and eight years of the General Missionary Baptist Convention's history, it met in Gainesville in 1978, invited and hosted by the First Baptist Church.

First Baptist is affiliated with the Northwestern Baptist Association, General Missionary Baptist Convention of Georgia, Inc., and National Baptist Convention, U.S.A., Inc.

Bibliography: Church history, and **The Eagle** newspaper of Gainesville, Georgia.

FIRST AFRICAN BAPTIST CHURCH
COLUMBUS, GEORGIA
1840

First African Baptist Church was organized in Columbus, Georgia in 1840, in a building located at what is now Twelfth Street and Third Avenue. In 1862, a lot was purchased on the corner of St. Clair and Front Streets, and a frame worship building was erected. Later to be destroyed by fire.

This church's next move was to erect a brick building under the pastorate of Rev. Green McArthur in 1881. It was located at Eleventh Street and Sixth Avenue.

The beautiful building, decorated with meaningful Christian symbols of which the congregation presently worships in, was built in 1915. Rev. J.H. Smith was the pastor. After having been burdened with indebtedness for over twenty-five years, Rev. T.W. Smith led them in liquidating the debt in 1938.

Rev. Fred Lawson led this Christian family in constructing a Christian Education annex in 1967, costing eighty-two thousand dollars.

First African Baptist Church pastors since 1862 are:

1862 -		Rev. Harry Watson
		Rev. Rucker
1870 -	1884	Rev. Green McArthur
1884 -	1889	Rev. Ramsey
1889 -	1893	Rev. J.S. Kelsey
1893 -	1899	Rev. McNeal
1899 -	1907	Rev. R.W. Smith
1907 -	1910	Rev. Carter
1910 -	1911	Rev. S.W. Batchelor
1911 -	1919	Rev. J.H. Smith
1919 -	1920	Rev. J.T. Brown
1920 -	1925	Rev. B.H. Hogan
1925 -	1938	Rev. T.N. Brown
1938 -	1964	Rev. T.W. Smith
1964 -	1972	Rev. Fred Lofton
1972 -		Rev. Frank Beauford

First African Baptist Church has entertained the General Missionary Baptist Convention three times, 1876, 1895 and 1922. It is affiliated with the Mount Calvary Baptist Association, General Missionary Baptist Convention of Georgia, Inc. and National Baptist Convention, U.S.A., Inc.

Bibliography: Church history.

THANKFUL BAPTIST CHURCH
AUGUSTA, GEORGIA
1840

On April 26, 1840, members of the Springfield Baptist Church organized what they stated in "regular order", the Independent Baptist Church. Rev. Samuel Bell became the first pastor.

Springfield was the only Black church in the city, located in the extreme northwest section. Many complaints had been expressed by slave owners, who operated large plantations and brickyards in the southeast area of the city, and their slaves having to travel so far to worship.

A sight at the corner of Walker and Lincoln Streets was selected to build the first building. Brothers Edd LaBoyd, Burney, Sharper Gray, Thomas Clarke, Cy Walker, Alford Johnson, Sandy Long and James Talbert were some of the first deacons.

After serving four years, Rev. Bell had purchased his freedom and resigned to emigrate to Liberia, Africa. There were few Black Ministers who were free or could read and write. They looked to the Mother Church to recommend a shepherd to them. In 1844, Rev. Henry Johnson, a member of Springfield, became their pastor. The two churches mutually agreed, "Independent" was not the best name. God had now sent them a pastor, there was much to be thankful for. The name Thankful Baptist Church was chosen.

Under Rev. Johnson's administration, the Provident Baptist Church and Macedonia Baptist Church (1869) were organized. He passed July 26, 1870. Rev. James T. Talbert, one of the first deacons, by now was a gospel minister and was called to pastor the church. The church was remodeled, many members united, the first choir organized and organ purchased. The Hale Street Baptist Church was organized.

Overcome with age, this third pastor resigned in 1890 and became Pastor Emeritus. Rev. Cyrus S. Wilkins of Atlanta was his successor. The church saw tremendous growth and in 1893 the present cathedral style building was begun. It was completed in 1898. A fifteen hundred dollar pipe organ was installed, being one of the first black churches in the city to do so.

August 21, 1904, Dr. Wilkins resigned. For the next forty years, numerous ministers served, all making splendid contributions:

1905 - 1911 Rev. Fred R. Wallace
1912 - 1924 Rev. L.P. Pinkney
1925 -　　　 Rev. H.H. Coleman (five weeks)
1925 - 1932 Rev.A.C. Davis
1933 - 1938 Rev. T.W. Smith
1939 - 1945 Rev. M.J. Sherard

Rev. Nathaniel T. Young, Pastor of First African Baptist Church, Dublin, Georgia, was called on the first Sunday of June, 1945. He is a graduate of Morehouse College. His record as pastor and preacher prior to arriving at Thankful was superb. His thirty-five years as pastor of this church is a testimony of his ability. His accomplishments have been legion.

Thankful Baptist Church is affiliated with the Walker Baptist Association, New Era Baptist State Convention, and Progressive National Convention.

Bibliography: Church history, and **History Book** of Springfield Baptist Church.

CENTRAL AFRICAN BAPTIST CHURCH
AUGUSTA, GEORGIA
1856

Rev. Peter Johnson was the organizer of the Central Baptist Church of Augusta, Georgia on June 17, 1856. Eighteen members from Augusta and one hundred and thirty from Old Storm Branch Baptist Church in South Carolina, comprised the charter members. Rev. H.H. Tuper delivered the dedicatorial sermon. His text was Psalms 122:1, "I was glad when they said unto me, let us go into the house of the Lord". He was assisted by Rev. W.J. Handy.

In September 1868, Rev. Henry Jackson was ordained to the Gospel Ministry and became pastor. Serving for sixteen years, more than nine hundred additions were received during this period. Rev. C.T. Walker was called in 1884, serving for one year. A group withdrew and organized the Tabernacle Baptist Church. Because of the turmoil that occured, the court was forced to sell the property and divide the proceeds equally between the two factions. Each received two thousand dollars. She is the mother of three other churches, Mount Olive, Liberty and Good Hope Baptist. Her list of pastors from July 27, 1894 are:

1894 - 1900 Rev. Henry Jackson (second pastorate)
1901   Rev. A. Wilson
1908 - 1915 Rev. Roman J. Johnson, sold the church on Walker Street for seven thousand dollars and erected present edifice.
1916 - 1944 Rev. R.B. Mabry
1944 - 1945 Rev. B.B. Felder
1945 - 1947 Rev. Moses C. Thomas
1948 - 1960 Rev. J.D. Williams
1961 - 1969 Rev. J.H. Sims, Jr.
1970 - 1974 Rev. J.A. Bryant
1974 -   Rev. M.E. Stokes

In May 1870, the General Missionary Baptist Convention of Georgia, Inc. was organized in the Central Baptist Church. She retains membership in the Convention and the National Baptist Convention, U.S.A., Inc.

Bibliography: Church history.

FRIENDSHIP BAPTIST CHURCH
ATLANTA, GEORGIA
1862

Twenty-five Black members of First Baptist Church (white) received their letters in April, 1862 and organized the Friendship Baptist Church. Rev. Frank Quarles was called to pastor them.

Their first place of worship was a boxcar sent them from the Ninth Street Baptist Church of Cincinnati, Ohio. After Emancipation, the congregation experienced rapid growth and moved into larger quarters, at Markham and Haynes Streets. They remained there until 1871, when construction began for their new church and moved into the basement of the present building.

Friendship has played a significant role in the total development of Atlanta since her beginning. She is the Mother of Black Baptist Churches in Atlanta because of harmoniously forming other congregations, Wheat Street, Providence (South

Atlanta), Union, Zion Hill (Lynhurst and Sewell Road), Little Friendship, Second Mount Zion, and Shiloh (Jonesboro). The boxcar of which housed the first church, Atlanta University began. What later became E.A. Ware Elementary School, had its beginning in the second building. Spelman College was founded in the basement of the uncompleted church in 1881. When Augusta Baptist College moved to Atlanta in 1879, becoming Atlanta Baptist College (now Morehouse College) its first classes were in the uncompleted church basement. Those initial ties with the institutions have never been severed.

Her first pastor, Father Frank Quarles, was instrumental in the organization of the Missionary Baptist Convention of Georgia in Augusta, in 1870. Father Quarles became the first president. On four occasions, this Christian family hosted the annual session, 1871 and 1879, Frank Quarles, host pastor, 1884 and 1893, Edward R. Carter, host pastor.

In 1894, the Foreign Mission Convention met in Montgomery, Alabama. A committee was appointed regarding uniting the existing Black Baptist bodies with National scope, to report in the next meeting in 1895. Dr. Carter extended an invitation for that meeting to be held in Atlanta, at the Friendship Baptist Church. The committee's report was in favor of uniting the groups to ensure a stronger stanze in foreign missions and domestic outreach. The name National Baptist Convention was chosen.

Without a doubt, no other Black Baptist church in the world has such a rich legacy as the Mother of Baptist Churches, Baptist related schools, public and higher education, and denomination-alism, as Friendship Baptist Church on Mitchell Street in Atlanta, Georgia.

Only five ministers have served as undershepherds of this flock:

1862 - 1881 Rev. Frank Quarles
1882 - 1944 Dr. Edward R. Carter
1945 - 1953 Dr. Maynard H. Jackson, Sr.
1954 - 1970 Dr. Samuel W. Williams
1971 -   Dr. William V. Guy

Affiliations are Atlanta Baptist Association, New Era Baptist State Convention of Georgia, Progressive National Baptist Convention.

Bibliography: Church history, oral testimony of Mr. Andrew J. Lewis, II, grandson of Dr. E.R. Carter, and minutes of the General Missionary Baptist Convention of Georgia, Inc.

THANKFUL BAPTIST CHURCH
ROME, GEORGIA
1863

Rev. Jefferson Milner, commonly called Father Milner acclaimed throughout North Georgia as "The King", was born July 22, 1820 in Laurens District, South Carolina. Before he died on March 16, 1895, he baptized more than thirty-three hundred souls, founding the Thankful Baptist Church and most of the churches organized in his era from Acworth on the southeast to the Alabama line on the west and the Tennessee line on the north, also founding the Rome High and Industrial School.

In 1863, Father Milner led a small following of believers in Jesus Christ in organizing, they cleaned off a spot of ground, and erected a bush arbor from the growth that had been cut. This was their first place of worship. Later it was destroyed by fire. The First Baptist Church (white) offered their basement as a meeting place.

After much work, sacrifice and saving, the land that is presently occupied was purchased in 1868, from Mr. Perry Chisholm. Another bush arbor was erected, and plank pews made. That building was used until the present edifice was built.

Thankful to be on their land purchased by their sweat, toils and sacrifices. To be in their building, built by their hands. Sitting on pews made by their labors. They changed the name of the church to Thankful Baptist Church.

This church has not merely been a light in Northwest Georgia, it has been a search light mainly because of the "Lights" who have shined from the pulpit. Rev. Holmes was the successor. A conflict occured and a few members withdrew, bringing to birth the

Springfield Baptist Church. His successor was Rev. John Poindexter. A larger group left the church to organize the Broad Street Baptist Church. Many of those members returned and Broad Street is no longer in existence. Its remanent is known as the Baptist Center.

The following served briefly:

Rev. John H. Laster
Rev. Waits
Rev. F.A. Harris

Rev. J.H. Gadson, who was the first principal of Rome High and Industrial School, a scholarly theologian became the next pastor. Serving efficiently and faithfully for eighteen years. He made an impact upon the total community, black and white. His immediate successors whose tenures were brief:

Rev. J.C. Gaffney - one year
Rev. J.H. Brown - two years
Rev. O.C. Thomas

For six years, Rev. Ralph Riley was the pastor. Many memorable accomplishments were achieved. Around thirty-five more members from Broad Street Baptist Church returned, with others going in other directions. He gave birth to the idea of an annex. He was succeeded by Rev. Frank L. Sanders, who served commendably. He was also one of the writers for the National Baptist Training Union. Rev. Obie M. Collins followed, whose emphasis was developing financial sovereignity and creating a building fund for the annex. Rev. J.N. Hollis served next for two years.

On the third Sunday of August, 1957, Rev. Clarence Tuggle became Thankful's pastor. Under his guidance, the old parsonage renovated, the annex built, and a new parsonage constructed. Many other significant contributions were made during his pastorate. His era ended by resignation the fourth Sunday of December, 1974, after serving seventeen years.

Since July, 1975, Rev. O.B. Yates has been the spiritual leader. Many tangible results of his leadership can be seen, over three hundred additions, old organizations revived, new ones organized, weekly broadcast. Thankful has assumed its rightful place in community leadership as the first black Baptist Church in every imaginable way.

Three times, Thankful has entertained the General Missionary Baptist Convention of Georgia, Inc., 1874, Rev. Jefferson Milner, Pastor; 1918, Rev. J.H. Gadson, Pastor; 1937, Rev. Ralph Riley, Pastor. Her affiliations are North Georgia General Missionary Baptist Association, General Missionary Baptist Convention of Georgia, Inc., National Baptist Convention, U.S.A., Inc.

Bibliography: Church history and convention records.

FIRST AFRICAN BAPTIST CHURCH
BAINBRIDGE, GEORGIA
1865

Little written record was kept on First African Baptist Church prior to the pastorate or Rev. E.G. Thomas in 1919, who was a writer and historian.

Both black and white citizens stated that members of color withdrew from the First Baptist Church (white) and organized the First African Baptist Church in a section of Bainbridge, known as Fort Hughes near the Old Riverside Hospital in 1865. Rev. Ben Munson and Rev. McIntyre, who were never called as pastors, did the preaching until the first pastor, Rev. John Thornton, was called.

Later the church moved to North Webster Street near the white cemetary. Shortly after this move, a disruption arose over the call of a pastor and a group withdrew to form the Greater Macedonia Baptist Church.

This church was coerced to move to the present location by a Mr. Patterson, who offered a number of bricks for their building if they didn't locate on Water Street near his residence. The membership accepted the offer.

Dr. N.B. Williamson was called to pastor in 1900, serving until 1904. During his pastorate the present structure was begun. His successor was Rev. J.B. Davis, who left the First African Baptist Church to assume the pastorate in 1905. He completed the construction of the church and celebrated it by entertaining the

41

Missionary Baptist Convention of Georgia in 1909. This was the first worship service in the new building.

Rev. H.F. Taylor, a youthful, scholarly preacher succeeded him. Rev. H.H. Coleman was the next pastor, a gifted preacher. He was succeeded by Rev. E.G. Thomas, author, historian and scholar.

By 1924, the church again sought a shepherd. Their choice was Rev. C.S. Ellington of Athens. Before his resignation in 1926 an organ costing five thousand dollars was installed. Rev. W.W. Weatherspool, Rev. W.W. Roberts and Rev. J.W. Mapson were the next pastors. Under these gospel stalwarts, the church experienced spiritual and numerical growth, with its influence being felt community wide. Under Rev. Weatherspool's pastorate, the General Missionary Baptist Convention of Georgia was hosted in 1931.

In 1940, the church again searched for a pastor, this time choosing Rev. I.S. Powell, Sr., who was serving the First African Baptist Church in Dublin, Georgia. He picked up the mantle in June 1940. Many improvements are credited to him. The young people's department was organized, debts were cleared, and mortgage was burned on the church. His tenure ended by death, February 19, 1946. His son, Rev. I.S. Powell, Jr., who was a ministerial aspirant when his father became pastor of the church was called. His contributions were installing the public address system and the Crucifix. His departure came in April 1950 when he resigned to accept the pastorate of the Mount Zion Baptist Church in Pensacola, Florida.

Rev. Henry Grady Neal, pastor of the Eureka Baptist Church of Albany was next. Serving from August 1950 to April 1954. He sowed the seed for the erection of the annex. Rev. W. Owen Devaughn of Birmingham, Alabama served from 1954 until September 1956.

Ebenezer Baptist Church of Athens, Georgia provided the next pastor, Rev. J.H. Sanders, who served from 1957 until his death in 1961. The annex was built during his pastorate and the General Missionary Baptist Convention of Georgia was entertained. Rev. Mose Pleasure, Pastor of Mount Olive Baptist Church of Brunswick, Georgia began serving in June, 1961. remaining until June 1964. Rev. Henry Grady Neal returned in 1965 and remained until April, 1979. Rev. John Giles is the present pastor of this historic Southwest Georgia Church.

Other pastors who served prior to 1900 but exact tenures are unknown are Rev. Fleming Fiveash and Rev. Thomas J. Bellinger.

This church is a member of the Flint River Baptist Association, General Missionary Baptist Convention of Georgia, Inc. and National Baptist Convention, U.S.A., Inc.

Bibliography: Church history.

BETHESDA BAPTIST CHURCH
AMERICUS, GEORGIA
1866

Out of the need for the blacks of Americus, Sumter County, Georgia to have their own church, so their spiritual, educational and civic course could be charted, the Bethesda Baptist Church was formed. This church has made phenomenal contributions to Christendom and its denomination throughout the years. Bethesda has provided great influence and challenge for the youth of her locale. It has been the training ground for many leading pulpiteers, such as the silver tongue orator of the twentieth century, Peter James Bryant, the distinguished administrator-scholar, James Madison Nabrit, pastor-educator, J.L. Lomax.

The Missionary Baptist Convention of Georgia was hosted in 1900 by this church under the pastorate of Rev. C.H. Young. Since first becoming a member of the convention, she has never withdrawn her support or identity.

Those ministers who have served faithfully as pastors, are:

1866 - 1869	Rev. John Bull
1869 - 1880	Rev. J.C. Bryan
1880 - 1881	Rev. J.S. Brown
1881 - 1885	Rev. J.S. Strong
1885 -	Rev. J.T. Browder (six months)
1885 - 1887	Rev. Jerry Davis
1887 - 1890	Rev. W.S. Ramsey
1890 - 1891	Rev. Jeremiah Jones
1891 - 1898	Rev. S.A. McNeal
1898 - 1899	Rev. Peter James Bryant, D.D.
1899 - 1902	Rev. C.H. Young
1902 - 1905	Rev. R.L. Darden
1905 - 1906	Rev. J.T. Latimer
1907 - 1913	Rev. J.M. Nabrit, D.D.
1913 - 1914	Rev. Hardy
1914 - 1915	Rev. Boliver Davis
1915 - 1916	Rev. W.C. Cartwright
1916 - 1929	Rev. W.M. Reddick, D.D.
1929 - 1930	Rev. J.L. Lomax
1930 - 1934	Rev. G.P. McKinney
1934 - 1939	Rev. P.H. Jackson
1941 - 1942	Rev. O.M. Collins
1942 -	Rev. L.B. Brown (until October, 1942)
1942 -	Rev. A.G. Davis (two months)
1943 - 1945	Rev. T.J. Pough

Rev. Robert L. Freeman was called to this pastorate in 1946. His thirty-four successive years are almost one-third of the church's life. He has broken all of his predecessors records. Only two others remained thirteen or more years, Rev. J.C. Bryan, eleven years, and Rev. M.W. Reddick, thirteen.

Pastor Freeman has made many significant contributions. Among the many milestones made, constructing an educational building. Recognizable, spiritual and civic guidance has been provided by him. He was one of the foremost civil rights leaders of the city during the height of the movement.

This church is affiliated with the Southwestern Georgia Missionary Baptist Association, General Missionary Baptist Convention of Georgia, Inc., National Baptist Convention, U.S.A., Inc.

Bibliography: Church history and records of the General Missionary Baptist Convention of Georgia, Inc.

FIRST AFRICAN BAPTIST CHURCH
DUBLIN, GEORGIA
1867

Assisted by the First Baptist Church (white), the First African Baptist Church was organized at its present location, on the corner of what is now known as Church and Telfair Streets, Dublin, Georgia.

Rejoicing over the opportunity to worship God under their own vine and fig tree, Rev. Fred Roberson was chosen as first pastor. Brothers George Washington, Callie Smith and Crawford were the first deacons. After Pastor Roberson's death, Rev. Samuel Reynolds succeeded him.

Under the pastorate of the third shepherd, Rev. N.G. McCall, the Sunday School was organized, with him being the Superintendent. During this administration the church became affiliated with the Missionary Baptist State Convention of Georgia.

After Rev. McCall's death, Rev. J.S.P. Watson was called to pastor, followed by Rev. S.D. Rozier, a possessor of spiritual power and social culture. The Sunday School was further developed and the foundation of the church was laid. After resigning to accept another charge, Rev. Boliver H. Davis assumed leadership. Adding dimensions to the Sunday School until its growth became the largest in the area. He is also accredited with the laying of the cornerstone. Rev. R.W. Walker became the next pastor, completing the present edifice. The present parsonage was constructed under Rev. P.W. Wrenn, the next pastor, who was an enviable spiritual leader and organizer. Rev. J.C. Adams became the next spiritual leader, utilizing the opportunity to display the ways of Christ through the examples of his life. His tenure ended with death.

Rev. C. Nathaniel Ellis, a native Tennessean, and graduate of Morehouse College, received the mantle during the lean years of the depression. He injected new life into many of the existing organizations, revived the membership and led the church to higher spiritual heights. Rev. J.C. Brown was inspirationally and spiritually enlightening, but only remained briefly because of his hunger for the academic setting of Benedict College. The services of Rev. I.S. Powell, Sr. was sought. He displayed great skills as an organizer, administrator, by organizing the Mission Circles, Matron's Club and Junior Missionary Department, both boys and girls, and purchasing the present pews. Rev. N.T. Young, the youthful spiritual son of Rev. C.N. Ellis, was given the staff of leadership. His commitment was felt by the total membership, and is remembered for purchasing the pulpit lectern, covering the floor, globes in the sanctuary and lighting throughout. Rev. T.T.R. Ball of Macon, Georgia was his successor, experiencing a brief pastorate, to be succeeded by Rev. E.L. Griffin, whose failing health prohibited him from serving long or fruitful.

A call was extended to Rev. E.J. Mason in December, 1950. His record reflects organizational skill shown by organizing the Junior Church leadership training, Trustee Board, the purchase of property adjacent to the church, and an electric Hammond organ. Plans for erecting an educational building, and playground instituted. Exterior and interior of the church decorated, safety wiring installed, and floor covering laid. He resigned on June 2, 1967.

A search was made for another pastor. A native of Florence, South Carolina, who had matriculated at Benedict College and Virginia Union Theological Seminary was found in the person of Rev. Hezekiah B. Johnson, Jr. He assumed his post after being called in November, 1967. He has organized the Junior Choir, Pulpit Aide, H.B. Johnson, Jr. Gospel Choir, Sunbeam Choir, Missionary Circle No. 3, Day Care Center, erected educational building, remodeled vestibule, renovated parsonage, and purchased fifteen acres of land.

Pastor Johnson has led the church to affiliate with the Second Rehoboth Association, the General Missionary Baptist Convention of Georgia, Inc., and the National Baptist Convention, U.S.A., Inc. He is the editor of *The Georgia Baptist* paper, the official organ of the State Convention.

First African Baptist Church of Dublin, Georgia is one of the brightest denominational lights of that area of our state.

Bibliography: Church history.

SPRINGFIELD BAPTIST CHURCH
WASHINGTON, GEORGIA
1868

This is the mother black Baptist Church of Washington, Wilkes County, Georgia. Organized in 1868. Rev. Lewis Williams was among her early pastors, if not the first.

Springfield was one of the early supporting churches of the Shiloh Baptist Association. Lent great support to the Shiloh Baptist Academy, influencing it greatly toward establishing the school in Washington.

Much support has been given the state convention by this church in the early years. In 1875, she hosted the Missionary Baptist State Convention. One of her sons, Edward James Grant was the Convention's president from 1971 to 1975.

Rev. J.P. Turner, Rev. J.H. Geer are some of the past pastors. Since 1962, Rev. Moses A. Lee has served as pastor. During his administration, the church has been remodeled, and an educational building constructed.

The church is affiliated with the Shiloh Baptist Association, and General Missionary Baptist Convention of Georgia, Inc.

Bibliography: Oral testimonies and convention minutes.

ANTIOCH BAPTIST CHURCH
LITHONIA, GEORGIA
1869

The oldest Black Baptist Church in DeKalb County, was organized in 1869, on what is now Covington Highway, with seven charter members. Rev. Matthew Mitchell was the first pastor, serving but one year.

Their first place of worship was a bush arbor, constructed at a cost of around two dollars and fifty cents, by a membership of twelve.

Rev. J.C. Center became pastor in 1870. Within two years, three acres of land where the church now stands, was purchased, for approximately one hundred and fifty dollars. This site is about one mile east of the initial place. Plans were made to erect a permanent building on the acquired land. Its construction cost was eight hundred dollars.

Pastor Center was among the first Moderators of the Atlanta Baptist Association. Before his demise in 1915, the foundation of the present structure was laid.

His successor was Rev. A.D. Williams, who completed the present edifice and increased the church membership. He is the grandfather of Dr. Martin Luther King, Jr.

Pastor Williams served from 1915 to 1919 and was succeeded by Rev. L.M. Glenn, whose pastorate was from 1919 to 1923, when he resigned to accept the call to pastor the First Bryan Baptist Church of Savannah, Georgia. Rev. A.D. Williams returned in 1924 to remain until 1926.

In 1927 a call to pastor was extended to Rev. J.T. Dorsey, one of the most gifted preachers of his day. He rendered efficient service until his health began to fail and his resignation was submitted in 1945.

The Corp of Gospel Ministers to serve since are:

1945 - 1948	Rev. A.G. Davis
1949 - 1953	Rev. O.L. Jackson
1953 - 1958	Rev. A.G. Belcher
1958 - 1978	Rev. Sim McIver
1978 -	Rev. Robert E. Glass

Antioch is affiliated with the Atlanta Baptist Association, General Missionary Baptist Convention of Georgia, Inc., and National Baptist Convention, U.S.A., Inc.

Bibliography: Church history.

Chapter 5

PROFILES OF BLACK GEORGIA BAPTIST
ASSOCIATIONS

An association is a group of Missionary Baptist Churches who have agreed to associate together for a common bond, usually missions, education, fellowship and upholding the doctrines of their persuasion.

The presider of the association is known as a Moderator. It usually has auxiliaries which are Women's Department, presided over by a President; and Sunday School and Baptist Training Union Congress, whose presider is a President, (originally called, Sunday School Convention; Baptist Training Union Convention) each had presidents. All of these are subject to the Moderator's directions.

Associations have no jurisdiction over the membership churches. Each Missionary Baptist Church is its own sovereign power and is governed only by its membership.

Many of the associations listed, existed prior to the organization of the Missionary Baptist Convention of Georgia. They were not a part of the organization of the state body and remained apart from it until the missionary preachers won their confidence. Others were organized after 1870, after converts were won to Christ, organized into Missionary Baptist Churches and subsequently into associations by the missionary preachers or through their influence.

These associations agreed to associate with the Missionary Baptist State Convention of Georgia and its successor, The General Missionary Baptist Convention of Georgia, Inc. to further perpetuate the Kingdom of God on earth. Likewise their association has been with the Foreign Mission Convention and its successor, The National Baptist Convention, U.S.A., Inc.

Their support and relationship with the state and national bodies is purely out of love, loyalty and denominational commitment. As the local church, the association is a democratic body and no outside body or individual has any jurisdiction over it.

Normally the association has certain bounds within a state. Sometimes its boundaries are geographical, bounded by rivers, county lines, mountain ranges or church composure, usually specified by the constitution.

Its purpose is further defined in the constitution. Most of the associations listed in this writing main objective was education. Many as you will see during their formative years, operated a school or joined with other associations in operating schools. After their schools were closed, they diverted their efforts toward scholarships. Their first move of course was to buy land to locate the school. Do not forget, some were just a matter of months removed from slavery, others a few years, but all less than a score. The founders and early leaders by the most part were unlearned, unlettered, uncultured - but determined. They knew God, and had faith.

Before the first building was constructed on the land for a school, the first teacher hired, the first students enrolled, valueable lessons were already taught. They taught their congregants and community to be industrious. They taught them self-confidence, not to doubt their abilities. They destroyed inhibitions and intimidations by instilling somebodiness. By the mere acquisition of land and initiating the endeavor to build a school.

Schools founded and operated by the associations were forerunners of public education for Blacks in Georgia and throughout the south. The student received Christian education and secular education. They learned to be good Christians, good Baptist and good Citizens, simultaneously.

With the loss of these denominational schools, our denomination, our Christian faith, our churches, our moral fibers have weakened. Those crude schools did not possess the light, glitter and beauty of many of the current educational plants, neither did they possess their sinful lust and darkness. Their teachers were committed to educate the students, they majored in quality education.

We have a rich legacy in our associations. The following represent a cross section of these associational bodies, that cover at least all of the regions of the state of Georgia. They represent in organization the immediate era after the Civil War. Only a few no longer exist, but all contributed greatly. Spiritually, Evangelistically, and Educationally toward the development of an undeveloped people, toward the freedom of a burdened people.

"And they were continually devoting themselves to the Apostles' **teaching** and to **fellowship**, to the **breaking of bread** and to **prayer**." Acts 2:32.

FIRST SHILOH MISSIONARY BAPTIST ASSOCIATION
1864

In 1864, a group of churches in the east central Georgia area united to form an association. They chose to name it, Shiloh Missionary Baptist Association.

By the mid 1870's, it had grown so large in numbers a large tent was required for satisfactory accommodations. Its boundaries had extended as far west as Walton, Barrow and Clarke counties, and as far north as Hall and Jackson counties.

It grew so large, members couldn't hear the speakers and didn't know each other. Because of this, many churches began pulling out in the 1870's to form other associations.

Seeing the need to educate their youth and others who hungered to feast from the table of knowledge, they operated a school, known as the Shiloh Baptist Academy, located in Washington, Wilkes County, Georgia.

Unfortunately, the names of the Moderator and charter officers, churches, and place of initial meeting are not available.

The present officers are holding the helm of responsibility, tenaciously and continue to stern her into the sea of fruitfulness. They are: Rev. Nathaniel Irvin, Moderator, Augusta, Georgia; Rev. C.W Huff, Vice Moderator, Atlanta, Georgia; Rev. C.I. Bennefield, Clerk, Midville, Georgia; Deacon C.L. Tapley, Assistant Clerk, Greensboro, Georgia; Rev. R.V. Sims, Chairman of Executive Board, Augusta, Georgia.

First Shiloh is a member of the General Missionary Baptist Convention of Georgia, Inc. and the National Baptist Convention, U.S.A., Inc.

Bibliography: Association minutes.

THOMASVILLE MISSIONARY BAPTIST ASSOCIATION 1865

Missionary Baptist churches of Brooks, Thomas and Lowndess counties organized the Thomasville Missionary Baptist Association in 1865. According to Article II of their constitution of 1922, their objective was to, "do missionary work and educational work. . .the cultivation of moral and fraternal union, the organization of new churches, the aiding of weak ones, the spreading of Bible principles, and the protection of the churches within its bounds".

The first annual session of the association met in Thomasville, Georgia at the First African Baptist Church in 1866. Rev. L. Blue preached the introductory sermon.

Rev. Jacob Ward was the first Moderator, serving until 1871. His successors are Rev. Charles Anderson, 1872-1873; Rev. John Thornton, 1874-1877; Rev. E. Forest, 1878-1883; Rev. N.W. Waterman, 1884-1887; Rev. G.L. Taylor, 1888-1894; Rev. E. Forest, 1895-1898; Rev. M. Young, 1899; Rev. S.S. Broadnax, 1900-1944; Rev. I.E. Washington, 1945. Other Moderators were Rev. J.J. Strickland; Rev. A.B. Sanders and the present Moderator, Rev. E.S. Sheffield, Pastor of Providence Baptist Church, Thomasville, Georgia.

Thomasville never operated a school according to reliable sources, but as indicated in the constitution, they have always had a strong commitment to education. They have been a very strong supporter toward the operation and projects of renovation, furnishings of the existing buildings and contributing toward the building now under construction, at Bryant Theological Seminary in Fitzgerald, Georgia, the main objective of the Convention.

Its affiliations are the General Missionary Baptist Convention of Georgia, Inc. and National Baptist Convention, U.S.A., Inc.

Bibliography: Association minutes and oral information.

ZION MISSIONARY BAPTIST ASSOCIATION
1865

On July 14, 1865, Rev. John Cox, Pastor of Second African Baptist Church of Savannah, Georgia; Rev. Ulyses L. Houston, Pastor of First Bryan Baptist Church, Savannah, Georgia; and two other pastors from churches in Savannah, and three from South Carolina, met at Hilton Head Island, South Carolina to organize an association.

Rev. John Cox, Pastor of Second Baptist Church in Savannah was elected first Moderator, Brother K.S. Thomas, Clerk, Rev. U.L. Houston, Treasurer. Rev. Houston presided until the officers were elected and then preached the first sermon. His text was Exodus 33:14, "My presence shall go with thee, and I will give three rest".

First African Baptist Church of Savannah hosted the first session of the association, July 13, 1866. The second session met in Florida. For a period of time churches in three states were members of this association until the churches in South Carolina withdrew to organize their own association. As late as 1942 there were still churches from Florida represented.

Zion's geographical range now runs along the eastern seaboard, from Brunswick to Savannah encompassing the following counties, Chatham, Bryan, Liberty, Glynn, McIntosh, Camden, Charlton, and Wayne.

Rev. J.F. Mann of Brunswick, Georgia is the current Moderator and has served for many years. This association holds membership in the General Missionary Baptist Convention of Georgia, Inc. and the National Baptist Convention, U.S.A., Inc.

Bibliography: Association minutes and **First Colored Baptist Church in North America**, J.M. Simms.

MIDDLE GEORGIA MISSIONARY BAPTIST ASSOCIATION
1868

In 1845, the Ebenezer Baptist Association (white), whose boundaries were Jones, Baldwin, Washington, Johnson, Laurens, Bleckley, Peach, Bibb, Twiggs and Wilkinson counties, appointed a committee to consider educating slaves.

Teaching blacks to read or write, free or slave, was a violation of the Georgia law and punishable by fines or imprisonment. This committee reported back to the association with a recommendation that all ministers, who were members of the association, spend a part of Sunday afternoons on their appointment days, with special religious instructions for the Negroes belonging to their congregants.

Many, who received this religious training, were converted and became members of the churches of their masters. Some became deacons assigned to the Black members, others were called to preach.

Some churches were organized for Blacks in this area during the Civil War. Others were organized by Blacks after the Civil War. A few retained membership in the churches of the Ebenezer Baptist Association until they were encouraged to withdraw their membership.

Around 1868, some of the pastors of the Ebenezer Baptist Association, assisted the Black pastors and lay people in organizing an association. It became known as the Middle Georgia Missionary Baptist Association.

The Ebenezer Baptist Association manifested an interest in the development of the Middle Georgia Association. In 1870, they invited Brother Powell Thompson of the Middle Georgia, to present to them such things of interest of his association they would consider proper. Whether Brother Thompson was a clergyman or layman is unknown.

Middle Georgia in the outset, at least covered the same geographical outlay as the Ebenezer Baptist Association.

Middle Georgia Orthodox Association as it is known, is a member of the General Missionary Baptist Convention of Georgia, Inc. and the National Baptist Convention, U.S.A., Inc. Rev. Marshell Stinson is current Moderator. His immediate predecessor was Rev. E.S. Evans.

Bibliography: Minutes of Ebenezer Baptist Association.

WALKER BAPTIST ASSOCIATION
1868

Seven churches, all under ten years old except one, met in the fall of 1868 in Burke County, Georgia to organize an association. This organization did not take place in a town or city, but in the rural. All of the constituents were rural people without any formal training, most could neither read nor write.

Although they were unlettered, they placed a high value on scholarship. They desired to learn more, but especially wanted their young to receive the best education possible. Scholars were also welcomed in their ranks and would be utilized to enable them to reach their goals.

The veil of their illiteracy did not rob them of hope to establish a school that would enlighten the future of their off-springs.

Their endeavor to organize an association was not in vengeance, neither were they alone. Their white Christian brothers, former church members and former pastors joined them. Most had been members of churches with mixed membership. After the Civil War, the blacks willfully withdrew their membership, without requesting any portion of the property. Their only request was for their white Christian brothers to help them organize their own churches, teach them in areas needed, and counsel them when called upon. The whites agreed to this.

The blacks had held membership in the Hephzibah Association. Members of this association were present at Ways Grove Baptist Church, Stellaville, Georgia in the fall of 1868 to help organize an association. Rev Joseph Walker, the first black pastor of the mixed membership, Franklin Covenant Baptist Church, was honored to have the association named after him. He was held in high esteem among whites and blacks, having served as a deacon of this church before being called to preach. After his ordination into the gospel ministry, the church called him as pastor in 1861.

This display of Christian brotherhood, fellowship and unity gave birth to the Walker Baptist Association. Like the seven churches of Asia Minor, she had her seven, namely, Ways Grove Baptist Church, Stellaville, Georgia, Rev. Alford Young was the first pastor of which knowledge is obtainable. He was probably the pastor at this time. Franklin Covenant Baptist Church, Hephzibah, Rev. Joseph Walker, pastor; Smith Grove Baptist Church, Noah, Rev. Alford Young, pastor; McKinnie Branch, McBean, Rev. Peter Walker, pastor; Hopeful Baptist Church, Burke County; Springfield Baptist Church, Jefferson County, Rev. Peter Walker, pastor.

The first officers were Rev. Peter Walker, Moderator, Brother Edward Young, Clerk, and Brother Charles Young, Treasurer. Rev. Peter Walker served only one year as moderator, declining to serve in 1869 in favor of his senior, Rev. Nathan Walker.

Walker Baptist Association's roots were planted deep in the fertile soils of Jefferson, Burke and Richmond Counties, of which the original seven churches were located. These roots rapidly spread into the soils of Jenkins, Screven, Emanuel, Johnson and Columbia Counties.

Although located in east Georgia, these early founders were determined not to be enslaved to geographical boundaries. Their influence and effectiveness was to transcend into the four corners of the world. After this association's roots were deeply anchored into the soil its growth was evidenced above the soil, branches spread in all directions with full foliage. Its seeds were scattered and they reproduced, more believers in Christ, churches, preachers and pastors.

Ten years later in 1878, the first dollar was given toward the school of which they labored and hoped for. This was the year the annual session met at Franklin Covenant Baptist Church in Hephzibah. Harper Grove Baptist Church sent twenty-five cents by their pastor, Rev. James Kelsey, along with Murphy Ebenezer, twenty-five cents by their pastor, Rev. J.C. Kelley, and Kelsey Chapel sent fifty cents by their pastors, Rev. James Kelsey. Thus one dollar was given to begin a school.

Three years later, this dollar having grown to a sufficient amount, inspired others and stirred momentum, that the Walker Baptist Institute was opened in Waynesboro, Georgia in 1881. Thomas Grove Baptist Church opened their doors, to house this beginning institution, where the sons and daughters of the Walker

Baptist Association would learn reading, writing and arithmetic. Professor H.B. Garvin was principal, assisted by Professor P.C. Watts and Miss M.A. Grant. The school term was for only three months. Rev. Nathan Walker was moderator when this was initiated.

Eighteen years after the Emancipation Proclamation, sixteen years after the close of the Civil War, thirteen years after the organization of the association, four years after the federal troups were ordered out of the south to protect the rights of blacks and reconstruction ended, these former slaves began a school. No greater testimony could be given of God caring for His own when they have faith and are faithful in their service to Him than this.

They were unselfishly selfish. They were not selfish to the extent they felt everyone should go to Walker Baptist Institute, but they were selfish to the degree they felt all Baptist children should go to a Baptist school or not any at all. A committee's report at their 1890 annual session best reflects how they felt. "We urge our people to send their girls to Spelman, as it costs but little more than it does to send them to schools of other denominations. If the children are educated in these schools, they will make very poor Baptists, if Baptists at all. We further urge our people to secure, if possible, Baptist teachers in their schools. Better not be educated at all than to be educated wrong".

Some of Walker Baptist Association and Walker Baptist Institute's reknown and respected products are Charles Thomas Walker, known as the "Black Spurgeon". Roman John Johnson, preacher, pastor, administrator, educator and author. Silas X. Floyd, educator, administrator, author, whose literary abilities were sought by national periodicals in the early years of the twentieth century. Some being *Sunday School Times, The International Evangel, The New York Independent, Lippincott's Magazine, The World's Work, The New York Herald, The Southern Workman,* and *The Augusta Sentinnel* of which he was editor. William Gilbert Johnson, preacher, organizer, traveler, scholar, Baptist leader, state and national, educator and church builder. All of whom were born within the geographical boundaries of the association. Early they were influenced in Christian belief, training and service in their local churches. They were sent by their churches as youths to the Walker Baptist Association. Almost from its inception they were a part of the Walker Baptist Institute. At one time, all of them pastored in the Walker Baptist Association, making a tremendous contribution toward her development.

Today the Walker Baptist Association is very much alive and flourishing, under the capable, forthright leadership of Moderator J.S. Wright, pastor of the Macedonia Baptist Church, on Lacey-Walker Boulevard, Augusta, Georgia. Under his leadership, ten acre tract of land has just been purchased. Their intent is to broaden the scope of Christian service. Through developing this land, the association will further be developed.

Rev. Wright holds many distinctions, having preached during the 96th Annual session of the National Baptist Convention, U.S.A., Inc. in Dallas, Texas. Currently he is president of the Augusta Baptist Minister's Conference, Treasurer of the Congress of Christian Education of the General Missionary Baptist Convention of Georgia, Inc., and member of the Convention's Executive Board. He serves in many other areas of civic and Christian efforts.

Many others whose names were not mentioned made an indelible contribution toward this association's development, growth and outreach during its one hundred and twelve years of existence. They remain alive as long as their influence continues to inspire. Walker Baptist Association is and will always be, because they have a mind to serve.

"So, we built the wall and the whole wall was joined together to half its height, for the people had a mind to work". Nehemiah 4:6.

Bibliography: History of **Walker Baptist Association,** written by Roman J. Johnson, 1908.

WESTERN UNION BAPTIST ASSOCIATION
1868

The Western Union Baptist Association takes in Coweta, Troup, Merriweather, Harris, and Heard counties. Baptist churches in these counties met in 1868 to organize an association.

Rev. J. Freeman was elected first Moderator, serving until 1870. His successors were: Rev. Charles Scott, 1871-1874; Rev. T.H. Sims, 1875-1880; Rev. C.T. Walker, 1881; Rev. J.H. Level, 1882; Rev. T.H. Sims, 1883-1884; Rev. E.J. Fisher, 1885-1887; Rev. P.M. Mobley, 1888-1891; Rev. E.J. Fisher, 1892-1896; Rev. J.W. Gore, 1898-1913; Rev. W.J. Smith, 1914-1940; Rev. W.C. Amos, 1941-1947; Rev. Tom Davidson, 1948-1978. Rev. C.R. Sheridan became Moderator in 1979, and still serves.

Western Union has made provisions for scholarships for what they determined as worthy students. Nominal contributions have been given to educational institutions.

This association is a member of the General Missionary Baptist Convention of Georgia, Inc. and the National Baptist Convention, U.S.A., Inc.

Bibliography: Association minutes.

CABIN CREEK BAPTIST ASSOCIATION
1869

This association was organized in 1869, probably somewhere in Henry County. Possibly one of the churches at either Locust Grove or McDonough, Georgia, in as much as the Cabin Creek runs in this area. It was their custom during this time to name churches and associations after creeks and rivers, and their boundaries be drawn from the same.

Its first Moderator or officers are unknown. Some of the Moderators during the Twentieth Century have been Rev. John Henry Moore, Rev. I.S. Mack, Rev. Adam M. Reeves, Rev. H.M. Alexander, and presently, Rev. W.M. Willis.

This association operated a very prominent school, known as the Cabin Creek Baptist Association School. Many of its graduates went on to higher education and achievements. Such as medical doctors, preachers, lawyers, politicians, school teachers, college presidents and good Christian citizens.

Originally her boundaries included Henry, Spalding Pike, Lamar, Upson, and Merriweather counties. There are churches in Fulton, DeKalb and Clayton counties that are members now.

Cabin Creek holds membership in the General Missionary Baptist Convention of Georgia, Inc. and the National Baptist Convention, U.S.A., Inc.

Bibliography: Minutes and conversations.

SOUTHWESTERN GEORGIA BAPTIST ASSOCIATION
1869

A number of churches in Dougherty, Sumter, Macon, Randolph, Early, Calhoun, Quitman, Terrell, Schley and Taylor Counties united to form an association in 1869. The name chosen was Southwestern Georgia Baptist Association.

The place of their first meeting was unavailable for this writing. Their first written record begins in 1871 at Jackson Grove Baptist Church in Dougherty County. Rev. D. Hines was Moderator.

Early in the association's operation, the administration recognized the importance of operating a school. It was located in Americus, Georgia, and was known as Americus Baptist Institute.

Rev. D. Hines was the first Moderator, serving until 1879; Rev. George Jones, 1881-1885; Rev. L.B. Simpson 1886-1892; Rev. A.W. Williamson, 1893-1897; Rev. R. Monson, 1898-1908; Rev. A.S. Staley, 1909-1925; Rev. S.J. Lane, 1926-1929; Rev. A.J. Allen, 1930-1941; Rev. R.H. Shepherd, 1942-1958; Rev. W.B. Mathis, 1959-1970. The present Moderator, Rev. W.D. Hatchett, was elected in 1971.

Although the association no longer operates a school, it contributes very heavily to educational institutions and scholarships.

Southwestern Georgia Baptist Association is one of the consistent contributors to the Bryant Theological Seminary, the main objective of the General Missionary Baptist Convention of Georgia, Inc.

This body is a member of the General Missionary Baptist Convention of Georgia, Inc. and the National Baptist Convention, U.S.A., Inc.

Bibliography: Minutes of the association.

FIRST NORTH GEORGIA MISSIONARY BAPTIST ASSOCIATION
1870

This body was located in northwest Georgia, covering the entire region. It was organized in 1870 with Rev. G.W. Wheeler as first Moderator; Rev. A.B. Nichols, First Vice Moderator; Deacon A.B. Nichols, Secretary; Professor W.F. Wheeler, Corresponding Secretary; and Deacon G.W. Salmon, Treasurer.

Immediately after organization, they got under way with missionary endeavors. These Nineteenth Century preachers and lay people traveled throughout the northwest Georgia mountains to all the communities, preaching and witnessing in the name of Jesus. Many converts were won to Christ, and churches were organized.

Within five years, after the association was organized, it had grown to such a capacity, both numerically and geographically, to be effective another association was needed. Thus came to birth in 1875, the North Georgia General Missionary Baptist Association.

Bibliography: History of North Georgia General Missionary Baptist Association's Centennial History.

MOUNT CALVARY MISSIONARY
BAPTIST ASSOCIATION
1870

Hamilton, Georgia is about twenty miles north of Columbus. This is where the Mount Calvary Baptist Association was organized, at the Friendship Baptist Church. Rev. E.B. Rucker, preached the introductory sermon. He holds the distinction of preaching the introductory sermon of the Missionary Baptist State Convention the same year. Rev. N.W. Ashurst, preached the Missionary sermon.

Rev. E.B. Rucker was elected the first Moderator and Rev. W. Brookins, Clerk. They only served one year, 1870 to 1871. The succeeding Moderators are:

1871 - 1872	Rev. N.W. Ashurst
1873 - 1876	Rev. Green McArthur
1877 -	Rev. D. Griffin
1878 - 1883	Rev. Green McArthur
1884 - 1884	Rev. H.O. Jackson
1885 - 1886	Rev. Green McArthur
1886 - 1887	Rev. Z.A. Jones
1887 - 1890	Rev. O.H. Jackson
1891 - 1894	Rev. Green McArthur
1895 - 1926	Rev. W.R. Forbes
1927 - 1940	Rev. Tom Simpson
1940 - 1949	Rev. J.H. Carter
1949 - 1966	Rev. S.A. Harvey
1966 - 1978	Rev. R.C. Gates

Rev. John Parkman, Pastor of Rose Hill Baptist Church of Columbus, Georgia, is the present Moderator, and is providing wholesome leadership to this body.

Mount Calvary covers the Chattahoochee Valley on the extreme western boundaries of the state. Most of the representing churches are in Muscogee County and a few in Harris County.

This association is affiliated with the General Missionary Baptist Convention of Georgia, Inc. and the National Baptist Convention, U.S.A., Inc.

Bibliography: History of Association and minutes of General Missionary Baptist Convention of Georgia, Inc.

NEW HOPE MISSIONARY
BAPTIST ASSOCIATION
1873

Rev. Richard Hern Burson was born in Morgan County, Georgia in May, 1840, to Matilda Sheets on Elijah Maddox's plantation; later to be sold to Seaborn Burson of DeKalb County.

He was converted to Christianity in 1865 and baptized by Rev. William Henry Strickland into the Salem Baptist Church in Gwinnett County, Georgia.

On December 14, 1873, Rev. Andrew Jackson, Pastor of Wheat Street Baptist Church, Rev. Thomas M. Allen, Pastor of Zion Baptist Church, Marietta, Georgia, and Rev. Matthew Mitchell ordained him into the gospel ministry.

This pioneer preacher pastored Hopewell Baptist Church, Norcross, Georgia; Bethlehem Baptist Church, Atlanta, Georgia; Bethsada Baptist Church, Stone Mountain, Georgia. For a number of years, he was engaged in missionary work, before being appointed missionary for the Missionary Baptist State Convention by Dr. C.H. Lyons, Corresponding Secretary.

While serving as a voluntary missionary in 1873, he was one of the founders of the New Hope Missionary Baptist Association. Churches located in Fulton, DeKalb and Cobb counties comprised its early membership.

Macedonia Baptist Church, Atlanta; Antioch Baptist Church, Atlanta; Mount Calvary Baptist Church, Adamsville; Second Mount Olive Baptist Church, Atlanta; Zion Baptist Church, Scott's Crossing; First Baptist Church, Reynoldstown; Zion Baptist Church, Marietta; Traveler's Rest Baptist Church, Edgewood; St. John Baptist Church, Adamsville; Mount Vernon Baptist Church, Atlanta; Springfield Baptist Church, Atlanta were among the early churches that made up her membership.

Rev. Cyrus Brown, Pastor of Macedonia Baptist Church was one of the early Moderators. Others to serve were Rev. J.W. Williams, Rev. E.D. Florence, Rev. G.W. Jordan, Rev. Andrew Bell, and Rev. Roy W. Williams.

Its objectives were to carry the gospel of Jesus Christ. Though it operated no school, educational contributions were made to students and institutions.

Bibliography: Associational minutes and files of Dr. D.D. Crawford, Executive Secretary of the General Missionary Baptist Convention of Georgia, Inc.

NORTH GEORGIA GENERAL MISSIONARY BAPTIST ASSOCIATION
1875

A group of pastors and churches withdrew from the First North Georgia Missionary Baptist Association in 1875 because it had grown so large, numerically and geographically. They met difficulty in traveling. Once there, found it difficult to enjoy the closeness of Christian fellowhsip.

They chose the name for their new organization, North Georgia General Missionary Baptist Association. Rev. W.J. White was elected first Moderator. Rev. C.H. Richardson was elected first Secretary.

Moderator W.J. White served from 1875 to 1924. His successor was Rev. J.L. Vaughn, Pastor of Lovejoy Baptist Church, Rome, Georgia. Rev. Vaughn also served as president of the Moderators Auxiliary of the National Baptist Convention, U.S.A., Inc. for a number of years. His tenure as Moderator was from 1925 to 1972. Rev. Clarence Tuggle, Pastor of Thankful Baptist Church, Rome, Georgia was elected Moderator in 1972, serving until his departure as pastor of Thankful Baptist Church. Rev. Calhoun Sims was elected Moderator in 1976, becoming the youngest person ever to be elected as leader of this historic association.

Under W.J. White's administration, a parcel of land was purchased on Blossom Hill in Rome, to operate a school. Rev. J.H. Gadson was chosen as first principal and the school got under way as Rome High and Industrial School. It became possible for Black youths of that region of the state to have an opportunity for education.

Its missionary outreach continued, lending greatly toward the spiritual development of all people within her bounds.

North Georgia General Missionary Baptist Association is a member of the General Missionary Baptist Convention of Georgia, Inc. and the National Baptist Convention, U.S.A., Inc.

Bibliography: Centennial Souvenir Book.

FLINT RIVER MISSIONARY BAPTIST ASSOCIATION
1876

Somewhere in Decatur County, Georgia in 1876 the Flint River Missionary Baptist Association was organized. Unfortunately little was written about it in those early years.

For a number of years, this association operated the Flint River School, later named, Union Normal School, in Bainbridge, Georgia. Rev. H.F. Taylor who pastored the First African Baptist Church of Bainbridge, was its first president. Rev. James Graves was his successor. In September 1927, Professor H.S. Dixon became the president and remained until 1952 when it merged with the Hutto High School of the Decatur County Board of Education.

After the discontinuance of the school the association's educational emphasis was directed to scholarships. When the centennial was observed in 1976, more than twenty-three thousand dollars had been given in scholarships since its inception.

The following are a list of her known Moderators: Rev. L. Montgomery, Rev. Jack Warren, Rev. Paul White, Rev. Ned Brock, Rev. I.C. Williams, Rev. S.D. Hopson, Rev. W.J. Jackson, Rev. J.L. Huffom, Rev. V.H. Donehoe, Rev. R.O. Glover. Rev. H.B. Jeffery now serves as Moderator.

This association's bounds are Decatur, Seminole, and Mitchell counties. Its affiliations are the General Missionary Baptist Convention of Georgia, Inc. and the National Baptist Convention, U.S.A., Inc.

Bibliography: Centennial Souvenir Book.

FRIENDSHIP MISSIONARY BAPTIST ASSOCIATION
1877

This association takes in the area west of Atlanta, portions of Cobb, Paulding, Douglas and Carroll counties.

Its membership was never large, because of the area it covers, until recently it had a sparse black population.

In 1877, it was organized by some of the key preachers and lay people of that region. Its purpose being no less than all of the other associations and churches given birth during that time, by the Black Baptist Missionary preachers. To win the lost to Christ and enlighten the minds of their people.

Bibliography: Association minutes.

NORTHWESTERN MISSIONARY
BAPTIST ASSOCIATION
1877

Nine churches organized by Rev. Green Hunter, formerly held membership in the Stone Mountain Baptist Association, withdrew to organize the Northwestern Baptist Association. The first Moderator was a resident of Gainesville, Georgia, organizing some twenty-nine churches in all, throughout northeast Georgia during his lifetime.

An attempt was made to establish a school in Gainesville in 1883. This initial effort failed, because of unenlightenment on the part of the people.

Moderator Hunter served until 1908 and was succeeded by Rev. Harrison Vincent. Green Hunter became Chairman of the Building Committee to build a school. The association was receiving from four to six-hundred dollars annually. Land was purchased in Gainesville on what is now Myrtle Street, and the school was opened in 1911 and named Northwestern Baptist School. Its operation was terminated in the late 1950's.

Rev. Harrison Vincent was a farmer, owning some eight hundred acres of land. He often mortgaged his total acreage so the school could operate. He served faithfully until his death in 1946. The next Moderator was Rev. Hosea H. Fortson, Pastor of St. John Baptist Church, Gainesville, Georgia. He served from 1947 to 1956, until his death.

In 1957, Rev. E.T. Smith, Pastor of New Salem Baptist Church in Jackson County, became Moderator. With the demise of the school, Moderator Smith established a scholarship fund for worthy college and technical school students, who are members of membership churches. In excess of three thousand dollars is given to scholarships annually.

A monument was erected during the centennial celebration on the remaining associational property in Gainesville, in memoriam of the three past Moderators and in recognition of the present Moderator.

Northwestern Missionary Baptist Association holds membership in the General Missionary Baptist Convention of Georgia, Inc. and the National Baptist Convention, U.S.A., Inc.

Bibliography: *Life and Times of Green Hunter,* and Centennial Book of this association.

NORTHWESTERN BAPTIST ASSOCIATION NO. I
1877

Rev. Charles Thomas Veal was born in Madison, Georgia, August 20, 1852 to Cope Veal and Annie Thomason. His mother was owned by P.R. Thomason, and his father was a boarder in the home of his master.

After leaving home, at fourteen years old, and hiring out at fifty dollars a year, he was priviledged to study at night under Miss Lera Lanier. For one term, he was a student at Atlanta Baptist Seminary, studying under Dr. Grave. When seventeen, he departed Madison to reside in Athens, Georgia and gained employment as a general laborer.

He accepted Christ in 1875 and joined Hills First Baptist Church and was called to preach almost immediately. His pastor, Rev. Floyd Hill, licensed and ordained him. Within three years of his call to the ministry, Pierce Chapel Baptist Church of Clarke County called him as pastor, followed by Shady Grove Baptist Church, Watkinsville, Georgia; Sprey Creek Baptist Church, Green County and Mount Sinai Baptist Church, Bogart, Georgia.

The Shiloh Baptist Association had grown to such proportions geographically which caused its members to travel so far, and so large numerically a large tent was needed for services. Hearing the speakers became difficult for those at a distance. Members who lived in the Northwestern part of the associational boundaries withdrew and formed the Northwestern Baptist Association.

62

One group wanted Rev. Green Hunter of Gainesville to serve as Moderator, another group wanted Rev. C.T. Veal to serve as Moderator. This was solved by Rev. Green Hunter organizing the Northwestern Baptist Association No. II with the number later being dropped. Rev. C.T. Veal became Moderator of Northwestern Baptist Association No. 1.

This association was supported spiritually and financially by her membership churches. As he traveled throughout the associational region, Moderator Veal saw the need for an associational school. Passing his feelings on to the members, soon Northwestern Association No. 1 made plans to organize, Northwestern High School in Monroe, Georgia. During the February 1910 term of Walton County Superior Court, Rev. C.T. Veal, H.H. Haygood, Robert Moncrief, Joe Moncrief, I.J. Jackson, and G.W. Williams were instrumental in a charter for the school being granted.

Rev. E.J. Thompson of Gainesville, Georgia, was the first principal, serving from 1910 to 1917. With a years absence in 1918 to serve as chaplain in the United States Army in 1918, he returned to serve until 1921.

When the association convened with the Macedonia Baptist Church in Monroe, Georgia, in 1921, Rev. W.M. Jackson ran against Rev. Veal. Rev. Veal won by five votes. Keeping a promise made earlier in the association's life, that if any man ever ran against him, even if he won, he would step down. Rev. Veal is reported to have said, "Boys, I am a man to my word. I said when you got tired of me and run someone against me, I would step down, even if I won. So I am stepping down."

Rev. W.M. Jackson became the second Moderator, remaining only one year. Rev. Robert Moncrief was elected the third Moderator in 1922 at the Mount Enon Baptist Church in Monroe, Georgia.

Because of the approaching depression, they were forced to close the school and merge with ten other associations in 1927 to operate the Jeruel High School in Athens, Georgia, later to be named Union Baptist High School. This school had been organized in 1881. Rev. J.H. Brown was its first headmaster and served until 1921. His successor was Professor C.H.S. Lyons, who served until death. Clarke County eventually took over the school and Rev. J.H. Geer became the first principal and remained until consolidation. The land was eventually sold to the University of Georgia, and though once owned by blacks until the early 1960's, they were prohibited by law to attend the university. The proceeds from the sale was used to build the Union Baptist Center in Madison, Georgia, co-owned and operated with the First Shiloh Baptist Association.

Another opportunity was given in 1934, to elect a Moderator. They wanted one with training and the ability to lead them during the crucial times. Rev. Hampton C. Moon was chosen as their fourth leader, until 1937. An apparent lack of appreciation for educated people developed, and Rev. Robert Moncrief was elected for his second time, to serve until his death in 1939.

There were two pastors contending for the moderatorship in 1940, Vice Moderator, Rev. W.M. Mitchell and Rev. E.D. Thomas, Pastor of Shady Grove Baptist Church of Watkinsville, Georgia. Rev. Thomas was elected, becoming the sixth Moderator but fifth man. He immediately encouraged the association to establish a scholarship fund to assist boys and girls pursuing a higher education. He lived to see the association give one thousand dollar scholarships in 1977. Before his death three thousand, eight hundred and seventy-five dollars were given to thirty-one students for scholarships. Rev. Thomas was Moderator until January, 1979.

Rev. J.H. Geer of Athens, Georgia is the present Moderator, and the association continues in the service of the Lord.

This association is a member of the General Missionary Baptist Convention of Georgia, Inc. and the National Baptist Convention, U.S.A., Inc.

Bibliography: Centennial Souvenir Book.

JERUEL BAPTIST ASSOCIATION
1879

A group of Baptist churches in Clarke, Elbert, Greene, Jackson, Oconee, Madison and Oglethorpe counties, formed an association in 1879. They named it Jeruel Baptist Association.

Although many of the churches were located within the shadow of the University of Georgia in Athens, many of their members were upstanding taxpaying citizens. A number of them were connected with the university; by employment or worked for people who had contact there. They and their offsprings were prohibited, by law to attend because of the pigmentation of their skin.

They were also forbidden to attend the schools of their community. They refused to stand by idly and allow their young to grow up in an informed world, in academic darkness.

Their purpose of uniting in the Jeruel Association was for strength to meet their purposes. Their purpose of tearing down the walls of oppression. To win the lost to Christ. To educate their young.

In 1881, two years after they organized their association, the Jeruel Baptist Association School was opened in Athens, Georgia. In 1924 it was consolidated, when the following associations pooled their financial resources: Atlanta, Carrollton, Union, Jeruel, Kennesaw, Madison, Northwestern No. 1, Savannah River, Shiloh, Union Middle River, Yellow River and the General Missionary Baptist Convention of Georgia, Inc. It became known as the Union Baptist High School. In 1927, Union became an accredited High School.

Bibliography: Associational minutes, General Missionary Baptist Convention minutes and records, **The Rugged Pathway,** Beulah Rucker Oliver, author.

Chapter 6
MISSIONARY BAPTIST CONVENTION OF GEORGIA
1870

Augusta, Georgia was the Black Baptist Citadel in 1870, having at least ten churches in the city, that many if not more in Richmond County. The adjoining counties were well populated with churches also. There were at least two associations, whose bounds covered this area, Walker and Ebenezer. Plus one of the first denominational schools, Augusta Baptist College was domiciled there. This city was accessible from any part of the state by rail, it was a transportation center of that day.

No wonder it was chosen for the convening place for Black Baptist pastors and delegates from their churches to assemble on May 13, 1870, at the Central Baptist Church, Rev. Henry Jackson, Pastor. Their purpose was to organize a state convention. The name, Missionary Baptist Convention of Georgia was chosen. Rev. E.B. Rucker of Columbus, Georgia, preached the Convention sermon, selecting II Peter 2:1-3 as his text.

This message, burned into their hearts with such deep convictions their convention's main objective would be to establish churches and Sunday Schools throughout the state and promote theological education. Therefore, they drew up the constitution to read:

1. To employ missionaries to travel through the waste places of our State, and gather the people and preach the gospel to them, and aid them in every way possible, and especially in organizing Churches and Sunday Schools.

2. To establish a Theological institute, for the purpose of educating young men and those who are preaching the gospel and have the ministry view, or any of our brethren's sons that sustain a good moral character, and to procure immediately, some central place in Georgia, for the establishment of same.[1]

Rev. Frank Quarles, Pastor of Friendship Baptist Church in Atlanta, Georgia was chosen as first President. Rev. George H. Dwelle of Augusta was first Corresponding Secretary.

President Quarles and others fulfilled their commitment of organizing churches. No less than five were organized by him during his eleven years as the leader of this organization in the Atlanta area.

Their Sunday School Convention was organized and by 1877, two hundred such schools had been organized with one thousand teachers and fourteen thousand students.

In 1881, two years after it moved from Augusta to Atlanta, Atlanta Baptist Seminary had eighty students, fifty of which were aspirants for the Gospel Ministry. It is estimated there were around eight hundred and fifty black ministers in the state at this time.

---

[1]Constitution of the Missionary Baptist Convention of Georgia.

It must be noted there was a fraternal Christian relationship between this group and its white counterpart, Georgia Baptist Conventon, the Northern Home Mission Society and Home Mission Society of New York.

Emanuel King Love, who was then employed by the American Baptist Publication Society of Philadelphia, Pennsylvania, in an executive board meeting in Milledgeville, Georgia apprized them of the approaching centennial of the Black Baptist Church in Georgia, and offered a resolution to celebrate it in 1888. In the annual session in Cartersville, Georgia in May, 1885, the following committee was appointed to prepare for a notable celebration: Revs. W.J. White, J.C. Bryan, E.K. Love, G.H. Dwelle, C.T. Walker, C.H. Lyons, E.R. Carter, T.M. Robinson, S.A. McNeal and Deacon J. H. Brown.

This committee seemed to have been given a large degree of freedom, or because of its powerful composure took it. J.C. Bryan was elected traveling agent; W.J. White, compiler; E.R. Carter and J.H. Brown, Gathers of historic facts; and E.K. Love, Editor-in -Chief. When the Convention met in Brunswick in 1887, all of the Moderators of associations who were members of the Convention were added, totaling around fifty.

During this same session, the Program Committee was appointed. The members were: Revs. Alexander Harris, Chairman, W.J. White, E:K. Love, J.M. Simms, O. Waters, J.C. Bryan, U.L. Houston, C.T. Walker, E.R. Carter, S.A. McNeal and Deacon J.H. Brown.

First Bryan Baptist Church of Savannah, contending to be the oldest church, because of its occupancy on the original grounds invited the Convention to meet with them during the Centennial. Their invitation was rejected and First African of Savannah became the host church.

When the State Convention met in May, 1888, in Brunswick, Georgia, Rev. W.S. Ramsey of Columbus, Georgia, motioned that since the Centennial in June of 1888 must be held in recognition of one of the oldest churches in Savannah, First African Baptist, Franklin Square or First Bryan Baptist, Bryan Street, Yamacraw, a committee of brethren be appointed, before whom, both claimants should appear with documents, in order for the right church to be determined. The motion was carried, and such a committee was appointed, of the following persons: Revs. E.M. Simmons, Stone Mountain, Chairman; E.J. Fisher, LaGrange; W.S. Ramsey, Columbus; N.B. Williamson, Quitman; H.B. Hamilton, Walthourville; S.A. McNeal, Augusta; and C.H. Brighthard, Milledgeville.

On June 6, 1888, one hundred years, five months, and sixteen days after the First Black Baptist church was organized on Georgia soil, Baptist of color began one of the most elaborate celebrations experienced before or since, almost within shadows of where the First Church was organized.

A large tent was erected on the Fairgrounds, the only means available to accommodate the people. All of the sessions were held here. Many organizations and churches had booths. This was a jubilee to recount, the founding and development of the First Colored Baptist Church and its subsequent growth into a militant denomination, state, national and international.

The committee's announcement and invitation below portrays its importance, the widespread participation depicts the caliber of State and National denominational leaders attracted.

Baptist Centennial 1888
Centennial Celebration of The Negro
Baptists of Georgia. To be held in
Savannah, Georgia. Commencing
Wednesday, June 6, and Closing
Monday, June 18, 1888

Committee: Rev. Alexander Harris, Chairman, Savannah, Georgia; Rev. U.L. Houston, Savannah, Georgia; Rev. J.M. Simms, Savannah, Georgia; Rev. E.K. Love, D.D., Savannah, Georgia; Rev. C.T. Walker, Augusta, Georgia; Rev. E.R. Carter, Atlanta, Georgia; Rev. J.C. Bryan, Americus, Georgia; Deacon J.H. Brown, Secretary.

CENTENNIAL PROGRAM

Wednesday, June 6, 9:00 to 10:00 a.m., Praise Service, led by Rev. Henry Way, Hawkinsville, Ga.

I. 10:00 A.M. Welcome Address, Rev. E.K. Love, Savannah, Ga.

II. 11:00 A.M. Opening Sermon, C.T. Walker, Augusta, Ga.

III. 12:00 M. History of the church, C.A. Clark Brunswick, Ga.

IV. 3:00 P.M. Baptist Doctrine, Rev. C.H. Lyons, Atlanta, Ga.; Rev. S.A. McNeal, Augusta, Ga.; and Rev. J.M. Pendleton, D.D., Pa.

V. 4:30 P.M. New Testament Policy, Rev. E.M. Brawley, D.D., Greenville, S.C.; Rev. W.E. Holmes, A.M., Atlanta, Ga.; Rev. A.F. Owens, Mobile, Ala.

Night Session. VI. 8:00 P.M. "Peculiarities of Baptist That Distinguish Them From All Other People," Rev. W.J. Simmons, D.D., Rev. C.H. Parrish, A.B., Louisville, Ky.; and Rev. C.S. Wilkins, West Point, Ga.

Thursday, June 7, 9:00 to 10:00 A.M., Praise Service led by Rev. E.W. Walker, Dawson, Ga.

VII. 10:00 A.M. Baptist Church History, Rev. W.J. White, G.H. Dwelle, Augusta, Ga.; and Rev. W.H. Tillman, Atlanta.

VIII. 11:30 A.M. "Reminiscences of the Baptist Fathers and the Church During One Hundred Years," Revs. Levi Thornton, Greensboro, Ga.; J.M. Simms, Savannah, Ga.; and Alexander Harris, Savannah, Ga.

IX. 3:00 P.M. "The Wants of the Colored Ministry." Rev. W. H. McIntosh, D.D., Macon, Ga.; Rev. Alexander Ellis, Savannah, Ga.; and Rev. W.G. Johnson, Augusta, Ga.

X. 4:30 P.M. "The Relation of the White and Colored Baptists in the Past, Now, and as It Should Be in the Future," Rev. T.J. Hornsby, Augusta, Ga.; Rev. G.S. Johnson, Thomson, Ga.; and Rev. J.B. Hawthorne, D.D., Atlanta, Ga.

Night Session, 8:00 o'clock, Sermon by Rev. E.R. Carter, Atlanta, Ga. 9:00 to 10:00 A.M., Praise Service, led by Rev. C.A. Johnson, Americus, Ga.

XI. 10:00 A.M. "The Home Mission Society and Its Work for the Colored People," Dr. A.E. Williams, Crawfordville, Ga.; Prof. S.Y. Pope, Waynesboro, Ga.; Rev. G.A. Goodwin, Gainesville, Fla., and Rev. S. Graves, Atlanta, Ga.

XII. 12:30 P.M. "Woman, Her Work and Influence," Misses S.B. Packard, Atlanta, Ga.; J.P. Moore, New Orleans, La.; and Rev. L. Burrows, D.D., Augusta, Ga.

XIII. 3:00 P.M. "The American Baptist Publication Society and Its Work for the Colored People," Rev. E.K. Love, Savannah, Ga.; Rev. N.W. Waterman, Thomasville, Ga.; Rev. G.B. Mitchell, Forsyth, Ga.; and Rev. B. Griffith, D.D., Philadelphia, Pa.

Night Session. XIV. 8:00 P.M. "Education," Dr. J.H. Bugg, Lynchburg, Virginia; Rev. J.A. Metts, Hightown, N.J.; and Rev. J.A. Battle, D.D., Macon, Ga.

Saturday, June 9, 9:00 to 10:00 A.M., Praise Service, led by Rev. John Williams, Brunswick, Ga.

XV. 10:00 A.M. "The Bible as Believed by Baptists, Revs. J.C. Bryan, Americus, Ga.; H.N. Bouey, Columbia, S.C.; G.M. Sprattling, Brunswick, Ga.; and P.S. Henson, D.D., Chicago, Ill.

XVI. 12:00 M. "The Authenticity of the Bible," Rev. David Shaver, D.D., Atlanta, Ga.; and Rev. H.H. Tucker, D.D., Atlanta, Ga.

XVII. 3:00 P.M. "The Dignity of the Ministry and the Necessary Qualifications To Fit Them for their Work," Revs. E.R. Carter, Atlanta, Ga.; C.H. Brightharp, Milledgeville, Ga.; E.V. White, Thomson, Ga.; and Dr. J.B. Broadus, Louisville, Ky.

Sunday, June 10, Divine Services.

Monday, June 11, 9:00 to 10:00 A.M., Praise Service, led by Rev. Floyd Hill, Athens, Ga.

XVIII. 10:00 A.M. "The Duty of Baptists to Home Missions," Revs. W.H. McAlpine, Montgomery, Ala.; J.M. Jones, C.O. Jones, Atlanta, Ga.; and E.J. Fisher, LaGrange, Ga.

XIX. 12:00 M. "Temperance," Hon. J.W. Lyons, Augusta, Ga.; and Rev. S.D. Rosier, Midville, Ga.

XX. 3:00 P.M. "The Duty of Baptists to Foreign Missions," Rev. J.E. Jones, W.W. Colley; and J.H. Pressley, Virginia.

XXI. 4:30 P.M. "Baptist Newspapers and Their Influence," Revs. S.T. Clanton, D.D., New Orleans, La.; J.T. White, Helena, Ark.; and Deacon W.H. Stewart, Esq., Louisville, Ky.

Night Session. XXII. 8:00 P.M. "Scriptural Divorce," Revs, A.S. Jackson, New Orleans, La.; and C.O. Boothe, Selma, Ala.

Tuesday, June 12, 9:00 to 10:00 A.M., Praise Service, led by Rev. Henry Morgan, Augusta, Ga.

XXIII. 10:00 A.M. "Are We Advancing as a Denomination?" Deacon J.H. Brown, Savannah, Ga.; Prof. M.J. Maddox, Gainesville, Fla.; Prof. M.P. McCrary, Valdosta, Ga.; and Rev. T. Nightingale, Memphis, Tenn.

XXIV. 12:00 M. "The Bible as Suited to the Elevation of Mankind." Revs. J.E.L. Holmes, D.D., Savannah, Ga.; and W.W. Landrum, D.D., Richmond, Va.

XXV. 3:00 P.M. "The Duty of the Pastor to the Church," Revs. J.W. Dungee, Augusta, Ga.; J.G. Phillips, Aiken, S.C.; and Rev. E.W. Warren, D.D., Macon, Ga.

XXVI. 4:30 P.M. "The Duty of the Church to the Pastor," Prof. Isaiah Blocker, Augusta, Ga.; Deacon R.H. Thomas, Savannah, Ga.; and Rev. J.L. Underwood, Camilla, Ga.

Night Session, XXVII. 8:00 P.M. Sermon by Rev. T.M. Robinson, Macon, Ga.

Wednesday, June 13, 9 to 10 a.m., Praise Service, led by Louis Williams, Washington, Ga.

XXVIII. 10:00 A.M. "What Is Our Duty to the Baptist Institutions of the Country?" Rev. A. Binga, Jr., Col. A.R. Johnson, Prof, H.L. Walker, Prof. T.M. Dent, Augusta, Ga.

XXIX. 12:00 M. "The Importance of Pure Baptist Literature," Revs. E.P. Johnson, Madison, Ga.; J.G. Ross, Jacksonville, Fla.

XXX. 3:00 P.M. "The Purity and Work of the Church," Rev. C.G. Holmes, Rome, Ga; Henry Jackson, Augusta, Ga.; and J.B. Davis, Atlanta, Ga.

XXXI. 4:30 P.M. "The Deacons and Their Duty," Revs. J.H. DeVotie, D.D., G.R. McCall, D.D., Griffin, Ga.

Night Session. XXXII. "Money as a Factor in Christianizing the World." Revs. W.R. Pettiford, Birmingham, Ala.; R.N. Counter, Memphis, Tenn., and Prof. J.G. Mitchell, Malvern, Ark.

Thursday, June 14, 9:00 to 10:00 A.M., Praise Service, led by Rev. U.L. Houston.

XXXIII. 10:00 A.M. "Baptist Church Government, Revs. J.L. Dart, Charleston, S.C.; H.J. Europe, Mobile, Ala.; H.A.D. Braxton, Baltimore, Md.

XXXIV. 12:30 P.M. "God as Revealed in Nature, "Rev. H.H. Tucker, D.D., Atlanta, Ga.

XXXV. 3:00 P.M. "Christian Baptism," Rev. J.H. Kilpatrick, D.D., White Plains, Ga.

Night Session. 8:00 o'clock preaching.

Friday, June 15, 9:00 to 10:00 A.M., Praise Service, led by Rev. C.T. James, Baconton, Ga.

XXXVI. 4:00 P.M. "Independence of a Baptist Church," by Rev. W.L. Kilpatrick, D.D., Hepzibah, Ga.

XXXVII. 10:00 A.M. "The Duty of Baptists To Give the World the Gospel," Rev. W.L. Jones, Atlanta, Ga.; John Marks, New Orleans, La.

XXXVIII. 12:00 M. "The Final Perseverance of Saints," Rev. E. Lathrop, D.D., Stamford, Conn.

XXXIX. 3:00 P.M. "Our Duty as Citizens," unassigned.

Night Session, 8 o'clock, preaching.

Saturday, June 16, devoted to Sunday school.

Afternoon, Sunday, 3:00 P.M. Dedication First Bryan Baptist Church.

Monday and Tuesday devoted to miscellaneous subjects.

The persons to whom this is sent, whose names appear on the program for an address or sermon, will please signify their acceptance by addressing

REV. A. HARRIS,
William Street, Savannah, Ga.

A LIVING WITNESS TESTIMONY OF THE CHURCH'S ORGANIZATION

The following is a verbal statement received from a centennarian during the celebration, Mrs. Mary Jackson, baptized by Rev. Andrew Bryan, almost a hundred years before the date was presented by Rev. E.K. Love, as a living witness of the organization of the First Colored Baptist Church:

When she was asked, did you know any thing about when the First African Baptist Church started, she replied, "Yes; I was there the very first Sunday evening it first started". "Well, mother who baptized you?" asked Rev. Alexander Harris. "Daddy Bryan", was the prompt reply. "Where did he baptize you?" "In the river. If you carry me there I will show you the place." "Who baptized old Daddy Bryan?" "A young man who was his friend, but things are so tangled up now I can't get 'em straight" - meaning she could not remember his name. Mr. George Licle is the young man referred to, who was then about thirty-seven years old. This is not at all strange, when it is remembered that he was not located permanently in Savannah. He was at work down the River, and very soon left for Kingston, Jamaica, in the West Indies. This old lady, has a vivid recollection of the organization of the church, being seventeen years old at the time. She is well preserved for one her age. She can remember and tell of every pastor the church has ever had. She was born on Bull Island in South Carolina, in 1771, and belonged to Mr. John McQueen. Some of the old members were called, that it might be learned if they knew anything about her. They testified that they knew her over forty years ago, and thought she was dead forty years ago, as she then looked old enough to them to have been dead from old age. Many things tended to corroborate the old lady's statement. When she was asked where did father Bryan

70

live, she replied, "right on the way as you go to the baptizing ground". She could tell of many old people who lived in that day. She could tell of Father Bryan's wife and his brother Sampson.

There are several persons still living who remember the old man. Among them are Mother Bryan and Mother Delia Telfair. The latter was fifteen years old when Father Bryan died. Rev. Bryan Neyler was eight years old when the old man died, and remembers him quite distinctly.

But to Mrs. Jackson the subject of the sketch. She is living about fourteen miles from the city, a member of the First African Baptist Church, but she is unknown to the majority of the members. Even the old members thought she was dead over forty years ago. This, perhaps, is due to the fact that she lived in the country. It is possible that in a church of five thousand members that many would not be known. So far as can be known she has lived a consistent, Christian life for one hundred years. Having never been disciplined by the Church, she however, would never become distinguished but for her age, she cannot be noted for great intellect, her greatest blessing being that God has spared her life for one hundred and seventeen years.

. . .It was a source of great joy for the Church to have a living witness of its organization and an eye witness to its organization and an eye witness to its eventful career for one hundred years. She spoke of Rev. Father Marshall as "Young Marshall, who took old Daddy Bryan's place when he died". She knew nothing of dates, when certain things which proved conclusively that she was a centennarian. She remembers the trouble of 1832, and when "Young Marshall", as she called him, carried the church from Yamacraw.

At this Centennial Meeting there were two great questions passed upon as to priority. The first and most important was to decide as to which branch of the 1832 division of this First Church was the original First Church.

The other question which was not formatable at this time and which was brushed aside with ease because its claim had such little merit, was the Silver Bluff Church at Dead River, South Carolina. At this time (1888) the Silver Bluff claim was new and no one paid serious attention to it. It should be stated here and now the Silver Bluff claim began more as a joke and afterwards some took it seriously.

The fact is the Silver Bluff Church was organized after the Revolutionary War. The members constituting this Church had been taken to Augusta from the Beach

Island plantations for fear the English Army would take them off and liberate them. But while they were in Augusta, Abraham Marshall (white) and Jessee Peters organized the Springfield Baptist Church (1793) and this is where they got their pattern of organization. They began worshipping and finally secured permission to organize themsleves into a Church.[2]

SPECIAL COMMITTEE REPORTS

We, your committee, to whom was referred the matter of priority of the First Bryan Baptist Church on Bryan Street, in Yamacraw, or the First African Baptist Church at Franklin Square, beg to submit the following report:

Having the facts in the case, which we think are conclusive, we earnestly state that the conclusion to which your committee has arrived was caused soley from the facts at their command. We regret to state that one of the parties refused to appear before your committee, not withstanding being urged upon, namely, Rev. J.M. Simms; for the First Bryan Church in Yamacraw. It does strike us that men feeling that they had a good case would not refuse to be examined. These brethren have openly and defiantly refused in the presence of the convention to lay their case before you or the committee, declaring that you have nothing to do with it, and they had nothing for you to decide. Your committee to perform their work, having seen the book written by Rev. J. Simms purporting to be the true history of the oldest colored Baptist church in North America, feels that the book makes their case as strong as they could possibly make it. We find that the church organized at Brampton's barn, three miles southwest of Savannah, January 1788, is the same First African Baptist Church today. This fact is admitted by the book which Rev. Simms has written. Until 1832 there was no dispute about the first African Baptist Church, but in the year, 1832 a great trouble occurred which continued for several months. Many councils were called, who advised again and again a course, which, if pursued, would restore peace to the grand old army, then numbering 2,795 members divided into parties, the one led by Rev. Andrew Cox Marshall, and the other by Deacon Adam Arguile Johnson; two thousand six hundred and forty following Rev. Marshall and one hundred and fifty-five following Deacon Johnson. It appears to your committe, from the evidence found, that before this trouble the church had contracted to buy the white Baptist church located at Franklin Square, hence, when the trouble occurred, Rev. Mr. Marshall and his 2,640 members went to Franklin Square, still owning the site on Bryan Street, in

[2]Files of D.D. Crawford, Executive Secretary of General Missionary Baptist Convention of Georgia, 1915-1941.

Yamacraw. The white Baptist church of this city took a lively interest in the church, and tried to spare it of all this bitter pain and heartache, an accurate account of which has been carefully preserved in their church records, which have been in the hands of your committee and carefully read, which we now offer in testimony. We read from the minute book of the white Baptist church:

"In the conference of the white Baptist church, Dec. 24, 1832, an application was made that the minority of the First African Church be received as a branch of this church, when it was decided that it was proper that they first be formed into a church and afterward would come under the supervision of a committee."

They being refused admittance under the supervision of the white Baptist church, it appears quite clear that the white brethren began to labor with both parties, hence the following petition of the First African Baptist Church, January 4, 1833. The First African Baptist Church addressed the following letter to the Savannah Baptist Church, white:

"We, the subscribers of the First African Baptist Church, do solicit the aid and protection of our brethren, the Baptist church of Savannah. We propose to come under the supervision of a committee of your body, provided you will receive us on the terms and conditions following:

"1st. That we be independent in our meetings; that is, that we receive and dismiss our members, and elect and dismiss our own officers, and finally manage our own concerns, independently; however, with this restriction: In case any measure is taken by us which shall seem to militate against our good standing as a church of Christ, we shall submit it to a committee of five members, whom we shall choose out of the Baptist Church of Savannah, whose counsel we bind ourselves to follow, provided it be not contrary to the precepts of the gospel.

"2nd. We agree to hold no meetings for discipline or other purposes until we have duly notified by writing, one member of the Baptist church, selected by said church, to be present and agreeing not to pursue any measure such delegated member shall deem improper until we shall have had council of the above named committee.

"3rd. We agree to relinquish to the minority of this body all our rights and title to the old church so soon as they shall agree to give up and do relinquish to us all rights and title to the newly purchased one, and when we are put in full and free possession of it and our trustees, William H. Stiles, Peter Mitchell and John Williamson, shall satisfy us that they have good and sufficient titles.

"4th. We agree to dismiss all members and such as have been members of our church, that they may either join another or form a new Baptist church, and as soon as such church shall be satisfied with and receive them, they shall be dismissed from us."

This being accepted by both parties, the minority of the First African Baptist Church was organized into the Third Baptist

Church, for in the minutes of the white Baptist church, January 28, 1833, appears the following resolution:

"Resolved, That, inasmuch as the minority of the First African (now the Third) Church have conformed to the requirements of this church in constituting themselves into a church, be received under the supervision of this body upon the same terms as the First African Church."

The 155 was always after the trouble of 1832 called the minority of the First African Church until they were organized into a church, when they became the Third African Baptist Church. To this name they offered no objection, nor for thirty years was the slightest protest offered of their being known and called the "Third African Baptist." In 1833 they entered Sunbury Baptist Association as such, and their church was always recorded in their minutes as the Third African Baptist Church." The Sunbury Association expelled the First African Church in November, 1832, as the First African Baptist Church. Every reference to this church in public or in the minutes of the Savannah Baptist Church book is as the First African Baptist Church. The Third Church themselves complained against the First African Baptist Church as the First African Baptist Church. Reverend Simms in his book admits that the 155 above mentioned were organized as the Third Church, that is he admits the reorganization. Your Committee has seen a sketch of the First African Baptist Church from its organization in 1788 till toward the close of the administration of Rev. W.J. Campbell about 1877, in Rev. Simms' own handwriting, without any reference to the First Bryan Baptist Church. It appears passing strange to your committee that if the First Bryan Baptist Church is the First African Baptist Church that they do not and have not called themselves by that name. The pastor of the First African Baptist Church has shown your committee the deed of the First African Baptist Church to the spot of ground which the First Bryan Baptist Church now occupies. With all of these facts and as many more which have come before your committee as candid, God fearing men, we feel in honor bound to decide that the First African Baptist Church at Franklin Square is the original First African Baptist Church, organized at Brampton barn, January 20, 1788, by Rev. Abraham Marshall and Rev. Jesse Peters, whose centennial anniversary we have gathered to celebrate. We decide, therefore, that the claim of priority of the First Bryan Baptist Church, which has given itself this name since the Emancipation and the claim of the book written by Rev. J.M. Simms, of being the oldest church (colored) in North America is without foundation.

Signed, you committee,

REV. F.M. SIMMONS,
Chairman.[3]

---

[3]Records of Missionary Baptist Convention of Georgia.

On June 3, 1888, The *Savannah Morning News* carried the following article:

FIRST AFRICAN BAPTIST CHURCH OF SAVANNAH HAS THE HONOR

"There was some show of feeling in the final settlement in the African Missionary Baptist State Convention yesterday of the question as to which is the oldest church organized in the state, and the First African Baptist Church of Savannah carried off the honors.

"Last Thursday the question was presented to the convention and on Friday it was referred to the following committee: Rev. F.M. Simmons, Stone Mountain; Rev. W.S. Ramsey, Columbus; Rev. H.B. Hamilton, Walthourville; Rev. S.A. McNeal, Augusta; Rev. E.J. Fisher, LaGrange; Rev. C.T. Walker, Augusta; Rev. N.B. Williamson, Quitman; Rev. G.T. Johnson, Arlington; and Rev. C.H. Brightharp, Milledgeville.

"Yesterday afternoon the committee presented a unanimous report in favor of the First African Baptist Church, in which it said: "We find that the church organized at Brampton barn, three miles southwest of Savannah, January 20, 1788, is the First African Baptist Church of today. This fact is admitted by the work which Rev. Simms has written. Up to 1832 there was no dispute about the First African Baptist Church, but in 1832 a great trouble occurred which continued for several months. Many councils were called, which advised again and again a course which, if pursued, would restore peace to the grand old army then numbering 2,795 members.

Two Factions

"This was divided into two parties, the one led by Rev. Andrew Cox Marshall, and the other by Deacon Adam Johnson, 2,640 following Rev. Marshall and 155 following Deacon Johnson and known as the Third African Baptist Church. It appears to your committee, from the evidence found, that before this trouble the church had contracted to buy the white Baptist church then located on Franklin Square; hence when this trouble occurred, Rev. Marshall and his 2,640 members went to Franklin Square, still owning the site on Bryan Street in Yamacraw. The pastor of the First African Baptist Church has shown your committee the deeds of the First African Baptist Church to the spot of ground which the First Bryan Baptist Church now occupies. With all these facts and many more which have come before your committee, as candid, God-fearing men we feel honor bound to decide that the First African Baptist Church at Franklin Square is the original First African Baptist Church organized at Brampton's barn, January 20, 1788, by Rev. Abraham Marshall and Rev. Jesse Peters, whose centennial anniversary we have gathered together to celebrate. We decide therefore that the claim of priority of the First Bryan Baptist Church (which has given itself this name since Emancipation) and the claim of the book written by Rev. J.M. Simms of being the oldest colored church in North America is without foundation.

"When the report was read, it brought Rev. Simms to his feet with blood in his eye. He said the committee had been packed in the interest of the First African Baptist Church, and that the committee had been prejudiced by the ex-bishop of Georgia, alluding to Rev. E.K. Love, Vice President of the Convention and pastor of the church. He spoke for half an hour with great vehemence and was frequently interrupted by indignant members of the convention. Calls for order and denials and interruptions flowed thick and fast. In vain, the President, Rev. J.C. Bryan of Americus, and Vice President Love appealed to the convention to hear Rev. Simms, but it howled him down, and the report of the committee was unanimously adopted.

"The President took the occasion to say that the only side which had attempted to pack the committee was the Simm's side, that Rev. Love had not suggested a single member of the committee, but that the Simms' side had suggested two persons, and one of these had been appointed to gratify them.

" 'This I would not have made public to the convention,' " said President Bryan, 'had not the charge been made that the committee had been packed, and I tell it now in vindication of the committee.'

Among the documentary evidence submitted by the First African Baptist Church was a deed, yellow with age and honeycombed by moths, dated July 3, 1797, being a deed by Andrew Bryan, a free black man, to the trustees of the First African Baptist Church of lot 7 in Yamacraw village for a consideration of 30 pounds, also a sketch of the church written by Rev. Simms when he was friendly to it."

ANALYSIS OF THE CONVENTION'S DECISION OF 1888

Composure of members of committees have much to do with committee decisions. Committee members are chosen often with the influence of others.

First Bryan was the first church to extend an invitation to entertain the Centennial. It was rejected and the convention chose First African as their host. Her pastor, E.K. Love, was now Vice-President of the Convention.

When he proposed such a celebration in 1884, he was not pastoring in Savannah. Rev. U.L. Houston, Pastor of First Bryan was Vice-President of the Convention. In 1886, J.C. Bryan became President with E.K. Love, Vice-President. Most likely, the Vice-President had influence in the place of meeting, committee appointments, committee persuasion and the bodies decision.

Alexander Harris, Chairman of the Program Committee was once a member of First Bryan. Serving first as Chairman of the board of deacons, then entering the ministry. He was not licensed by the church because of his intent to oust Pastor Houston. Through a plot, and presiding over a conference in the pastor's absence, was successful in terminating him. Then elected himself as pastor serving from August to December, 1871, until the church could have a proper conference, reelected Pastor Houston and dismissed him from the church. As Chairman of this committee, Harris wielded a satisfiable amount of influence. This could be an opportunity for him, to be revengeful of his past defeat. Why would he have been selected as a member and Chairman of the committee, with such a negative relationship with the church?

W.J. White, J.C. Bryan and C.T. Walker's relationship with E.K. Love had existed across the years. All were celebrated products of Augusta Baptist College, with Love being highly influential as a scholar and denominational leader. Would they decide in Love's favor? Without a doubt, he had done a thorough job in historic research to preserve the historic position of his church. Some very strong facts were presented in First African's favor. There is a conflict of dates with the deeds, July, 1793, or September, 1793.

What preacher of that date would go against C.T. Walker? He had preached the first sermon of the celebration. Certainly they were influenced by his revered ability to deliver a gospel message.

Most of the delegates had been influenced by W.J. White's pen. He was founder and editor of *The Georgia Baptist*. They were informed of the denominations movement through his paper.

Few delegates apprized of the movement of any organization go against the president. J.C. Bryan was President of the Convention.

There were only two who could give such representation for First Bryan. They were James M. Simms and U.L. Houston. When the celebration was held, Pastor Houston was dead. James M. Simms had just written a book, *The Oldest Colored Baptist Church in America,* 1888. Had forfeited any influence he could have rendered because of refusing to meet with the Committee. Therefore, there was no one in a key postion to speak for First Bryan.

Because of Simms' absence, his book could not be defended. This inconspicuous unavailability caused the committee to question the credibility of his historic writing. Therefore enabling greatly the committee's findings in deciding in behalf of First African Baptist Church.

For your own historic examination and appeasement, compare the presentation of this chapter and chapters, two and three. An acceptable answer for both churches will never be determined, and had it not been for the time involved would never occurred.

However, the following invalidates much of the evidence presented by the committee in favor of First African.

Whereas, by an act of the Legislature assented to by the Governor, on the 23rd. day of December, 1833, it is enacted, that no person of color, whether free or slave, shall be allowed to preach to, exhort, or join any religious exercise with any persons of color, either free or slave, there being more than seven persons of color present without a written certificate being first obtained, from three ordained ministers of the Gospel of their own order, in which certificate shall be set forth the good moral character of the applicant, his pious deportment, and his ability to teach the Gospel, having a due respect to the Character of those persons to whom he is licensed to preach. The said ministers to be members of Conference, Presbytery, Synod, or Association to which the Churches belong in which the said colored preachers may be licensed to preach. And also the written permission of the Justices of the Inferior Court of the county; and the counties in which the county town incorporated, in addition thereto, the permission of the Mayor or Chief Officer of Commissioners of such Corporation. Such license not to be for a longer term than six months, and to be revocable at anytime "by the persons granting it".[4]

Andrew Marshall was silenced to preach in 1832, by the Sunbury Association and did not regain permission until 1837. The Savannah Baptist Church (white) of which the committee referred to, did not have determing power over the association. The church itself was under the association.

According to the evidences presented by the committee, First African was permitted to operate only, by agreeing to submit to supervision by a committee of the Savannah Baptist Church. This had not been necessary prior to 1832, nor was it necessary for what was known as the Third African Baptist Church (First Bryan Baptist Church) at that time.

Like all committee reports and group decisions, some were pleased others displeased, but First African Baptist Church of Savannah, was sanctioned by the Missionary Baptist Convention in 1888, as being the Mother Church of the denomination. Many distinguished Baptist from the national arena, including W.H. McAlpine were present.

Over the next four years, the spiritual climate was invaded with turmoil that eventually led to a split. They had made many enroads toward forming their organizational structure to function effectively. In 1876, Dr. W.J. White became the first Sunday School Agent. To ensure communication with their constituency, the office of Corresponding Secretary was created in 1883, with William Holmes being the first to serve. None of these were strong enough balm to prevent a storm that would cause the Convention to split in 1892.

---

[4]Sunbury Baptist Association minutes.

MISSIONARY BAPTIST CONVENTION OF GEORGIA
AND
GENERAL STATE BAPTIST CONVENTION OF GEORGIA 1893-1915

A number of things triggered the first split in 1893. The position of Corresponding Secretary was among them. C.H. Lyons had held the position from 1886 to 1892. J.C. Bryan was President the second time, from 1886 to 1891. J.C. Bryan became Corresponding Secretary in 1893. E.K. Love had been his Vice-President and was not permitted to succeed him. So from 1891 to 1893 there was no President. The Convention was led by two Corresponding Secretaries, C.H. Lyons, 1892; J.C. Bryan, 1893.

Another apparent reason was one group could not see how they could possibly begin a school as proposed in their constitution and maintain missionaries on the field and not destroy the Convention. Others diametrically opposed the idea of a women's auxiliary.

All of these came to a boiling point, provoking a split. The newly organized Convention was named the General State Baptist Convention of Georgia with, George H. Dwelle becoming the first president. As mentioned earlier, the Missionary Baptist Convention had been unable to decide on a president in 1891 and 1892. Now in 1893 they were still undecided, waiting until 1894 to select a president. Their choice was Dr. W.J. White of Augusta.

Ironically, both presidents were from Augusta. Dwelle was pastor of Springfield Baptist Church, White was pastor of Harmony Baptist Church. They both were baptized, licensed and ordained to preach as members of the Springfield Baptist Church, by Pastor Kelly Lowe. Now they are both presidents of state conventions and White succeeding J.C. Bryan who had the same relationship with their Augusta church.

During White's administration, *The Georgia Baptist* paper, founded by him in 1880, became the official organ of the Convention in 1895.

E.K. Love was finally permitted to serve as president in 1896. He is responsible for selecting the site in the central part of the state as stipulated by the contitution to establish a school. In 1899, the Central City Baptist College began operation in Macon, Georgia. Contrary to the prediction of the opposition, the Convention continued her missionary thrust.

Her counterpart organized their women's auxiliary in 1901. Mrs. Sylvia C.J. Bryant, wife of Dr. Peter J. Bryant of Atlanta, was first president.

Under President William G. Johnson, a Reformatory for delinquent boys and girls was founded in 1903. This letter bears out both Conventions objectives:

Macon, Ga., Feb. 7, 1904

Rev. D.D. Crawford
Savannah, Ga.,

My own dear Brother: Both of yours is received. I have been to Rev. Mr. Polloc several times, but his place is still closed. I will go and see if I can find him today. Perhaps he has smallpox or is quarentined. I can't tell. As to my former letter you try to make me accuse you of infidelity. Infidelity! There is not a man living whom I regard as more loyal to our cause than your own dear self. I have said that everywhere, I repeat it here, that I regard you as one of the most loyal *original* New Convention men in Georgia. I wrote in that strain because I felt that I was writing to a man who had the best interest of our Convention at heart; and would not wilfully do any thing that would hinder its progress. The letter I wrote you was designed to get you and me to see alike, what is best for the Convention. Great Generals differ as to methods of attack and to expediencies etc. Perhaps you read the charges made against General Longstreet. They say he did not carry out General Lee's orders, but Mrs. Longstreet goes to the record and proves that it is true that General Longstreet, did not carry out Lees order, minutely; but that Lees orders were impractiable, and when he so explained, Lee agreed that Longstreets views were best. My letter was an effort to get us to see alike and reach like conclusions. Thats the only way we can hold our own. If those of us who are attempting to mould sentiment for our cause, are not ageed, even as to methods, there will be but little accomplished. Your "imagination" was a little acute, when it lead you to believe that I was acusing you of infidelity. One thing is true - There is in Georgia some oppostion to our project, -- Am I correct? Some of that opposition is in our own quarters. Is that true? That opposition is really trying to muddy the waters, and make us all feel that we are unequal to the task that we have undertaken. That opposition has already weakened a number of us. If we feel that we can't do a thing it won't be done. The Central City College has no opposition from any of the Old Convention leaders. I don't know this, and yet I believe, that, that opposition weakend you. You remember stating in Atlanta at the "Old Folks Home" that the Central City College had killed the Mission work of the old Convention and that you feared that the Reformatory would kill our work"? Now old friend you didn't have those fears some months ago. You urged the beginning of some project that would give our forces some thing around which to rally. You told me that we must have something to rally around. You suggested to me the propriety of starting this scheme; which you said had been suggested to you by Dr. Carter, I had this Reformatory movement in mind but never thought of having the Convention to espose it. I wrote you because I thought it would not do to have our *biggest gun Our Sherman* -- our *Stonewall Jackson* to weaken. I felt strong and encouraged all along when I had you at my back, because I knew you didn't dread the noise of cannons or mind the scent of powder. But when you seemed to be discouraged and hopeless, I could imagine my whole army retreating. It is running time when a bull dog hollows. I know you have not received just compensation for the service rendered, but remember "All things come to them that wait". As to districting of the state. You said at the Wheat Street meeting that you feared complications would arise that would hinder rather than help the work. I thought you were mistaken. I mentioned the fact that the White Baptist had done the same thing and as I see it, there is no need of complications. You remember that just before you spoke, it had been stated that even that etc was wrong and could not be carried out. I wrote to try to get you to agree that it can be carried out. I was laboring to harmonize our views upon these issues that meets opposition in our own ranks. You and the other missionaries do not understand each other, but you and I should. We must be together in principles and doctrines. If you preach one thing and I another what will happen. You advise me to write no more such letters for fear of alienating some one from the work. Let me say just here: if you find a man that, that kind of letter would alienate he was already gone and was only waiting a pretext to make the announcement. I wrote you without ill feeling but I wrote out of the depth of my heart. I was only anxious to have our party republican adopt the same platform and advocate the same principles. I am surprised to find that you regarded my letter as an insult. You have been to brave a fellow for me to stoop to such a thing. You seem not to appreciate how easily a man who is all most fallen and discouraged can discourage others. You have had hitherto an iron will. I pray that you keep it. The world honors a brave man.

W.G. Johnson

Both conventions had churches throughout the state. They rallied together toward supporting Morehouse and Spelman Colleges. Many of them had fellowships and relationships other ways, but conventionally they were separate.

Serious negotiations were undertaken in the early teens toward merging these bodies who were born of the same womb, soldiers of the same army carrying the same standards, exhorters of the same Word. Such togetherness occurred in 1915. They were reunited to do a more effective job together than had been done separately. The concept of districting the state for district conventions was conceived.

Bibliography: Minutes of the Missionary Baptist Convention of Georgia and records of the General Missionary Baptist Convention of Georgia, Inc.

Chapter 7
GENERAL MISSIONARY BAPTIST CONVENTION
1915 - 1945

After twenty-two years of separation, Black Baptist of Georgia were reunited, dropping the banners of Missionary Baptist of Georgia and General Baptist State Convention in exchange for, General Missionary Baptist Convention of Georgia.

Their slate of officers were:

Rev. M.W. Reddick, A.M., Americus, President
Rev. C.T. Walker, D.D., Augusta, Vice President-at-Large
Rev. W.M. Gray, Savannah, 1st Vice President
Rev. W.F. Satterwhite, Albany, 2nd Vice President
Rev. O.F. Green, 3rd Vice President
Rev. W.J. Smith, Newnan, 4th Vice President
Rev. R.R. Smith, Atlanta, 5th Vice President
Rev. J.H. Moore, D.D., Griffin, 6th Vice President
Rev. J.H. Gadson, B. Th., 7th Vice President
Rev. J.T. Johnson, Athens, 8th Vice President
Rev. L.T. Jones, Atlanta, 9th Vice President
Rev. R.J. Johnson, Augusta, 10th Vice President
Rev. John William, Brunswick, 11th Vice President
Rev. G.B. Burney, Eastman, 12th Vice President
Rev. J.H. Brown, A.M., Athens, Recording Secretary
Rev. D.D. Crawford, D.D., Atlanta, Corresponding Secretary
Rev. W.R. Forbes, D.D., Macon, Treasurer

Their pragmaticism may be noticed in the preservation of proven structure and workable objectives of either convention. The twelve vice presidents were presidents of the twelve conventional districts, initiated by the General Baptist State Convention. They were vehicles by which close contact could be made with the local churches, Associations and to reach others that were not conventionalized.

Both conventions had objectives, the Missionary Baptist had Central City College. The General Baptist had a reformatory. Both institutions were located in Macon. Now they have two objectives, along with their Missionaries.

The following resolution informs us of their relationship with the National Baptist family:

Resolutions

Whereas, At the last National Baptist Congress held in Memphis, Tenn., our state was bound by the election of Dr. D.W. Cannon as President of that great body and for other reasons best known to the loyal supporters of the National Baptist Convention, therefore, be it.

Resolved, That it is the sense and request of the General Missionary Baptist Convention now in session that the next annual session of the Congress be held in Atlanta, Ga.; 1917[1]

---

[1]General Missionary Baptist Convention of Georgia minutes, 1916.

They refused to allow a mere invitation to suffice the entertaining of the National Congress. Much planning was made at home and proper groundwork done as reflected in this document to the leaders of the state.

A CALL TO THE BAPTIST LEADERS OF GEORGIA

Atlanta, Ga. Feb. 15, 1917

My Dear brother:

I am sure that you have heard of the National Baptist Sunday School and B.Y.P.U. Congress which is to meet in Atlanta, June 6-11, 1917. It is expected that fully 5000 delegates will be in attendance upon its sessions. These delegates are coming from every state in the Union and many of the very best scholars and thinkers of the country will be among them to take part upon the program.

We are sending you this letter that you may line up your Sunday School and B.Y.P.U. workers and have them send the pastor with the superintendent or president of the B.Y.P.U. or both, that they may meet these great leaders and get all the new methods of doing young people's work. Don't fail to be represented, for nothing inspires young people as do these young people's gatherings which bring together young Baptists from all over the United States.

At Memphis last June there were enrolled nearly 2000 delegates who elected Rev. D.W. Cannon, D.D., one of Georgia's own sons to the office of president of that great congress, and now you owe it to Georgia and to President Cannon to help his own state show up well at the June meeting here in Atlanta.

It will be worth much to any pastor or other worker to be present and hear all that is said.

There will be on hand experts to give instruction along the following lines.

(a) Sunday School Methods.
(b) B.Y.P.U. Methods.
(c) How to Study the Scriptures.
(d) Social Service.
(e) Home and Foreign Mission Work.
(f) How to be a good Superintendent.
(g) Baptist Doctrine and History.
(h) Women's Work.

Besides the above, able ministers from every section of the country will preach official sermons. Come and hear such speakers as:

Rev. E.C. Morris, D.D., Pres. of the National Baptist Convention
Rev. L.K. Williams, D.D., of Chicago, Ill.
Rev. W.M. Taylor, D.D., of Baton Rogue, La.
Rev. D.V. Jemison, D.D., of Selma, Ala.
Rev. W.H. Moses, D.D., of Philadelphia, Pa.
Rev. W.B. Johnson, D.D., of Washington, D.C.
Principal R.R. Morton, LL.D. of Tuskegee, Ala.

Special rates will be given by all railroads coming into Atlanta on the certificate plan. Elect your delegates at once and begin making arrangements to send them.

Send all names of delegates elected to Rev. D.W. Cannon, D.D., 40 Tatnall St., Atlanta, Ga.

Board during the Congress will be $1.00 per day.

THE GENERAL COMMITTEE ON ARRANGEMENTS,
P. James Bryant, Chairman
E.P. Johnson, Secretary
A.D. Williams, Treasurer
D.W. Cannon, Cor. Sect.
Cyrus Brown

The Corresponding Secretary's report, gives a good statistical report of the Convention, along with the depth of his thinking.

REPORT OF DR. D.D. CRAWFORD, CORRESPONDING SECRETARY OF THE GENERAL MISSIONARY BAPTIST CONVENTION OF GEORGIA FOR THE YEAR ENDING OCTOBER 31, 1916

To the General Missionary Baptist Convention of Georgia:

Dear Brethren: Seventeen months have elapsed since this Convention launched out upon the sea of time, steering as she is towards the port of glory and insisting on landing at the haven of rest. Others have sailed this sea before. Some have pulled through safely while others have been wrecked on the rock of hard trials. We are striving to profit by their mistakes to steer clear of danger. God's guiding hand has been impleaded at all times. That he has been with us admits of no doubt. We have seen wonderful things transpire in the last few months, and all to the glory of God. The Baptists of Georgia have been knitted together as with heavenly cement and brotherly love is flowing from heart to heart. Great and marvelous are thy works, Thou King of saints.

Launching our Convention in the midst of these panicky times has worked a hardship for all of your field workers such as few man have ever been called upon to bear. We had not money to start with and yet we were commanded to do the work and to do it better than it had been possible to do it before. Our churches were poor and hard hit by the panic. Our pastors had not been trained to lift collections, though small, and send up so as to keep the work from suffering. So we had to do the work and get the money to do the work with, too, somehow. This was a bitter experience. We were compelled to make keen sacrifices, and all benefactors must suffer for those they serve. If sacrifice and suffering will cause this Convention to succeed, she ought to go forward in leaps and bounds.

We have always had good credit, but it has been strained this year to the breaking point. We have been ashamed to call upon our friends repeatedly for favors, but there was nothing else to do. And yet the will of this Convention has been done. Your work has been accomplished, your commands have been obeyed and your every interest has been conserved as sacredly as if your eyes were immediately upon our every action.

You told me to collect denominational data, facts and history. I have done so. We have secured 534 minutes, 67 catalogues, 173 books, booklets, etc. We have gathered from these the following facts: We have in this State 118 associations, fully as many District Sunday School Conventions, 8 B.Y.P.U. Conventions and 84 Women's District Conventions. With reports from 103 associations we have 2,779 churches, 3,038 ordained preachers and equally as many licensed preachers. We have 408,624 members, 2,460 Sunday schools, 6,796 teachers, 93,518 scholars. We have 52 denominational schools and efforts with 189 teachers and about 5,000 pupils in attendance. Our school property is valued at $2,500,000 and our church property at $10,000,000. We now have our Baptist Year Book ready for the press; it would have been out but for the lack of money. We are working on a Baptist history and hope soon to have it ready for the press. We have unearthed things from the beginning of our denominational creation till now. We have written a short denominational sketch which will come out in a history of the Negro by Mr. A.B. Caldwell.

We wish to state, too, that much constructive work has been done. Every nook and corner of this state has been touched either in person or by correspondence. Thousands of letters have been sent out to all parts of the state. All sorts of helpful information has been given to the people. Associations have been listed and all other organizations have been listed likewise. So that we can tell you where every association is and anything you may want to know about it. All of the churches have been listed alphabetically by counties, with the clerks of each and their post office addresses. We have fitted up our headquarters as best we could with the means at our disposal. Our books, though properly kept, are open to all. All papers and documents are properly filed and almost any information can be given at a moment's notice. We have harmonized several associations and quite a number of churches. We have helped to settle a number of pastors in vacant churches. We defended our doctrine and our denomination at all times and at all hazards. We have pushed every plan and policy of this convention and its Board unflinchingly. We thank God that we have been the means in his hands of heralding the prospects of a better day for our Zion in this State.

I wish to commend most of our moderators for the assistance they have rendered. The Georgia Baptist cannot be commended too highly for its efficient and loyal service. We ought to give the paper a collection at least as a token of our appreciation. We most cheerfully commend the Standard, Albany Era and Tribune for loyal support gratis.

Besides running the headquarters and looking carefully after its every detail, I have traversed every part of the state, met several hundred thousand of the brethren face to face and pressed the claims of the convention to their hearts. I have done the following work besides: Miles travelled, 15,940; letters written, 6,846, literature distributed, 5,000; families visited, 794; churches visited, 220; Sunday school visited, 50; associations visited, 57; district conventions 12; National Convention, 1; State Sunday School Conventions, 2; State B.Y.P.U. Conventions, 2; Prayer meetings attended, 132; other meetings, 67; sermons preached, 110; addresses delivered, 345; funerals preached, 9; Lord's Supper administered, 4; conferences held, 124; schools visited, 18; B.Y.P.U.'s visited, 15; church taken out of court, 1; deacons ordained, 1; revivals assisted in, 6; institutes held, 1; conversions, 33; restored, 3; by letter, 2; articles written, 17.

In conclusion, we appeal to all our brethren, official and laymen alike, to stand together and pull together for our common cause. Let us lay aside all bickering and honestly seek mutual understanding on all questions affecting brotherhood. The success of this year are only an inkling of what they will be when we get our machinery oiled well and every part running in harmony. God is in this movement and he approves our course. Let us act wisely and play our part well. Half a million eyes are upon us. They look for help and guidance. They are depending upon us for future prosperity.

And now, my brethren, thanking you for the faith you have reposed in me, and having the satisfaction of my own conscience, together with the approval of high heaven that I have done my best unselfishly, I remain,[2]

The 1920 statistics gives a clear picture of Baptist growth, by their united efforts, with wholesome leadership and oneness of purpose.

---

[2]1916 Journal of the General Missionary Baptist Convention of Georgia.

STATISTICS OF THE NEGRO BAPTISTS OF GEORGIA

It may be refreshing and encouraging to know something of the progress being made by the Negro Baptist of Georgia. The harder the times the greater our progress seems to be. We have just compiled the following from the 1920 Associational records.

Number of Associations in the state 116
Number of Churches in the state 3408
Number of Ordained preachers in the state 4391

Increases
By Baptism 43200
By Letter 12412
Otherwise (by restoration and experience) 5243

Decreases
By Death 8352
By Letter 3480
Otherwise (by exclusion and strayed) 8120
Net Increase 40903
Present membership............................. 568454
Number of S.S. in the state 3132
Number of Officers and Teachers 10440
S.S. Scholars enrolled 268200
Woman's Missionary Societies...................... 2088
No. of Women enlisted in these 12064
No. of B.Y.P.U.'s in the state 580
No. of Young People enrolled 3248
Value of church property $9,595,354.12
Money raised for church expenses including salaries, building and improvement, current expenses and for charity
.... $1,711,624.88
Money raised for Missions, Home, Foreign and state, Woman's Work, Christian Education and Ministerial aid
.... 171,244.20

Making a grand total $1,882,869.08
The average salary paid pastors $288.65

An explanation

Doubtless all of these figures would be larger had we been able to secure the records from all Associations and District Conventions.

One encouraging thing about this report is the average salary paid to our pastors has increased since last year from $246.00 to $288.65 no withstanding the present financial depression. This shows what the proper kind of aggitation can do. Last year we mildly but earnestly advocated better salaries for our preachers and we are gratified to note such a large increase so early.

It is easy to see from these figures that quite a number of our churches have no Woman's Societies, S.S.'s or B.Y.P.U.'s. Many of these churches are small and feeble but if they deserve the right to exist at all they should be properly organized. The weaker the church the more effective should be the organization. The stronger churches should exercise a sympathy for and interest in the weaker churches. Too often it is just the opposite the stronger seek to strangle and destroy the weaker ones. The bruised reed should not be broken nor the smoking flax quenched.

The value of our church property has decreased One Million Dollars since last year. The value of all property has shrunken.

The total amount of money raised for all purposes is near Two Million, but we were unable to get it all for lack of records. It is however no mean showing especially for the times through which we have been passing. If we only had the proper cooperation on the part of District Workers our showing would be far more commendable. It is a tremendous task to keep up with the doings of people who care so little about them.

D.D. Crawford, Corresponding Secretary

A new era of Black Baptist power was certainly underway. The convention had now established a headquarters on Auburn Avenue in Atlanta. They were now about the total needs of mankind, there were no unsurmountable barriers for them to attack. In all of their endeavors, they were respected. This letter from Dr. D.D. Crawford in 1922 to the Governor and the dispatch of his reply is an example:

"August 14-1922

Hon. Thomas W. Hardwick, Governor,
State Capitol
Atlanta, Georgia
Dear Governor:
The Colored people are leaving the rural sections of our state so rapidly and are coming to the large cities and going into - other states at such a rate that our economic conditions in these sections are greatly affected, and the health and morals of these people are worse affected than the communities from whence they come. I am wondering if you could not do something about this. Could you not call the best White and Colored citizens of the various Counties together and have them confer on ways and means of keeping these people on the farms and inducing others to return to the farms? They are at a great advantage in the crowded cities from any view point. It presents a question so grave that I believe it claims your attention and all those in authority. Our rural churches and schools are suffering. Then too, there are too many consumers and not enough producers. The situation is serious to say the least.
Trusting you may see your way clear to solve this problem, I am

Most respectfully yours,
Corresponding secretary
DDG/WLG."

Rev. D.D. Crawford,
Corresponding Secretary,
132 Auburn Ave.
Atlanta, Ga.
Dear Sir:

I have yours of the 14th instant, and have carefully noted its contents.

I am deeply concerned in the subject-matter of your letter, and am anxious to do something to aid in the proper solution of this question. I am afraid that for the next three or four weeks my time will be so much taken up with pressing public affairs and with the pending election that I cannot go into the subject now; but if you will call up the matter at any time after September 20th, I shall be glad to see what, if anything, I can do to aid in its proper consideration, and possible solution.

With best wishes, I am

Very truly yours,
Thos. W. Hardwick
Governor"

The Convention met with the First African Baptist Church, Columbus, Ga., in 1922, Rev. B.H. Hogan, host pastor. President Reddick has served seven full years now, over against the persuasion of his friends and many conventioners does not desire to serve any longer.

Vice President T.J. Goodall, Savannah, Ga., presented President Reddick to deliver the annual address. Song "Oh God Our Help in Ages Past". Then the President delivered his eighth annual message. The President proceeded in his calm way to deliver the address with fitting style and eloquence which touched the hearts of the brethren perhaps as never before. He reviewed the history of unification among Georgia Baptists. Education and missions was ably defended. Suggestions: 1. Hold sacredly the organization of the General Missionary Baptist Convention. 2. That swearing as to your honor to guard the honor of the Convention. Keep a bank rating. 3. Provide largely in finance for convention purposes. 4. Do not allow the offices of Convention to be a denominational football to be kicked around during the year. 5. Never try to run the Convention without the Holy Spirit and prayer.[3]

Election of Officers
For President Nomination: Rev. A.D. Williams, Atlanta, Ga., Rev. J.M. Nabrit, Atlanta, Ga., Rev. S.S. Broadnax, Thomasville, Ga., declining in favor of Dr. Nabrit. Motioned that

[3]1922 Journal of the General Missionary Baptist Convention of Georgia.

nomination close upon names presented. Tellers on election, Dr. Ernest Hall, Dr. C.H. Young, Professor Hubert, B.W. Warren. The nominees were ably represented by Dr. W.F. Paschal for Williams and H.F. Taylor for Nabrit. The tellers announced the results of the election which resulted in the election of Dr. J.M. Nabrit who received 154 votes. Thus Dr. Nabrit was elected by a majority of 43 votes.

By motion of Dr. A.D. Williams the election was made unanimous:
The other officers elected were:

Rev. T.J. Goodall, D.D., Savannah, Vice President-at-Large
Rev. W.M. Gray, D.D., Savannah, 1st Vice President
Rev. S.S. Broadnax, D.D., Thomasville, 2nd Vice President
Rev. O.C. Green, Americus, 3rd Vice President
Rev. W.J. Smith, Newnan, 4th Vice President
Rev. R.R. Smith, Atlanta, 5th Vice President
Rev. R.A. Holland, Griffin, 6th Vice President
Rev. J.H. Gadson, Rome, 7th Vice President
Rev. R.G. Cash, Madison, 8th Vice President
Rev. L.T. Jones, Atlanta, 9th Vice President
Rev. W.W. Jones, Augusta, 10th Vice President
Rev. R.J. Sanders, Valdosta, 11th Vice President
Rev. G.B. Burney, Eastman, 12th Vice President
Daniel Wright, Macon, Recording Secretary
Rev. A.S. Staley, Americus, Assistant Recording Secretary
Rev. D.D. Crawford, Atlanta, Corresponding Secretary
Dr. W.R. Forbes, Macon, Treasurer[4]

Resolution of Thanks to our Retiring President, Dr. M.W. Reddick:
Mr. President:
Whereas, it was largely through the instrumentality of our Ex-President, Dr. M.W. Reddick, A.M., that the movement to Coordinate the opposing forces of Negro Baptists of Georgia into this great body was first laid upon the hearts of our people; and
Whereas his services as our President through the period of seven years were so wise, efficient, and constructive; and
Whereas his voluntary retirement despite the protest of his brethren evidenced a spirit of superior self-forgetfulness; therefore

---

[4]1922 Journal of the General Missionary Baptist Convention of Georgia.

Be it resolved, That we, The General State Baptist Convention of Georgia, vote our most hearty and sincere appreciations and Commendation of his wise counsel and valuable services to this body,

Be it Resolved, further, That we cherish him as a peerless Christian statesman, and hold him high up before our youth as a model of goodness, honor, and service.

Respectfully submitted,
S.D. Ross
E.G. Thomas
J.T. Saxon[5]

Attention has been given to the calibre of ministers and women of the Convention. The following letter will vouchsafe the competence of the layman who was given an opportunity and became recording secretary. A position he held for more than twenty years.

"Savannah, Ga., November 11, 1927

Dr. D.D. Crawford, D.D.,
Herndon Building,
Atlanta.
Dear Doctor:-

This comes as a special request that I am making of you, for our State Convention Program. I have a deacon in my church who is thouroughly loyal to the State's program, treasurer of our district, and stands four square for the work. With regards to the place of Dr. Staley. I know it has to be filled and I am making this urgent request of you as my colleague to appoint Deacon Nathan Roberts as temporary secretary in Dr. Staley's place during the session of the convention with the hope of landing him permanently as one of the secretaries.

We haven't a better supporter of the State Convention work among the laymen, who gives his time and money for the furtherance of the work, than Deacon Roberts. Your influence to have him appointed, leaving it to me and the rest of the brethren to land him permanently will much appreciated, if you assist me in this matter. I will be in Macon Monday morning. I am,

Yours for a successful meeting,
Lawrence M. Glenn, D.D.

amr/lmg"

Corresponding Secretary Crawford continued to distinguish himself through his pen, mental acumen, administrative skill, persuasive politics and experience as a Baptist leader. This general letter is a panorama of his denominational activities:

------

[5]1922 Journal of the General Missionary Baptist Convention of Georgia.

MY BELOVED BROTHER IN CHRIST:

I have been in the gospel ministry 43 years. I have given 13 of those years to the pastorate, and the other 30 have been given to our Baptist Zion on the field as Education Missionary or as Secretary. The best years of my life, the best of my energy and efforts have been given unselfishly to my Denomination.

I can truthfully say that I have done my best for my people, and for the Cause and Kingdom. I have looked well to their every interest and welfare. Not one trust have I betrayed. Since being Secretary for the last 15 years, some $140,000.00 have passed through my hands, all of which have gone straight. I have traveled nearly 400,000 miles in the discharge of my duties and the cost to the Convention has been almost nothing.

I have given the Denomination from 12 to 24 hours per day, working night and day, Sunday and Monday. Every bit of my time has been given to the Denomination. I have had no vacations and holidays. I have been on the job. I am still carrying on.

I am anxious to make this the crowning year of my service for the Baptists of Georgia. I will greatly appreciate your help and co-operation.

The Convention directed me to ask all the churches to pledge what they are going to give to the work this year, and to ask them to be kind enough to raise it in their own way and send it in monthly or as it best suits them and their local program. Will you please do this and sign the ticket herein and return the same to me right away? I will esteem it a personal favor. This will save the expense of my coming to collect it.

We were compelled to bring over some very pressing obligations from last year and some of them must be cared for at once. I am in duty bound to help take care of these obligations.

Please give your District President and county chairman your full co-operation and loyal support. This should be a banner year.

Yours for the Master,
D.D. CRAWFORD, Secretary."

These letters, June 12, 1931 and August 22, 1931, show the rapport Dr. Crawford had with Dr. L.K. Williams, President of the National Baptist Convention. Also his forthrightness in speaking up and looking out for Georgians, the kind of esteem our state held because of him and the large array of forerunners that supported the National organization from its inception.

"June 12, 1931

Dr. D.D. Crawford
141 Auburn Avenue, N.E.,
Atlanta, Georgia.
Dear Dr. Crawford:

I am writing a few of the outstanding workers in our National Baptist Convention, submitting to them a questionnaire, the purpose of which is to form some conclusions and plans whereby the usefulness of the National Baptist Convention may be increased. Kindly answer me promptly, as we plan to incorporate some of these plans in the making of our program.

1. What could be done to increase the finances of our Convention?
2. What would you suggest be done that would increase the harmony and spirituality of the Convention?
3. Have you any suggestions to make in respect to the auxiliaries and boards of the Convention?
4. What changes would you suggest in the Constitution of the Convention?

I wish you would feel free to write me in full in respect to the departments of the Convention, and their activities.

Hoping to hear from you at once, I am

Yours truly,
L.K. Williams
President National Baptist
Convention.

LKW:LMP"

"August 22, 1931.

Dr. D.D. Crawford
141 Auburn Avenue, N.E.,
Atlanta, Georgia.

My dear Dr. Crawford:

I received your very kind letter a few days ago. I am writing, now, to ask that you do me a very special favor. In the introduction of my address, I desire to make some mention of Georgia's contribution to the nation, and especially to the National Baptist Convention. I would appreciate it very much if you would give me about 25 of the outstanding men of our race that Georgia has produced, and in connection with it, give a resume of their special fitness, power and achievements. Make it short, about one page of legal size paper.

Thanking you in advance, and hoping that you will give this to me at once, I am

Yours truly,
L.K. Williams
President National Baptist
Convention

LKW:LMP"

The Atlanta Baptist Minister's Union invited the National Baptist Convention to Atlanta in 1931, under the presidency of Dr. L.A. Pinkston. In fulfillment of the promise made in his letter of August 22, 1931, Georgians received much recognition by entertaining that session. Dr. J.M. Nabrit became Secretary of the National Baptist Convention in 1932, a position he held until 1946, Rev. Roland Smith, statistician, many others were brought into the denominational limelight.

This is the letterhead used by the entertaining committee:

The National Baptist Convention Entertainment Committee

Under the Auspices of the
ATLANTA MINISTERS' UNION
Office: 141 Auburn Ave., N. E.

J. A. Hopkins, General Sect.

L. A. Pinkston, Director
D. D. Crawford, Cor. Sec'y for Georgia
J. M. Nabritt, Asso. Director
J. T. Johnson, Treasurer

J. Raymond Henderson, Chmn. Program Committee
Mrs. L. L. Craig, Asso. Director for Women
Mrs. H. E. Harris, Asso. Sec'y for Women

Only providence would have directed the secretary to record this event that took place on Wednesday afternoon, November 14, 1934, in the annual session held at the Mount Vernon Baptist Church in Newnan, Georgia.

Master M.L. King, Jr. age five, accompanied by his mother, sang for the Convention and was given a rising vote of thanks.[6]

This may have been the first of a long line of successive standing ovations. Not as a singer but as orator and revered civil rights leader, that revolutionized the twentieth century. His grandfather, Dr. A.D. Williams, was a life long member of this convention, likewise, his father Dr. Martin Luther King, Sr. until the early 1960's. He was bred, born and reared in the General Missionary Baptist Convention. His brother, Rev. A.D. King, was later to pastor that church.

Another entry in the journal, the same afternoon, shows the constant contact with the National Convention,

Dr. J.H. Branham, representing Dr. L.K. Williams, President of the National Baptist Convention, was presented and gave words of greeting which were highly appreciated. He spoke of the work of the Transportation Committee which was enlightening.[7]

Excerpts from the Sixty-Fifth Annual Session of the General Missionary Baptist Convention of Georgia, November 13, 1936, at the Hills First Baptist Church, Athens, Georgia, "Address, Rev. R.C. Barbour, of the National Baptist Voice".

Many other obstacles were to be attacked by the pen of D.D. Crawford, supported by the strength of the five hundred thousand Black Georgia Baptist of whom he represented. The first two documents represent accolades of gratitude for his courageousness to speak out, the other was to the **Atlanta Constitution,** the most powerful southern press then and now.

---

[7]1934 Journal of the General Missionary Baptist Convention of Georgia.

"GEORGIA STATE INDUSTRIAL COLLEGE
INDUSTRIAL COLLEGE, GEORGIA
June 19, 1933.

My dear Dr. Crawford:
I read with a great deal of pleasure your article on the three Negro State Schools that appeared in the Constitution yesterday.

I really do not know how to express to you my appreciation for the very fine expression about the College and about me personally. I am only attempting to do what I think is a service to our group. It is quite heartening to have such strong men like yourself and Dr. Kelly Miller agree with us most emphatically that the future of the masses of the Negro race lies in farming.

It seems to me that we can render no greater service now than to re-educate the Negro so that he will think concretely and definitely, not in the air but practical things that confront us from day to day. Certainly much of our education has been mis-education.

It takes leaders like yourself with broad experience to start the wheel rolling in the right direction. I want you to count on me absolutely. I shall take every opportunity to cooperate with you in your drive for practical thinking in this our great hour of racial peril.

Again I thank you.

Very sincerely yours,
Benj. F. Hubert
President

BEF:JF
Dr. D.D. Crawford
Corner Fair and Ashby Street
Atlanta, Georgia"

"The Christian Index
owned and published by
Georgia Baptists
22 Marietta Street Building
Room 511-513
Atlanta, Ga.

November 16, 1937

Dr. D.D. Crawford
239 Auburn Avenue N.E.
Atlanta, Georgia
Dear Dr. Crawford:
It gives me pleasure to call your attention to the publication of your letter in this week's issue of The Christian Index, on the editorial pages under the heading: "Letters to The Index."

How I wish our people would do more to help you in your difficult task. I believe the clouds are lifting and I am really looking forward to a better understanding and a happier day for the races, especially in the South.

If at any time I can be of service to you, feel free to command me.
With best wishes, I am

OPG:M"

Sincerely yours,
O.P. Gilbert
Editor and Manager

HEADQUARTERS
GENERAL MISSIONARY BAPTIST CONVENTION
OF GEORGIA
D.D. CRAWFORD, EXECUTIVE SECRETARY—TREASURER
239 Auburn Avenue, N.E., Herndon Building
ATLANTA, GEORGIA

CHRISTIANITY'S HARDEST BATTLE

Editor Constitution,

My observation leads me to believe that Christianity is now faced with her hardest battle since the days of the Apostles. In the end, it may mean her "Armageddon". Sin and wickedness have always opposed God, the church and righteousness. The Christian Religion has been bested many times by governments, groups and individual atheists, but the opposition offered by Voltaire, Tom Paine, Darwin and Bob Inglesol fade into insignificance as compared to what we are up against today.

I make bold the assersion, that the most subtle enemies of Christianity to day are to be found in some of our colleges and our systems of education. There is said to be atheistic organizations in many of our colleges and in some cases they are said to be working through our Greek Fraternities. It looks like there is some truth in it for these Fraternities are doing all sorts of stunts these days. They are changing times and customs. They are making possible, passable and prominent mid-night balls, dances, drinking, gambling and dissipation. They are the type who decry the customs and habits of our fathers and urge upon the young to throw aside the old and get in style and keep pack with the times. The Bible and its teachings are antiquatic, they say, and keep one in a straight-jacket so they cannot have their way. They tell the young people that Jesus was a modernist and had no respect for the customs of his day. They say he was a revolutionist and thus justify Communism on the ground that it seeks to put all people on a level - no big and no little ones.

Verily, some of our educators and many of our young especially students, are headed in the wrong direction and need to be handled with an iron hand. If our government and our churches do not wake up, we will find ourselves in the worse hole we have ever been in, and if America fails the whole world will be shrouded in mid-night darkness, the outcome of which no statesman can forecast.

The time calls for sober thinking and definite actions, yea more, it is time to pray. We need a season of National prayer and fasting. "How be it this kind goeth not out but by prayer and fasting" Matt. 17:21. Let America turn to God. He is the remedy for all her ills, yea, He has the healing balm that the whole world needs.

D.D. Crawford, Executive Secretary"

Another convention split occurred in 1937. Dr. J.M. Nabrit was leaving the state to assume the presidency of the American Baptist Theological Seminary of Nashville, Tennessee. Dr. L.A. Pinkston was elected president, Dr. L.M. Terrill, Vice President.

The group that split, named their convention Georgia Baptist Missionary and Educational Convention, with Rev. R.D. Couch becoming their President.

Around this same time, Central City College property was lost due to foreclosure. The reformatory had long since ceased to operate. The Convention for a brief time had no objective.

During the 1938 annual session held at Macon's First Baptist Church, the Gum Creek and Willacochee Baptist Associations offered their property in Fitzgerald, Georgia, on which they once had operated a school, to the Convention if a Baptist School would be operated. The Convention accepted this offer, all arrangements were finalized in January 1939, and the school was opened in February 1939. Dr. J.H. Gadson, who had been president of Central City College, became president of the new school.

Because the geographical location was no longer in the Central city of the state, there was a need for a name change. Dr. Roland Smith submitted the name of Peter James Bryant, a highly respected Baptist leader, who at death was President of the Sunday School Convention. Thus the name of Bryant Theological Seminary was given.

A DYNASTY ENDS

When the Convention met in Albany, Georgia with the Mount Calvary Baptist Church, November 11-13, 1941, the dynasty of D.D. Crawford, that began in the early 1890's as Educational Missionary, next to serve as Corresponding Secretary, later Executive Secretary came to a close.

ANNUAL REPORT AND ADDRESS OF D.D. CRAWFORD EXECUTIVE SECRETARY - TREASURER TO THE GENERAL MISSIONARY BAPTIST CONVENTION OF GEORGIA

My Dear Brethren:

It is with joy and sadness that I come before you to deliver my Twenty-Sixth Report. I was elected June 11, 1915 and have been re-elected annually ever since. I have had no opposition during these twenty-five years and I thank you for such confidence reposed in me.

Yet it is with deep sorrow that I offer you my resignation, or rather declination from a position that has become an institution with Georgia Baptists. Before I was elected to this position, you never had an office or headquarters and your work was carried on in a rather haphazard way. You left it up to me without giving me a dime to start with, and I had to use my credit for the denomination, which was used to rent quarters, purchase equipment and to hire help.

My duties as outlined by the Constitution made me Statistation, Historian, Keeper of Records, Theological Advisor, Supervisor of Finances and all the duties incident to a General Secretary and a General Office or Headquarters. It was more than a one man job and still is.

I accepted and even now marvel at God's goodness when I tell you, that during these twenty-five years I have traveled from 33,000 to 40,000 miles annually, which subjected me to many changes in climate, weather, water, food and different types of cooking - sometimes on high land and sometimes on low land. It is a mystery that my life has been spared.

But I have had strong hands and willing hearts to encourage and help me. My friends have been legion, and with them we have accomplished almost super-human feats.

SOME THINGS DONE

I wrote a history of the Negro Baptists of Georgia, but you have made no effort to publish it. One among my first efforts was to create and build up an old ministers relief fund. Some money was raised but it has about all dissipated. I also tried to get you to buy or build a headquarters building of your own, but that effort failed. We ran a reform school for several years but it finally went down. We ran Central City College until recently when the holder of a mortgage sold it from under us without notice or a chance to redeem it. We helped to run nine other schools and we kept several missionaries on the field. We have helped in a very large way to build our Sunday School Publishing House at Nashville, Tennessee and we have rendered valuable aid in establishing and operating our Theological Seminary at Nashville. We stood hard by our foreign and home mission boards in supporting missionaries. We have also given our best men and leaders to most of the states in the Union and to the national convention.

OUR NEEDS

1. We need a fuller and larger cooperation with white Baptists - state and national.

2. We need a new educational program. We are going at it wrong. Our method gets us nowhere. We must learn the lesson of self-help. We cannot afford to become chronic beggars. We must do something for ourselves. It will take three denominational schools in Georgia to satisfy Negro Baptist psychology - one major near the center of the state and one secondary in South Georgia and one in North Georgia. The one at Fitzgerald should be paid for first and then operated. The Union Normal at Bainbridge should be closed and her teachers, as far as possible, should be provided for at Bryant Theological Seminary.

3. A Mission Program on a reconstructed basis, is a crying need. The idea of placing men on the field who cannot help, but who themselves become an object of charity has served its day. Missionaries should be constructive and they should carry a heartening message

to the people. When collecting money becomes the prime object instead of help for the people, the missionary is placed in the light of a beggar, rather than an uplifting agent of the Lord.

Rev. Marshburn is doing, through his institutes, untold good in strengthening pastors and church workers. We should enlarge and strengthen this phase of our work. Rev. Marshburn should have a helper. We need a woman to give special attention to our woman's work and we need Sunday School and B.T.U. specialists, so as to give us efficient trained workers.

4. We need to do more for outside causes. As Dr. Branbrell said, "Baptists are many but they are not much." He referred to their lack of giving. We have thousands of orphans in this state but we are doing nothing to help them. We should operate an orphan home. There are thousands of sick and wounded. We should open a hospital. We have hundreds of aged and used up preachers but we do very little for them. Jesus enjoined upon us the care of all the unfortunate. From the government down, used up men and women are cared for, but Negro Baptists do not give them a thought.

5. Our District Vice-Presidents should understand their places and opportunity more than they do. The office is not intended to glorify and magnify them. They should magnify the office and make it a useful asset to the denomination, or the office should be abolished.

All money raised by one representing the convention from any source should be accounted for and reported to the proper one, and become a permanent part of the convention's records. Graft should never be known in a religious organization and neither slack handling of money.

We should strive to pay our debts and obligations promptly and be careful about making debts. None but absolutely necessary debts should be made. Notes and mortgages should be paid first and salaries should be taken care of. A religious body should enjoy unlimited credit and the confidence of the business world. Slackness and unpaid debts are the burying grounds for debtors.

We are living in troublous times. The world is upside down and our country is on the verge of war. We cannot be neutral. We must stand with our country for freedom and humanity, for God and righteousness. We must also take a firm stand for church independence and for Bible orthodoxy. We must do our part to save a lost world. Evangelism must be emphasized. Sleepy churches should be awakened and idle preachers should get on the job. Church forces should be organized and properly trained to do their work efficiently and successfully.

An inventory will be made of all your physical property and left with the executive committee.

I wish here to thank from the bottom of my heart all who have helped me through the years to carry on successfully. Hundreds of our brethren and sisters deserve honorable mentioning. I wish I could shake the hands of each and every one, but instead, I will leave with you a prayer for God's benediction to rest heavily upon you.

I also thank God for the help and cooperation of our white brethren, both of Georgia and of the South and North. The State and Southern Baptists are doing a fine job. The local pastors and church workers, including their women and department heads, joyfully help us in all our work without charge. They are doing, more good than they realize at present.

RESIGNATION OF D.D. CRAWFORD AS EXECUTIVE SECRETARY — TREASURER, GENERAL MISSIONARY BAPTIST CONVENTION OF GEORGIA

Albany, Georgia
November 12, 1941

For reasons well known to you, I am offering you my resignation from the office you have entrusted to me since June 11, 1915. My health is not good and my strength is failing and I cannot do the work I once did nor carry on the load I have been carrying.

Yet I pledge you to help whomsoever you put in my place without charge till they get on their feet or as long as my services and advice are needed. I will help you in every way I can to keep the work going and that without charge.

Signed: D.D. CRAWFORD.[8]

Fully aware of their loss with this resignation, a resolution was offered:

General Missionary Baptist Convention of Georgia
By Dr. J.M. Nabrit, Acting Secretary

Officers and members of the General Missionary Baptist Convention of Georgia.

It is with deep regret and a sense of personal loss that your Executive Secretary - Treasurer, from the organization of the Convention to the present, because of failing health and desires to be relieved of the heavy responsibilities, duties and cares of this your major salaried office.

He has been faithful to every trust, loyal to all the interests of the Convention and always ready to carry out programs and direct the Campaigns of the board and the Conventions. We acknowledge with tender affection and services, the dignity, honor, efficiency and success of this officer, and pray a benediction of heaven upon him as he retires voluntarily, from this service he has loved so well and from a life's work which he has placed upon the highest pedestal.

Bowing reluctantly to his expressed wish and earnest desire, we recommend that he be retired:

1. With the title of Executive Secretary - Treasurer Emeritus.
2. That he be designated Historian and given such compensation

---

[8]1941 Journal of the General Missionary Baptist Convention of Georgia.

as the board may deem satisfactory, as a further token of esteem.
3. That he shall be granted a seat without vote in the board for the benefit of his wisdom and counsel.
4. That the Convention and its officers and the Executive Board and its officers be authorized to plan for the payment of the unpaid salary due our retiring officer, upon terms mutually agreeable at the earliest time possible, in keeping with the ability of the Convention and the condition of the officers.
5. That we give him a copy and a copy of this resolution be put on record.[9]

Dr. Crawford was succeeded by Dr. W.W. Weatherspool of Atlanta.

From the Journal of the Seventy-Third Annual Session of the General Missionary Baptist Convention, held at the Mount Zion Baptist Church, Atlanta, Georgia, November 16-18, 1943, from the Thursday 10:15 a.m. program, "Dr. Nabrit, Secretary of the National Baptist Convention, Inc., was called on to introduce, Dr. D.V. Jemison, President of the National Baptist Convention, Inc. In a fitting way, Dr. Jemison was introduced. Address Dr. D.V. Jemison of National Baptist Convention".

The Seventy-Fifth Annual Session of the General Missionary Baptist Convention was held in Atlanta, at the Zion Hill Baptist Church, 666 McDaniel Street, S.W., Dr. L.M. Terrill, host pastor, November 13-15, 1945.

Here are the first two paragraphs of Dr. L.A. Pinkston's eighth annual address:

"Mr. President, Officers, Messengers and Friends:

The Seventy-Fifth Annual Session of the General Missionary Baptist Convention of Georgia brings us to Atlanta, the Captial of the Empire State, Atlanta is more than New York of the South. It has the New York, Chicago, Philadelphia or a Boston within itself. It has all the aspects of our world's largest municipalities. Atlanta is the city of great churches, great schools, great businesses, great opportunities, in fact, it is a great convention-city. In 1895, the Baptist Foreign Mission Convention, the National Baptist Convention and the National Baptist Educational Convention met in Atlanta, and united themselves into what is now known as our great National Baptist Convention, U.S.A., Inc. This organization of Negro Baptist Believers met in Atlanta in 1931 under the auspices of the Atlanta Baptist Ministers Union, and next September this same organization will meet in Atlanta as the guest organization to the same host organization, the Atlanta Baptist Ministers Union.

---

[9]1941 Journal of the General Missionary Baptist Convention of Georgia.

The General Missionary Baptist Convention of Georgia was not organized in Atlanta, but held its second session in Atlanta, and has held several of its Annual sessions here ever since at several of our great Atlanta churches. In 1924, we met at this great church, Zion Hill, with the late Claud H. Robinson, Pastor. He later became the President of the General Missionary Baptist Sunday School Convention of Georgia."

Your humble President
(Signed)
Leander Asbury Pinkston
973 Mayson-Turner Ave., N.W.
Atlanta, Georgia

The diamond jubilee of the Convention ended in preparation of entertaining the National Baptist Convention in 1946. A thirty year era ends, having survived two World Wars, a depression and midnights of social horror.

Bibliography: Journals of Missionary Baptist Convention of Georgia; General Missionary Baptist Convention of Georgia; files and records kept by D.D. Crawford, Executive Secretary 1915-1941.

Chapter 8
GENERAL MISSIONARY
BAPTIST CONVENTION OF GEORGIA, INC.
1946 - 1980

Celebrations are always succeeded by important challenges. The road ahead after the Diamond Jubilee was to be one of bumps, ruts, curves, floods and sundried turmoils, within and without the convention walls. World War II, the war to end all wars, had ended. Unsurpassed boulevards and avenues of education would be opened to blacks and all other races whose economic conditions heretofore would not permit it, as a reward for their military services. Many whose background was rural before 1941 would never return. Suddenly our nation was to change from predominently agrarian to urban. There would also be attacks on the segregated and Jim Crow posture of the nation as a whole, but specifically the overt stance of the deep south.

Veterans whose lives had been placed on the line in far away places like Omaha Beach, Iwo Jima, Okinawa, Corregidor and others, in defense of America, would now demand full citizenship rights, such as voting, housing, educational privileges in the public schools and state university system.

What position would the church take in this new warfare? This warfare questing equal rights and human dignity. Its position would be the same as always, for this is but a continuous fight. There will be more troops to man the battle stations than before. Enlightened, brave troops to support the generals, who for so long had commanded and fought, frequently unsupported.

It is not strange at all, for the first annual session to return to Savannah, the birthplace of the Black Baptist Church and convene with the Mother Church, First Bryan Baptist Church, 475 West Bryan, Rev. N.E. Holsey, Pastor. In order for some portion of the Diamond Jubilee to be celebrated in Savannah, they had a parade.

These following are excerpts of the Journal of the Seventy-Six Annual Session of the General Missionary Baptist Convention of Georgia, November 12-14, 1946:

"Reverends J.H. Geer, R.E. Edwards and J.W. King were appointed to assist Secretary Roberts while he engaged in the other duties toward the welfare of incoming delegates."

When Rev. Richard Williams became Secretary in the early fifties, Rev. Geer was elected one of the assistants and after Rev. Williams death in the sixties, Geer became Secretary, serving faithfully until November 1979, when failing health caused him to retire.

Other entries from the same minutes are: "Dr. Louie D. Newton, Pastor of the Druid Hills Baptist Church, Atlanta, President of the Southern Baptist Convention, and Secretary of the World Baptist Alliance. Dr. Newton delivered a forceful and practical message from the 31st Chapter of Deuteronomy and the 25th verse."

A DAY OF PRAYER FOR GOVERNOR-ELECT
EUGENE TALMADGE

"Whereas, we, the members of the General Missionary Baptist Convention of Georgia assembled in Annual Session in Savannah, Georgia on this 12th day of November in the year of our Lord 1946, want peace, democracy, Christianity, and prosperity to prevail in our State; and

Whereas, we believe that these principles cannot function without the existence of goodwill and Christian love in the hearts of the citizens of Georgia, one toward the other, irrespective of race, class or religion; and

Whereas we know that the Governor-Elect Eugene Talmadge, was elected Governor on an anti-Negro platform in which platform there was an appeal to prejudice against one-third of the population of Negro descent; and

Whereas we believe that this attitude of racial ill will as expressed in the campaign, over the air, in public gatherings, in deeds, and in the press, is partly responsible for the revival of anti-Negro, anti-Jewish, and anti-Catholic forces in our State; be it

Resolved, that the members of the General Missionary Baptist Convention of Georgia assembled in Annual Session in Savannah, Georgia, this 12th day of November in the Year of Our Lord 1946, set aside Thursday noon, January the 9th, 1947, the day of Governor Talmadge's inauguration, as the day and hour of prayer for the Governor and his administration; and that we assemble in our respective churches and pray to the God of the Universe for Eugene Talmadge asking God to make of him a good, just, democratic and Christian Governor; an impartial administrator, an example of Jesus the Christ , and an embodiment of the spirit of the Federal Constitution; a Governor of all the peoples, Negroes and Whites, Jews and Gentiles, Labor and Management, Protestants and Catholics, "with malice toward none, and with justice for all;" and be it

Further resolved, that we call upon all Negro Baptists in the State of Georgia and all Christian bodies throughout the State and Nation, Negro and White religious bodies, Jewish and Gentile religious bodies, Protestants and Catholics groups to participate in this hour of prayer, Thursday noon, January 9th, 1947, and if they cannot assemble in church, we call upon them to stop for a few moments wherever they may chance to be; at work, at play, on their sick beds, in the air, on the sea, on the train, on the bus, in their homes, in the street and pray for Governor Eugene Talmadge and his administration, asking God to make an impartial administrator, an exemplar of Jesus Christ; a Governor of all peoples, Negro and Whites, Jews and Catholics, Labor and Management, Protestant and Catholics, "with malice towards none, and with justice for all," and finally be it

Resolved, that a copy of these resolutions be sent to the Governor Elect, Eugene Talmadge, to the press, and that a copy be spread on all the minutes of the General Missionary Baptist Convention of Georgia."

1959 PINKSTON ERA ENDS - TERRILL EPOCH BEGINS

In Bainbridge, Georgia during the 89th Annual Session held with the First African Baptist Church, the mantle of leadership was passed from Dr. Leander Asbury Pinkston, who had served as President for twenty-two years to Dr. Levi Maurice Terrill, who had been his Vice-President twenty of those years.

The official roster of the Parent Body was:

Dr. L.A. Pinkston, President Emeritus
Dr. L.M. Terrill, Atlanta, President
Rev. Charles Hamilton, Augusta, Vice-President-at-Large
Rev. Richard Williams, Savannah, Secretary
Rev. J.H. Geer, Athens, Assistant Secretary
Rev. E.D. Thomas, Hull, Treasurer

Excerpts from the Journal of the Ninety-First Annual Session of the General Missionary Baptist Convention of Georgia, held with the Hills Chapel Baptist Church, Athens, Georgia, Rev. M. Tate, Pastor, November 15-17, 1960: "Tuesday afternoon - 3:30 p.m., Vice President Hamilton officiating,. . .Rev. G.P. Bowman, Baptist Headquarters Commission Chairman, gave information regarding money raised for Baptist Headquarters Building. It was pointed out that $571.00 is in the treasuries of the association awaiting the call of the President,

Rev. W.W. Weatherspool offered a motion that the brothers who have come to be a part of the Convention be welcomed to the body. This motion was seconded by Rev. W.M. Jackson and approved by the House.

Wednesday afternoon - 3:45 p.m., President Terrill informed the Convention that he and Mr. Borders had met in a conference. Dr. Borders was then presented to the Convention by the President. Dr. Borders stated that the Georgia Educational Baptist Convention had come for "unification without qualification." He further asserted that he had paid his twenty-five dollars and others would do the best they could, under the circumstances. The President was also asked to meet to discuss further disposal of the cash money. Dr. Borders then introduced Rev. B.J. Johnson, who presented a list of names of the churches paying the Convention. An amount of $403, was reported. The members of the Georgia Educational Convention were then asked to come to the front by Dr. Borders, after which they were welcomed by President Terrill.

Rev. O.H. Stinson also gave words of welcome and offered a motion that the members of the Georgia Educational Convention be accepted, that their representation be acknowledged, and that they become members of the General Missionary Baptist Convention of Georgia. The motion was seconded by Rev. W.W.

Weatherspool and the House approved the motion."

This brought together again the Black Baptist of Georgia who had been separated for twenty-three years.

The program of that historic session continues, "Thursday Evening 7:30 p.m., . . . Rev. Samuel Williams, Chairman of the Social Action Committee was then asked to come forward. Rev. Williams presented Mr. Lonnie King, leader of the "Sit-ins" in Atlanta, who in turn presented a panel consisting of Rev. Otis Moss, Rev. A.D. King, Rev. Larry Moore, Mr. Robert Felcock and Rev. Bennett.

A great message was delivered by Rev. Otis Moss. The President awarded citations to Rev. Samuel Williams and Dr. Martin Luther King. Dr. King's citation was received by his brother, Rev. A.D. King, since he was away in Nigeria. Rev. Moss offered a motion, properly seconded and approved, that the text of the Citations be published and put on the records of the Convention. The Convention joined in singing 'We Shall Overcome Someday'."

From page twelve of Dr. L.M. Terrill's annual address to the General Missionary Baptist Convention of Georgia, November 17, 1960, "Therefore I am recommending a Convention Award to Dr. Martin Luther King, Jr. for distinguished service in the area of Civil Liberties and Human Justice and Dignity".

TEXT OF CONVENTION AWARD

"Child of Destiny, born the son of Dr. and Mrs. Martin Luther King, Sr., no one knew at your birth that in 1960 through a phone call by Mr. John F. Kennedy that you would be directly responsible for the election of the President of the United States of America (President John F. Kennedy), the most powerful nation on earth. Since receiving your Bachelor of Arts degree at Morehouse College, your B.D. degree at Crozier and your Ph. D. degree at Boston University, you have been the constant companion in thought, soul and deed of Jesus of Nazareth and Ghandi of India.

You have clearly proved that a Ph. D. degree did not blind you to the inner yearnings and longings for freedom and human dignity that is to be found in the souls of men around the world. While others talked and preached Love and Positive Non-Violence you lived it, acted it and you were even willing to die for it if need be. From a ready man meeting situation in Montgomery, Alabama, you took the love of Jesus and the positive Non-Violence of Ghandi and the humiliating abuses that go along with them, and shook the whole world into a new sense of direction and purpose.

From the capital city of Confederacy known as Montgomery, Alabama, where you walked the streets with dignity, to the capital cities of Nigeria and the world, you continue to walk as a spotless untouchable world figure.

You are too big to be little and you are too little to be big like Paul on the Mediterran; with God's help you have changed your position from a prisoner to a pilot on the ship of Human Freedom for black people of the world.

On behalf of the officers and members of the General Missionary Baptist Convention of Georgia, it is my cherished honor and privilege since I have known you since you were born to present you with this citation and award.

Rev. L.M. Terrill"

Minutes of the Mid-Winter Board meeting February 22, 1961, held at the New Pleasant Grove Baptist Church, Macon, Georgia, Rev. Cameron M. Alexander, Pastor.

. . ."The President introduced Rev. G.P. Bowman, who reported on the Building Fund for the Baptist Headquarters. The President also gave information regarding the purchasing of Baptist Headquarters, 244 Ashby Street, N.W., Atlanta, Georgia.

Thursday Morning, February 23, 1961, The secretary, at the request of the Chair, read the business transactions of the purchasing of Baptist Headquarters at 244 Ashby Street, Atlanta, Georgia. After much discussion for clarification, Rev. E.P. Perry offered a motion that the Board righteously accept and adopt the legal transaction of the purchasing of Baptist Headquarters. He urged that a rising vote of thanks be given the President. The motion was seconded by Rev. E.D. Lawson, and the Board approved the motion.

Rev. L.S. Stell offered a motion, seconded by many, that the minutes to be printed carry the picture of the newly purchased building. The Board approved the motion. Rev. M. Tate moved that the President with a special committee proceed to incorporate the Convention. The motion was seconded by Rev. E.P. Perry and the Board approved same.

The President proceeded to present a plan to wipe out the debt of purchasing Baptist Headquarters. Mr. Troy Goodwin served as Chairman of a special committee. His ideas were most warmly received. Rev. N.T. Young moved, seconded by Rev. G.H. Hunley, that the plan of the President be adopted. The House approved. The President made it clear that June 7 will be used as the dedication date for Baptist Headquarters and March 8 will be the date of 'Open House at the headquarters'."

For the first time in its history, the Convention owned its headquarters. All the years prior, the office facility was rented. In this same year, the Convention was incorporated.

A number of the churches from the Georgia Educational Convention, did not unite with the General Missionary Baptist Convention. They chose a new slate of officers and continued operating their Convention. Most of their churches are located in Macon or around the Central Georgia area. Today they have about nineteen churches, with Rev. Mills of Macon as President. Recently they purchased a building in Macon, and it is used as their headquarters.

From the Journal of the Ninety-First Annual Session of the General Missionary Baptist Convention of Georgia, Inc. held with the First Baptist Church, Macon, Georgia, November 14-16, 1961,

Rev. Van J. Malone, Pastor. "Wednesday Morning - . . .Rev. B.J. Johnson introduced Mrs. Primrose Funchess to the Convention. Mrs. Funchess brought greetings on behalf of Dr. Jackson and the National Baptist Convention.

Thursday Morning - . . .Dr. Terrill presented Dr. M.L. King, Jr. to the Convention for remarks and Vice-President Grant presented Rev. Ralph Abernathy for remarks. Both speakers were warmly received by the Convention."

A few churches in Georgia were persuaded by the outcome of the election of the National Baptist Convention in Kansas City, Missouri in September 1961. When Dr. J.H. Jackson won the election commandingly over Dr. Gardner C. Taylor. Some were disenchanted over the mandate of the people and withdrew to organize another National Convention. There were some in Georgia who joined them. Thus the New Era Baptist State Convention of Georgia was born, with Dr. O.H. Stinson of Griffin, Georgia, being the first President, Rev. R.H. Milner of Atlanta as Vice-President. Their heaviest church concentration is in Atlanta with a few churches in Augusta, Savannah and Macon. With rare exceptions, they have no churches in the other cities, communities or hamlets of the state. In the past five years, many churches have departed to return to the mother Convention.

In the late sixties, they purchased a building on Auburn Avenue in Atlanta for their headquarters. Presently Dr. Melvin Watson, Pastor of Liberty Baptist Church is President.

Another consolidation, was that of the Sunday School and Baptist Training Union Conventions, into a Sunday School and Baptist Training Union Congress. Both of those Conventions were led by strong Convention men. Meaning that at best, only one could be a leader of the educational and training wing of the Convention. As it was neither Dr. O.E.S. Cleveland nor Dr. J.L. Lomax, who had served as Presidents of the Sunday School and Baptist Training Union Conventions respectively, were elected as President of the Congress. Rev. A.M. Reeves of Griffin, became President, Rev. A.E. Hagins of Savannah, Vice-President, Rev. Mose Pleasure of Bainbridge, Dean, Rev. Cameron M. Alexander of Macon, Assistant Dean.

This was the first certified congress in Georgia to be accredited by the National Baptist Director of Christian Education in Nashville, Tennessee.

Later that same year, November 13-15, 1962, the Convention convened at the Zion Hill Baptist Church in Atlanta, President Terrill was host pastor. The Convention's program reads, "Tuesday Night - 8:20 Introduction of Speaker: Dr. E.C. Estell, President B.M. and E. Convention of Texas and Vice-President-at-Large of the S.S. and B.T.U. Congress. 8:30 Message of the Hour: Dr. J.H. Jackson, President National Baptist Convention, U.S.A., Inc. and Pastor of the great Olivet Baptist Church in Chicago, Illinois."

Headquarters of Georgia Missionary Baptist Convention of Georgia, Inc.

In 1969 an opportunity to purchase a larger facility for Baptist Headquarters at 155 Ashby Street, N.W., Atlanta, Georgia, was presented. The Convention accepted the President's proposal with great confidence since the first Headquarters had been paid for seven years in advance. The new Headquarters was dedicated in October of 1969, and paid for in 1970 during the Centennial.

Preparations were now being made to observe the Convention's Centennial in 1970. Again Zion Hill in Atlanta was to become the host church, just as it was for the Diamond Jubilee. Dates of the celebration were November 10-12, 1970. It was kicked off with a mass musical at the City Auditorium. The Centennial message was brought on Tuesday night by Dr. M.K. Curry, Jr., President, Bishop College, Dallas, Texas, Assistant Secretary of National Baptist Convention, U.S.A., Inc.

On Wednesday Night - at the

Civic Center Auditorium a Pageant-Pantomine (The History of our Convention) by the young people of our Convention, directed by Mrs. Emma Irwin, Mrs. C.M. Pearson, Miss Freddie Bason, Mrs. Ethel Henderson, Mrs. Della Pinkston, Mrs. Katie Grant, Mrs. Mary Denton, and others with appropriate music in background. . .[1]

This was the night for the President's annual address. Dr. Terrill

---

[1]1970 Journal of the General Missionary Baptist Convention of Georgia, Inc.

was present but due to illness was unable to deliver the address. His son, Levi Terrill, Jr., read it for him. The following excerpts from that Centennial address, "Rev. Frank Quarles of Atlanta who served as president of the Missionary Baptist Convention from 1870-1881 was president of the first convention organized in Georgia and then made his contribution and then passed on. Rev. J.C. Bryan of Americus, Georgia served from 1881-1883 and Rev. Alexander Harris of Savannah, Georgia was selected to succeed him for 12 months. Rev. J.C. Bryan of Americus, Georgia came back into the office of president and served from 1885-1891. From the period 1891 to 1895 the Missionary Baptist Convention was served by Dr. E.K. Love of Savannah, Georgia, Dr. W.J. White of Augusta, Georgia, Dr. E.K. Love of Savannah, Georgia once again and Rev. G.M. Spratling of Brunswick, Georgia; Rev. C.S. Wilkins of Columbus, Georgia; Rev. W.R. Forbes of Macon, Georgia who presided over the Missionary Baptist Convention through 1914 were wonderful leaders and did a very good job.

The General State Baptist Convention was in operation from 1893-1914 under the leadership of Dr. G.H. Dwelle of Augusta, Georgia; Rev. W.G. Johnson of Macon, Georgia, and Rev. J.H. Moore of Griffin, Georgia.

The Missionary Baptist Convention and the General State Baptist Convention consolidated into General Missionary Baptist Convention of Georgia with Dr. M.W. Reddick of Americus, Georgia as the first president, served until 1921 and gave up to Dr. J.M. Nabrit who served until 1937 in Rome, Georgia when Dr. L.A. Pinkston took over the reins of leadership until he gave up in Bainbridge, Georgia after serving long and well. All of these great leaders have passed on to a deserving reward except Dr. Pinkston and L.M. Terrill. Dr. Pinkston is serving now as President-Emeritus while L.M. Terrill is carrying on as active President of Georgia Baptist."

Terrill's eleven years and three months service to Georgia Baptists was filled with historic landmarks. His death on January 31, 1971, a fifth Sunday morning, terminated his physical earthly contribution.

E. JAMES GRANT OF ALBANY, GEORGIA
1971 - 1975

Dr. Grant chose Rev. Thomas G. Blue of Columbus, Georgia as his Vice-President. During his four year administration, six acres of land was purchased outside of Albany, two buildings at Bryant Theological Seminary in Fitzgerald were brick veneered.

The Constitution was revised, that all elected officers could not be reelected after four successive one year terms.

The Journal of the One-Hundred and Third Annual Session of the General Missionary Convention of Georgia, that convened at Mount Zion Baptist Church in Albany, Rev. E.J. Grant, Pastor,

November 12-15, 1973 reads, "Tuesday Night, Dr. E.J. Grant introduced Dr. J.H. Jackson, President of the National Baptist Convention, U.S.A., Inc., who preached on the theme 'Using old situations - Launch out into the deep'."

Because of the Constitution, there was an expected change in 1975, in the Parent body and Women's Convention. The waters were first tested on Wednesday afternoon, November 12, 1975 during the 2:00 p.m. session. The Journal of the One-Hundred and Fifth Annual Session of the General Missionary Baptist Convention of Georgia, Inc. held with the Mount Vernon Baptist Church, Atlanta, Georgia, Rev. S.A. Baker, Pastor, reports "President Dyar asked Mrs. Clara West to preside, and the Nominating Committee's report was asked for; the report is as follows:

President Emeritus, Mrs. L.S. Weatherspool, Atlanta, Ga.
President, Mrs. C.M. Pearson, Atlanta
Vice-President-at-Large, Mrs. Viola Robinson, Savannah
Vice-President, Mrs. Gertrude Dyar, Rome
Promotional Secretary, Mrs. Arvella Turnipseed, Atlanta
Recording Secretary, Mrs. Ruth Mallard, Ludowici
Assistant Recording Secretary, Mrs. Grace Huff, Columbus
Corresponding Secretary, Mrs. Elizabeth Johnson, Atlanta
Financial Secretary, Mrs. Clara West, Thompson
Treasurer, Mrs. Nettie Drummer, Atlanta
Historian, Mrs. C.B. Singleton, Americus
Parliamentarian, Mrs. Ollie Mae Hardy, Pine Mountain
Music Director, Mrs. Mary Murray, Fort Valley
Asst. Music Director, Mrs. Elizabeth Golden, Augusta
Pianist, Mrs. Carrie Simmons, Brunswick
Young People's Director, Mrs. A.T. Williams, Macon
Mission Study, Mrs. Mattie Hardaway, Columbus
Organist, Mrs. Ruby Moss, Atlanta

Officers were installed by Dr. W.W. Weatherspool, Pastor of Mount Olive Baptist Church, Atlanta, Georgia.

The same Journal gives the account of the Parent body, that began Wednesday evening and concluded, Thursday, 2:00 a.m.

ELECTION OF OFFICERS

"Dr. William Holmes Borders was appointed to preside over the election. Rev. J.H. Geer was appointed official time-keeper. It was motioned and carried that, five minutes would be allowed for nomination speeches.

The house was qualified by names on letters. Motioned and carried that, all persons whose name was not called would leave the main floor, and go to the balcony. A motion prevailed that, the Candidates be nominated alphabetically. It was motioned and carried that each Candidate would have three tellers.

The votes were as follows:

111

Rev. C.M. Alexander   424 votes
Rev. S.A. Baker   172 votes
Dr. E. James Grant   93 votes

Rev. C.M. Alexander was declared the winner by Dr. William Holmes Borders. Rev. G.E. Darrisaw of Brunswick, Georgia was elected Vice-President."

NEW DAY FOR BLACK BAPTIST OF GEORGIA

Between 2:00 a.m. and 2:30 a.m. at Atlanta's Mount Vernon Baptist Church on Martin Luther King, Jr. Drive, N.W., an unusual early morning light was shed upon the General Missionary Baptist Convention of Georgia, Inc. when they gave their overwhelming mandate for Cameron Madison Alexander, Pastor of Antioch Baptist Church-North of Atlanta, to lead this historic august organization.

His first official act was to set the date for the administrative transition of Convention business and records to be transferred from Albany, Georgia to Baptist Headquarters in Atlanta. He next asked Rev. Clarence M. Wagner, who had successfully managed him to a victorious campaign to serve as Executive Secretary. The Convention had not had one since 1959. A director was chosen for the Baptist Youth Convention, in the person of Mrs. Beverly W. Glover of Macon, Georgia. This would be one of many new auxiliaries in an effort to reach the total church, having its first session in 1976.

Executive Board appointments were made according to constitutional stipulations, based on positions, auxiliary, and location. A date was set and place established for such a meeting. Because of organizational structure, for the first time the women of the Convention became a part of policy making on equal basis of men.

This Board Meeting was in conjunction with the President's Inaugural Celebration and Banquet. Dr. J.H. Jackson, President of the National Baptist Convention, U.S.A., Inc. was the banquet speaker. Other distinguished participants were Dr. William Holmes Borders, Toastmaster, Atlanta Mayor Maynard H. Jackson, Dr. T.J. Jemison, Secretary of the National Baptist Convention, U.S.A., Inc. and others.

Since 1976, the Convention has a centralized treasure of which all auxiliaries operate from. A fully equipped Baptist Headquarters, that operates five days per week, 9:00 a.m. to 4:00 p.m., with a full time secretary-bookkeeper, in the person of Mrs. Ernestine Weems. All twelve District Conventions are functioning with President of Parent body and Women's Convention receiving a monthly stipend for their services rendered. The Annual Session and Mid-Winter Board Meetings are held jointly with the Parent body and Women's Convention.

Such new programs as Statewide Minister's Conference, Statewide Music Workshop, Mission in Action (ladies 26-46), Young Davids (boys 10-15), Statewide Vacation Bible School Workshop,

District Conferences, Women's Retreat, Camping Program, reviving of publishing the **Georgia Baptist** Paper all have been vehicles to generate a brighter light.

Plans are underway, to establish a Baptist Book Store, and halfway houses for first offender boys and girls.

Presently an all purpose building is being constructed at Bryant Theological Seminary in Fitzgerald, Georgia. When completed, its appraised value will be approximately one-half million dollars. Twelve In-Service Training Centers, one in each of the twelve Conventional districts, will operate out of Bryant.

Although the Headquarters is located in Atlanta, the Convention is not stationary. A 1978 Ford Chateau van enables the Convention to reach the remote areas of the state.

In five years, her annual receipts have soared from thirty thousand dollars to almost three hundred thousand. Many churches and associations, who once leaned toward one of the other two conventions have proudly united with this light bearing Convention.

The greatest five year period of the Convention's one hundred and ten years has been from 1975 to 1980.

YEAR	CITY	CHURCH	HOST PASTOR	CONVENTION SERMON	TEXT
1870	Augusta	Central	Henry Jackson	E.R. Rucker	2nd Peter 2:1-3
1871	Atlanta	Friendship	Frank Quarles	W.J. White	Matthew 2:36-37
1872	Macon	Second Baptist	J.A. James	Sylvanus Carter	Luke 1:78
1873	Savannah	Second Baptist	H.L. Simpson	Henry Jackson	Psalms 133:1
1874	Rome	Thankful	Jeff Milner	Frank Quarles	Romans 10:1
1875	Washington	Springfield	Lewis Williams	Alex Harris	2 Timothy 2:1
1876	Columbus	First Baptist	Green McArthur	T.M. Allen	1 Corinthians 3:2
1877	Augusta	Central	Henry Jackson	J.C. Bryan	Ephesians 4:1
1878	Brunswick	First Baptist	John Williams	George Dwelle	Isaiah 1:8
1879	Atlanta	Friendship	Frank Quarles	W.J. White	1 Corinthians 3:9
1880	Macon	First Baptist	Henry Williams	L.T. Smith	Romans 10:15
1881	Thomasville	First Baptist	N.W. Waterman	C.T. Walker	Songs of Solomon 6:10
1882	Savannah	First Baptist	George Gibbons	E.K. Love	Psalms 27:14
1883	Athens	Hills First	Floyd Hill	N.W. Waterman	Psalms 110:1-3
1884	Atlanta	Friendship	E.R. Carter	T.J. Hornsby	Deuteronomy 11:31
1885	Cartersville	Mount Zion	J.F. Bright	W.S. Ramsey	Hebrews 12:1
1886	Quitman	Beulah	G.H. Washington	C.T. James	Exodus 33:14
1887	Brunswick	First Baptist	John Williams	C.A. Johnson	1 Kings 2:2
1888	Savannah	First Baptist	E.K. Love	M.L. Thornton	2 Corinthians 10:4
1889	Atlanta	Wheat Street	W.H. Tilman	George H. Dwelle	Psalms 124:8
1890	LaGrange	First Baptist	N.B. Williamson	N.A. Johnson	Genesis 14:9
1891	Cuthbert	Friendship	Lawrence Solomon	W.G. Johnson	Phillippians 3:18
1892	Macon	First Baptist	T.M. Robinson	R.L. Darden	Hebrews 12:2

Year	City	Church			Scripture
1893	Atlanta	Friendship	E.R. Carter	C.G. Holmes	Daniel 9:25
1894	Columbus	Metropolitan	W.R. Forbes	R.J. Johnson	Nehemiah 4:18
1895	Brunswick	Bryant Baptist	G.M. Spratlin	G.S. Byrd	Psalms 119:105
1896	Washington	Springfield	Lewis Williams	J.W. Whitehead	Timothy 4:12
1897	Augusta	Thankful	C.S. Wilkins	E.R. Carter	1 Thes. 4:12
1898	Americus	Bethel	R. Monson	C.H. Brightharp	Joshua 13:1
1899	Atlanta	Mount Zion	W.H. Tuggle	E.V. White	Psalms 15:1
1900	Americus	Bethesda	C.H. Young	Cyrus Brown	Psalms 16:8
1901	Thomasville	First Baptist	J.B. Davis	C.H. Haralson	Nehemiah 4:9
1902	Brunswick	First Baptist	John Williams	W.L. Jones	Acts 2:22
1903	Washington	Springfield	Lewis Williams	M.J. Morris	Matthew 28:20
1904	Valdosta	Antioch	R. Munson		
1905	Hawkinsville	Springfield	S.M. Cook		
1906	Macon	Tremont Temple	W.R. Forbes		
1907	Fitzgerald	Salem	M.J. Morris		
1908	Albany	Mount Zion	T.J. Simpson	S.E. Rosier	Matthew 5:8
1909	Valdosta	Macedonia	A.W. Bryant		
1910	Atlanta	Macedonia	Cyrus Brown		
1911	Bainbridge	First Baptist	J.B. Davis		
1912	Brunswick	Bryant	J.W. Fisher		
1913	Savannah	First Baptist	J.W. Carr		
1914	Hawkinsville	Springfield	S.M. Cook	J.M. Nabrit	Phillippians 3:13
1915	Macon	Tremont Temple	W.R. Forbes	S.M. Cook	Psalms 63:8
1915	Atlanta	Wheat Street	P. Jas. Bryant		
1916	Augusta	Springfield	J.M. Nabrit		
1917	Columbus	Metropolitan	A.W. Bryant	T.W. Smith	Acts 4:23
1918	Rome	Thankful	J.H. Gadson	W.F. Paschal	Romans 13
1919	Macon	Macedonia	J.H. Evans		
1920	Savannah	First Bryan	Daniel Wright		

Year	City	Church		Preacher
1921	Macon	First Baptist	S.E. Piercy	W.W. Floyd	Matthew 5:16
1922	Columbus	First Baptist	B.H. Hogans		
1923	Thomasville	First Baptist	J.H. Brown		
1924	Atlanta	Zion Hill	C.H. Robinson	J.H. Moore	Romans 13:11
1925	Brunswick	Shiloh	J.L. Burney	R.H. Thomas	James 1:5
1926	Valdosta	Macedonia	T.A. Lomax		
1927	Macon	First Baptist	S.E. Piercy	C.H. Robinson	Matthew 28:19
1928	Augusta	Thankful	A.G. Davis	W.F. Strickland	1 Corinthians 13:8
1929	Cordele	Mount Calvary	H.F. Taylor	R.W. White	John 18:36
1930	Atlanta	Mount Olive	J.M. Nabrit	A.J. Allen	Acts 2:1-4
1931	Bainbridge	First	W.W. Weatherspool	J.M. Nabrit	2 Thes. 1:2
1932	Savannah	First African	J.A. Wilson	E.R. Carter	John 3:1-3
1933	Macon	Mount Olive	J.H. Evans	W.M. Pulliams	John 18:36
1934	Newnan	Mount Vernon	S.M. Weaver	W.R. Forbes	1 Cor. 14:20
1935	Athens	Hills First	A.W. Williams	C.N. Ellis	Acts 1
1936	Columbus	Metropolitan	W.W. Weatherspool	R.J. Johnson	Romans 1:15
1937	Rome	Thankful	R.W. Riley	J.T. Brown	2 Cor. 12:9
1938	Macon	First	F.N. Marshburn	P. James Bryant	Acts 1:8
1939	Atlanta	Ebenezer	M.L. King	T.L. Ballou	Isaiah 62:10
1940	Fitzgerald	Salem	E.A. Hargrove	C.N. Ellis	2 Cor. 1:12
1941	Albany	Mount Calvary	I.A. Harris	E.P. Johnson	Jude 1:13
1942	Waycross	Macedonia	J.M. Benton	J.H. Gadson	Romans 1:16
1943	Atlanta	Mount Zion	J.T. Dorsey	A.W. Vincent	Phil. 4:1
1944	Augusta	Springfield	J.H. Sanders	J.T. Dorsey	
1945	Atlanta	Zion Hill	L.M. Terrill	J.H. Sanders	
1946	Savannah	First Bryan	N.E. Holsey	L.M. Terrill	
1947	Cordele	Mt. Zion, 1st A.B.	C.B. Johnson	N.E. Holsey	
1948	Rome	Lovejoy	J.L. Vaughn	C.B. Johnson	
1949	Atlanta	Mount Vernon	Emory M. Johnson	J.L. Vaughn	

Year	City	Church			
1950	Griffin	Mt. Zion	O.H. Stinson	Emory M. Johnson	
1951	Columbus	Friendship	A.W. Fortson	O.H. Stinson	
1952	Augusta	Thankful Baptist	N.T. Young	A.W. Fortson	
1953	Atlanta	Ebenezer	M.L. King, Sr.	N.T. Young	
1954	Savannah	Tremount	J.M. Benton	M.L. King, Sr.	
1955	Columbus	Metropolitan	C.C. Cloud	J.M. Benton	
1956	Atlanta	Mount Olive	W.W. Weatherspool	C.C. Cloud	
1957	Atlanta	Mount Moriah	R. Julian Smith	W.W. Weatherspool	Ezekiel 1:1
1958	Augusta	Tabernacle	C.S. Hamilton	R. Julian Smith	
1959	Bainbridge	1st A.B.	J.H. Sanders	C.S. Hamilton	
1960	Athens	Hills Chapel	M. Tate		
1961	Macon	1st A.B.	Van J. Malone	M. Tate	Matthew 20
1962	Atlanta	Zion Hill	L.M. Terrill	Van J. Malone	
1963	Columbus	Friendship	A.W. Fortson		
1964	Atlanta	Tabernacle	E.H. Dorsev	A.W. Fortson	
1965	Valdosta	Macedonia	J.L. Lomax	E.H. Dorsey	
1966	Savannah	First African	Wm. F. Stokes		
1967	Albany	3rd Kiokee	R.B. Smith	Wm. F. Stokes	Numbers 13:30
1968	Savannah	Tremont Temple	J.M. Benton	R.B. Smith	
1969	Augusta	Macedonia	J.S. Wright	J.M. Benton	
1970	Atlanta	Zion Hill	L.M. Terrill	J.S. Wright	
1971	Atlanta	Mount Olive	W.W. Weatherspool	C.M. Wagner	Acts 8:26-40
1972	Athens	Ebenezer	Wesley G. Griffin	W.W. Weatherspool	Rev. 1:18
1973	Albany	Mount Zion	E. James Grant	R.L. Calloway	
1974	Brunswick	Zion	G.E. Darrisaw		
1975	Atlanta	Mount Vernon	S.A. Baker	G.E. Darrisaw	Joshua 24:14, 15
1976	Tifton	Mount Zion	J.F. Glover	S.A. Baker	
1977	Savannah	First Bryan	Arthur D. Sims	J.F. Glover	
1978	Gainsville	First Baptist	C.M. Wagner	Arthur D. Sims	
1979	Columbus	Fourth Street	J.H. Flakes	C.M. Wagner	Hebrews 13:8
1980	Dalton	Mountain Ridge	R.E. Henley	J.H. Flakes	

SEQUENCE OF GENERAL STATE BAPTIST CONVENTION OF GEORGIA
1893 - 1915

YEAR	CITY	CHURCH	HOST PASTOR	CONVENTION SERMON	TEXT
1893	Atlanta	Wheat Street	W.H. Tilman		
1894	Augusta	Springfield	G.H. Dwelle		
1895	Columbus	First Baptist	J.S. Kelsey	M.W. Gilbert	1 Kings 19:9
1896	Savannah	First Bryan	G.W. Griffin		
1897	Athens	Hill First	E.J. Fisher	M.W. Gilbert	1 Kings 19:9
1898	Atlanta	Mount Olive	J.G. Poindexter	W.J. Jenkins	Isaiah 6:8
1899	Rome	Thankful	C.H. Young	Ernest Hall	
1900	Americus	Bethesda	J.H. Moore		
1901	Griffin	Eighth Street	W.G. Johnson	G.W. Woodson	
1902	Macon	First Baptist	J.T. Latimer		
1903	Cartersville	Mount Zion	P.J. Bryant	W.F. Paschel	1 Chronicle 12:15
1904	Atlanta	Wheat Street	C.H. Holloway		
1905	Washington	Marks Chapel	J.J. Jenkins	E.G. Thomas	Isaiah 62:10
1906	Darien	First Baptist	J.H. Brown	D.D. Crawford	Rev. 15:3
1907	Athens	Hills First	A.D. Williams		
1908	Atlanta	Ebenezer	W.G. Johnson	J.H. Evans	
1909	Macon	First Baptist	Daniel Wright		
1910	Savannah	First Bryan	R.R. Smith		
1911	Atlanta	West Hunter Street	J.W. Whitehead		
1912	Augusta	Antioch	P. Jas. Bryant		
1913	Atlanta	Wheat Street			

CORRESPONDING AND EXECUTIVE SECRETARIES

1883	William E. Holmes
1884 - 1885	George H. Dwelle
1886 - 1892	C.H. Lyons
1893 -	J.C. Bryan
1894 - 1896	S.A. McNeal
1897 -	F.M. Simmons
1898 - 1901	N.B. Williamson
1902 - 1904	S.A. McNeal
1905 - 1909	G.M. Spratling
1910 - 1914	J.D. Davis
1915 -	A.W. Bryant
1915 - 1941	D.D. Crawford
1941 - 1944	W.W. Weatherspool
1944 - 1959	W.M. Jackson
1975 -	Clarence M. Wagner

One Century and a decade ago, the progenitors of our faith began this Convention with little more than faith, hope and love. It has endured squalls within and without. She has withstood the tornadoes of division, the whirlwinds of misunderstanding and the earthquakes of human injustice. Yet she has not bowed her head in disgrace nor surrendered in defeat, but set her anchors in the port of faith and humility to await the storms submission to the Controller of the elements. Her waiting has not been idly spent, that time has always been utilized to refuel, in prayer, song and Exhorting the Gospel of Jesus Christ.

From that meager beginning, the General Missionary Convention of Georgia, Inc., the successor of the Missionary Baptist Convention of Georgia is now the largest (five hundred and fifty thousand) and among the oldest Black organizations in the State of Georgia. There are many unreached horizons ahead of which her focus is upon.

Bibliography: Journals, records and files of the Missionary Baptist General State Baptist and General Missionary Baptist Convention of Georgia.

Chapter 9
PRESIDENTS FROM 1870

Acquaint yourself with the Presidents of the Missionary Baptist Convention of Georgia, General Baptist State Convention of Georgia and since consolidation in 1915, General Missionary baptist Convention of Georgia, Inc.

Each one has been a unique individual and rallied to the needs of his constituency for his day. Because of each one's contribution, the name of Jesus Christ has been lifted. Black Baptist philosophy spread, the denomination anchored to the table rock of faith, producing widespread growth and consequences.

REV. CAMERON M. ALEXANDER

On February 12, 1932, in Atlanta's Grady Hospital maternity ward, the vows of wedlock between Providence and Determination were consumated. The witnesses of this union were Homer Alexander, best man and Augusta Alexander, bridesmaid. The

initiator of matrimony and Creator of mankind, God pronounced the vows, after telling Providence and Determination, "I the wed". As usual He changed their names, hereafter to be known as Cameron Madison Alexander.

Whose walk in life would be deeply rooted in Jesus Christ, in the home of his Baptist preacher father, in Atlanta's Summer Hill section. During his formative years, he would travel with mother and father, to the rural churches, pastored by the Alexander patriarch, who served as many as four. These years were a part of the Christian education, deposited in his reservoir to be called upon in later years.

Joyously, he talks about the deep faith instilled by his parents. When quite young, assisting his mother preparing breakfast, his hand was severely burned with steaming grits. He was rushed to Grady Hospital, given emergency treatment and admitted. The burn was to such an extent the doctors thought they would have to amputate his right hand. They told the Senior Alexanders of this possibility, but they could tell definitely the next day. After an all night prayer vigil by their son's bed, in plea to God to save their son's right hand because, "someday he may need it", the doctors entered the room early the next morning and examined the burned hand.

Exasperatingly asked who has been in here attending to this child. With candid honesty on one hand and shaded truthfulness on the other, Mrs. Alexander answered, no one doctor. Recognizing what she had just said and remembering what she had been about all night, corrected her statement by saying, doctor "my husband

and I have been praying all night long, that it won't be necessary to amputate my child's hand, and Jesus has been here with us". Equally as happy, the doctor answered, "I knew someone had been here, there will be no need to amputate the hand". That hand is used and needed today, in baptism, fellowship, and gestures to preach the gospel of Jesus Christ.

His knowledge of the Bible and commitment to God's word cannot be attributed to seminary training solely. Each Saturday evening throughout childhood at his mother's knee, the coming Sunday's, Sunday School lesson was taught.

Another example of faith in the home was one Christmas. An ice storm came preventing Pastor Alexander from getting to his church. This left the house foodless and moneyless. This posed a dismal picture for Christmas, there would be no toys either. Christmas day arrived, the picture had not gotten any brighter. Understandingly, but chagrined, Mrs. Alexander asked her husband what are we going to do for dinner. Confidently, he said, set the table and call us to dinner. This done, the family gathered around the table and proceeded to offer thanks. Their prayer was interrupted by a knock at the door. In responding to this knock, there were two deacons from one of the churches, with a mule drawn wagon, loaded with food and toys. Happily the deacons said, "Reverened we knew you couldn't get to us, but these mules could get us to you, we didn't want you to be without".

One Thursday night during a revival at the Linsey Street Baptist Church in Atlanta, pastored by Rev. Davenport, Cameron accepted Christ as his Lord and Savior. Later to be baptized by the pastor.

Elementary and high school education was received from the public schools of Atlanta, the E.R. Carter Elementary and Booker Washington High School. While at E.R. Carter there was another Alexander enrolled, whose family was very prominent. Although Cameron's father was a minister and the family were Christians with character, many faculty members referred to him as, "the other Alexander". At Washington High, he excelled in band, playing the saxaphone. Upon graduating, a scholarship to Florida A&M University was received.

College was interrupted by the Korean War, with service in the United States Air Force. Being assigned for overseas duty in Thule, Greenland, he played in combos and served as a disc jockey. Up to this point his determination had excelled God's providence. As in everyone's life, God moves in His own due time. Now it was God's time to move. He did by speaking to Cameron, "go preach my Gospel!" He answered by laying the saxaphone down, turning off the record player, and started blowing for the Lord, and spinning the records of God's word.

With the tenure in Greenland over, and return home, his high school sweetheart, Barbara Jackson, accepted his proposal for marriage, and they were united in marriage, by his father, Rev. H.M. Alexander.

Recognizing the need to finish his education after being Honorably Discharged from the United States Air Force, he enrolled in Morehouse College in Atlanta, Georgia. Following graduation from there, he enrolled in the Morehouse School of Religion, earning the Master of Divinity Degree. While at Morehouse College, an effective friendship was developed with Dr. Melvin Watson, one of his professors, who made an indelible impression upon him.

While at Morehouse, his pastoral ministry began, being called to pastor the Mount Olive Baptist Church in Cartersville, Georgia. It was during this pastorate, he attended the National Baptist Convention the first time as a pastor, and undertook the first church improvement, the construction of two needed outside restrooms. The Flagg Chapel Baptist Church of Milledgeville, Georgia called him as their pastor. Following a brief tenure there, the New Pleasant Grove Baptist Church of Macon, Georgia sought his leadership. Many church and community improvements were made there. This was during the height of the civil rights movement. He was involved in the total community life. Because of the record now as pastor/preacher, the Saint John Baptist Church of Savannah, Georgia called him to the pastorate of their church. Following the same pattern as in Macon, his involvement was in the whole community. Saint John became known as the "Mighty Fortress", during this pastorate.

In July of 1969, God saw the need to bring him home to Atlanta to pastor. After preaching at Antioch Baptist Church-North, not as a contender for the church on the first Sunday of July. Later that week, he was called unanimously as their pastor. Antioch has not stopped moving since.

Throughout the pastorate, he has held denominational offices. For three years Assistant Dean of the Sunday School and B.T.U. Congress of the General Missionary Baptist Convention of Georgia, Inc. and Dean for twelve years. On September 21, 1975 at the Salem Baptist Church in Atlanta, Georgia, a campaign was initiated to elect Cameron Madison Alexander to the presidency of the General Missionary Baptist Convention of Georgia, Inc.

Three weeks earlier, I was asked to be his campaign manager. By now the campaign was organized and we were off running. Fifty-three days later, after traveling more than five thousand miles by car, plus air travel, Cameron was elected President of the General Missionary Baptist Convention of Georgia, at the Mount Vernon Baptist Church in Atlanta, around 2:30 a.m., November 13, 1975. At 5:00 p.m. on November 12, we polled the house for our votes, a total of 428 was counted. Our vote total during the election around 2:00 a.m. on the 13th was 424. Our campaign slogan had been, "New Frontiers of Christian Service".

Thus began his tenure as President of the 500,000 member, General Missionary Baptist Convention of Georgia, Inc. These four years, the convention has grown Spiritually, financially, numerically and has new meaning. It has programs that are addressed to the total church needs.

In Pittsburgh, Pennsylvania in June, 1979, Dr. J.H. Jackson appointed, "the other Alexander" to fill the unexpired term of one of the vice presidents who is now deceased. To my knowledge there are two Alexanders that are presidents of State Conventions, both of whom have been longer than Cameron. But it was "the other Alexander" chosen for that enviable position. On September 13, 1979 during the 99th Annual Session of the National Baptist Convention in Cleveland, Ohio, he was elected one of the vice presidents of this august body.

"The other Alexander" has baptized 2200 people, united 310 couples in marriage and preached 106 funerals during his pastorate. Two churches have been renovated during his pastoral career, and countless numbers counseled. Plans are being made at Antioch Baptist Church-North for an extensive building program.

Through it all, his high school sweetheart who became the bride of his youth, has been there. To this union were born Cameron Eric Alexander, Gregory Madison Alexander, Kenneth Lamont Alexander, Barbara Maria Alexander, Zeporia J. Alexander, wife of Gregory and their daughter, Shatevia. His parents, Reverened and Mrs. H.M. Alexander, who licensed and ordained him.

Solomon's Proverb fittingly describes Cameron Madison Alexander's pastoral career, "Commit your works to the Lord, and your plans will be established". Proverbs 16:3.

REV. J.C. BRYAN

J.C. Bryan was baptized, licensed to preach and ordained for the

Gospel Ministry by Rev. Kelley Lowe, long time pastor of the Springfield Baptist Church, Augusta, Georgia.

He pastored the Bethesda Baptist Church of Americus, Georgia from 1869 to 1880, and was President of the Missionary Baptist Convention of Georgia from 1882 to 1883 and again from 1886 to 1891. For one year, 1893, he served as Corresponding Secretary.

Like Enoch, J.C. Bryan, "walked with God". Genesis 5:24.

REV. GEORGE H. DWELLE

George H. Dwelle was born January 26, 1833. He was probably born in Augusta or Richmond County, Georgia. Rev. Kelly Lowe, Pastor of Springfield Baptist Church, Augusta from 1847 to 1861, ordained him.

From 1870 to 1884, he served as recording secretary of the Missionary Baptist Convention of Georgia. On two occasions, he preached the convention sermon. In 1878, when the convention met at First Baptist Church, Brunswick, Georgia, his text was Isaiah

1:8. The second time was in 1889, at the Wheat Street Baptist Church, Atlanta, his text was Psalms 124:8.

He came to Augusta in December, 1885, from Albany and Americus, Georgia to shepherd the historic Springfield Baptist Church. He is reported to have been upright of Character, pious and thrifty. Immediately after his pastorate began, the church took on new life, and growth, with many physical improvements being made.

Before resigning December, 1911 and preaching the farewell sermon in April, 1912, closing twenty-seven years of service, he left as a lasting monument the brick edifice constructed during his pastorate.

The Missionary Baptist Convention of Georgia suffered its first split in 1893. The split was named General Baptist State Convention and Dwelle was elected its first president, serving until 1901.

After resigning from Springfield, he moved to Atlanta, owned and operated the Dwelle Hospital at Edgewood and Auburn Avenue until his death, March, 1928.

He was funeralized at the Liberty Baptist Church, Atlanta, Georgia, March 28, 1928. Being eulogized in the custom of the day by the denominational leaders. He was buried in the Springfield Baptist Church yard, Augusta, Georgia.

Seriously he took David's command, "Serve thy people, and bless thine inheritance: be their shepherd also". Psalms 28:9.

REV. W.R. FORBES

Many men live a long time, but render little service. W.R. Forbes, Pastor of Macon's Tremount Temple Baptist Church, Moderator of Mount Calvary Missionary Baptist Association from 1895 to 1926, and President of the Missionary Baptist Convention of Georgia

from 1904 to 1915, was one who lived a full life and rendered great service to Christ, his denomination and race.

He and William Gilbert Johnson must be given credit for their unselfishness. Both pastored in Macon. Each was president of a state convention. Rather than becoming competitors, they were compatriots and made efforts to unite these two Baptist groups. They recognized they were serving for such a time as that. Possibly there was no one else who could have brought about reconciliation and arbitrated a merger so effectively as they.

Johnson died the year before the merger, his hopes and dreams came true in 1915. W.R. Forbes can be seen serving as treasurer of the General Missionary Baptist Convention until his death. Other known churches he pastored was Metropolitan Baptist Church, Columbus, Georgia.

Forbes was committed to service, willing to serve wherever and whenever called upon.

"Knowing that from the Lord, you will receive the reward of the inheritance. It is the Lord Christ whom you serve." Colossians 3:24.

REV. E. JAMES GRANT

A compassionate friend of blacks who had worked ardently with Andrew Bryan in Savannah, together they organized the Savannah River Baptist Association in 1802. Two years earlier, he had organized the Savannah Baptist Church, with twelve members, nine women and three men. The same year the association was organized, he was instrumental in organizing the Second Baptist Church of Savannah. These three churches, First Colored Baptist Church, Second Colored Baptist Church and Savannah Baptist Church, comprised the organizing bodies of the Savannah River Baptist Association. After laboring in the coastal

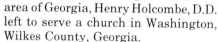

area of Georgia, Henry Holcombe, D.D. left to serve a church in Washington, Wilkes County, Georgia.

Whenever an accurate account of Georgia Baptist History, white or black is rendered, this pioneer made such an indelible impression, he must be mentioned.

In the next century after his arrival as a pastor in Wilkes County, a child was born in this same county to Edgar P. and Clara Julia Grant whom they named Edward James. This child would become equally as significant in the history of Georgia Baptist.

In 1864 when this nation was engaged in a Civil War, Black Baptist Patriarch's organized an association, that included Wilkes County. They named it Shiloh, with objectives to educate their young and win others to Christ through missionary endeavors. Their school was organized and named Shiloh Academy and located in Washington, Georgia. It was still in existence when Edward Grant became school age, becoming the site where his initial education was received.

In order to meet life's challenges and properly develop his abilities, E. James Grant continued the academic flight to the Georgia Industrial School in Savannah, Georgia. Then to Morehouse College in Atlanta, Georgia where he earned the A.B. Degree, and on to Atlanta University to receive the M.A. Degree. In order to be a workman that would not be ashamed as a gospel preacher the efforts of his studies at Union Seminary awarded him the B.D. Degree. This institution later bestowed upon him the Doctor of Divinity Degree (D.D.). In addition to the mentioned matriculations he felt a need for special studies at Gammon Theological Seminary, Atlanta, Georgia, Hampton Institute, Hampton, Virginia, and The University of Chicago, Chicago, Illinois.

One of Edward James first major decisions that gave his life such vital direction was when he accepted Christ as his Lord and Savior. Rev. F.M. Simmons who pastored the Springfield Baptist Church in Washington, Georgia was instrumental in this. It was by his hands young Grant was baptized and given the right hand of fellowship into the membership of the Springfield Baptist Church. Many years later and many miles from the land of his birth, there was another life directing decision to be made. This decision brought his life into proper focus and balance, that decision was his choice to accept God's call into the gospel ministry. He was in the state of Alabama at this time and the Rev. J.D. Harris, pastor of Montgomery's First Baptist Church is accredited with licensing and ordaining him to preach the gospel.

It seems the hand of providence dealt for E. James Grant a quadrilateral career assignment. During his life he has served well as pastor-preacher, educator-administrator, insuranceman, and businessman.

For the past thirty-four years he has pastored Albany's Mount Zion Baptist Church. During this time he has built a church plant costing nearly a million dollars. He is the president of Mount Zion Gardens Apartments, a seven million dollar low rent housing development in which he was instrumental in leading the church to sponsor. For twenty-five years he has provided tenacious and effective leadership of the Fowltown Missionary Baptist Association as Moderator. He has served as Vice President and for five years as President of the General Missionary Baptist Convention of Georgia, Inc.

Prior to pastoring Mount Zion, he pastored the New Salem Baptist Church of Jackson, Alabama and Montgomery, Alabama's First Baptist Church. He presently serves faithfully as President Emeritus and a member of the Executive Board of the General Missionary Baptist Convention of Georgia, Inc. Only a pastor-preacher could acquire such a record.

As an insuranceman he was Field Auditor and District Manager for Atlanta Life Insurance Company in the state of Alabama, also State Agent for Pilgrim Health and Life Insurance Company in Alabama.

He distinguished himself as educator-administrator as principal of East Baker Elementary and High School in Newton, Georgia. Also as director of Daughterty County Resources Development Association.

In business he owned and operated The Emporium Shoe Mart and served as interim manager of Harlem Drug Company in Albany. One probably wonders where he found the time, and from what source he drew his energy for such diversified careers.

Naturally one so involved receives many honorary positions and honors. While governor of Georgia, Jimmy Carter appointed him Lieutenant Colonel Aide De Camp on his staff. He served on the Administrative Board of the Phoebe Putnam Hospital; Citizen's Advisory Committee for Marine Logistics Supply Center; State Advisory Committee for National Guard. Albany State College has honored him with a plaque for outstanding contributions to the Religious Service of the Community. Another plaque for Outstanding Citizenship has been received from the Omega Psi Phi

Fraternity. The Mount Zion Baptist Church has recognized their Pastor for, "Outstanding Community Service and Friendship". The Delta Sigma Theta Sorority presented him their Outstanding Community Service Award. He is the recipient of Eta Omicron Chapter of Omega Psi Phi Fraternity's, Leadership in Greek Letter Franternities. The Mount Pilgrim Baptist Church has shown their appreciation for him by giving him their award in Church Community Cooperation and Leadership. The current President of the General Missionary Baptist Convention of Georgia, Inc. honored him for Leadership Rendered while president of this august body. Antioch Baptist Church of Waycross joins the others in bestowing upon him an award for Distinguished Service. He was listed in the 1970 edition of Personalities of the South". The City of Albany named, "Grant Place" in his honor. As an addendum to all that has been said, he is a smooth presider and thinks on his feet.

Dr. E. James Grant has had supporting him in these outreaches, Mrs. Ruby Brown Grant, the daughter of the late Dr. and Mrs. A.W. Brown of Richmond, Virginia. They are the parents of two daughters, Carolyn Juanita Grant Williams of Atlanta, Georgia, a Delta Airlines Trainee Instructor, and Sheryl Rosine Grant, a graduate nurse from Georgia State University, Atlanta, Georgia. Two grandsons, Tyler R. Hall of Montgomery, Alabama, and Perry E. Williams, Jr. of Atlanta and one sister.

E. James Grant was planted as a Baptist seed in the baptist forest. He outlived and outgrew other seeds. He surpassed other seedlings, shrubbery, and bushes. He caught up with some trees far his superior and over shadowed them. As he kept grasping for life, he reached for The Son. Now he stands towering far above the average and side by side the extra ordinary lofty pines. His rootage is deep in the mother earth to receive the needed nutriment for survival. The circumference of his faith is as broad as those he stands beside. Yet he possesses the agility needed to kneel in prayer to supply him with endless strength.

Our world is the better because of E. James Grant yielding himself for service to his total capacity. He took the spark of hope, fanned it with determination and illuminated the surroundings wherever he went. His stimulation could have come from the words of Solomon in this classic proverb, "Happy is the man that findeth wisdom, and the man that getteth understanding". Proverbs 3:13

REV. ALEXANDER HARRIS

Very little is known of Alexander Harris. He succeeded Adam Johnson as leading deacon of First Bryan Baptist Church of Savannah, Georgia. When Pastor U.L. Houston accepted a second term in the Georgia Legislature in the late 1860's, he was instrumental in creating a considerable amount of confusion in the church to oust the pastor.

During this upheaval, he began preaching and became an aspirant for the church. Successfully getting himself called as pastor from August of 1871 until December of the same year, when the church was permitted to have an uninterrupted conference to recall Pastor Houston.

He is next seen creating confusion in the Zion Missionary Baptist Association over his right to preach a sermon. Thus causing the first split, to organize the Mount Olive Baptist Association.

There is no available record of his pastoral career, but served 1884 - 1885 as President of the Missionary Baptist Convention of Georgia. Prior to this service, he had preached the convention sermon in Washington, Georgia in 1875.

"Blessed are the gentle, for they shall inherit the earth." Matthew 5:5.

REV. WILLIAM GILBERT JOHNSON
1861 - 1914

On June 4, 1861 during the heat of the Civil War, Gilbert and Frances Johnson were blessed with a son. They named him, William Gilbert Johnson. When nine years old, William accepted Christ and was baptized. Rev. Nathan Walker, his uncle, was pastor of Franklin Covenant Baptist Church in his native community, Hephzibah, Richmond County, Georgia.

When twelve years old he became a teacher in the Sunday School, and at fourteen was a messenger to the Walker Baptist Association, from his church.

He was a product of the public schools of Richmond County, Augusta Baptist Institute, Augusta, Georgia; Haven Normal School, Waynesboro; Payne College, Augusta; Greek and Hebrew studies under the private tutorship of Dr. O.C. Pope, a resident of Augusta.

For nine years he was a public school teacher. In 1880, was called to preach, licensed by Dr. C.T. Walker, pastor of Tabernacle Baptist Church of Augusta, and ordained by Rev. T.J. Hornsby, a life long friend.

Zion Baptist Church of Screven County called him as their pastor, the first Sunday of December, 1881. His next call was Murphy Ebenezer Baptist Church, Burke County. Followed a call to Thankful Baptist Church, Waynesboro as he rose rapidly in the forefront as an associational leader. Somehow, he managed to serve Palmer Grove Baptist Church, near Green's Cut, Georgia and Franklin Covenant, his membership church, at the same time. He did a commendable job and left an indelible mark upon all these churches during his pastorate.

In 1887, Elim Baptist Church of Augusta called him. This was his first station church. Although it was rocked with tremendous turmoil from the church it withdrew from, he stayed there for ten years. Many accomplishments were made.

First Baptist Church of Macon, Georgia called him in 1896. Again he found a chaotic situation. The church building was half completed, having stood that way for sometime. In his first year there, more than ten thousand dollars were raised. In a relative brief time the church was completed at a cost of sixty thousand dollars, with around fifteen hundred souls being baptized.

His travels were extensive, London, Paris, Gibraltor, Spain, Genoa, Italy, Pisa, Rome, Naples, Pompeii, Mount Vesuvius, Mileta, Venice, Cairo.

He served as president of the General Baptist Convention of Georgia, and one of the vice presidents of the National Baptist Convention.

He was a preacher of accomplished ability, administrator, founder of a Reformatory for delinquent youth, denominational leader, educator, respectable respresentative of his people in any circle.

Paul fittingly described W.G. Johnson,...."Devoted...in brotherly love;...preference...in honor...not lagging behind in diligence, fervent in spirit, serving the Lord; rejoicing in hope, persevering in tribulation, devoted to prayer, contributing to the needs of the saints, practicing hospitality". Romans 12:10-13.

EMANUEL KING LOVE
1850 - 1900

This child that was destined to become a denominational giant, a persuasive preacher, was born July 27, 1850 near Marion, Alabama. He accepted Christ under Rev. W.H. McIntosh in the church located in his native community.

Rev. McIntosh baptized him in July 1868, and he preached his trial sermon the same night. In 1871, he entered the Lincoln Institute in Marion, but stayed only a short while because of financial problems.

On November 18, 1872, he entered Augusta Baptist College (now Morehouse College) in Augusta, Georgia. He graduated in June 1877, head of his class.

The Home Mission Society of New York and the Mission Board of the Georgia Baptist Convention (white) appointed him State Missionary of Georgia in 1877. He retained this position until 1879 when the First African Baptist Church of Thomasville, Georgia called him as pastor.

During his pastorate there from 1879 to 1881, four hundred and fifty persons were won to Christ and baptized by him.

In 1881 the American Baptist Publication Society of Philadelphia, Pennsylvania sought him for a colporteur. He resigned the pastorate in Thomasville to accept this position.

First African Baptist Church of Savannah, Georgia, became vacant, and called him as their pastor. He assumed his pastoral responsibility there on October 1, 1885.

His call to this church was under adverse conditions. The church was badly divided in calling him. They had been severely fragmented over his predecessor, who had taken a group from the church to organize another church. To heal this wound and begin his pastorate in unity, he drew both his opposers and supporters around him and got started on a very effective and fruitful ministry.

Many physical improvements were made on the church building during E.K. Love's pastorate. A twenty-six and half foot addition onto the building, galleries in the sanctuary on both sides and back, memorial windows and a one thousand and sixty-seven pound bell was purchased in 1888, all costing eighteen thousand dollars.

E.K. Love was among other Georgians who were present in founding the Foreign Mission Convention in 1880. He became president of the Missionary Baptist Convention of Georgia in 1896.

After the National Baptist Convention was organized, there had been much discussion on the need of the convention having a publishing board. E.K. Love had been one of the prime movers in favor of it. In a message to the convention in St. Louis, Missouri in 1896, delivered by Love, he furnished the necessary fuel for such a move and offered the motion to establish a publishing board. In Boston in 1897 during the convention session, such a board was established.

His untiring labors were not extended only away from home, but at home as well. He was a leader in establishing the Georgia Industrial College for Negroes, with determination for it to be in Savannah, and Professor R.R. Wright its first president. He was the initiator of the sentiment for Atlanta Baptist College (Morehouse) to have a black president. Central City College in Macon, Georgia, the denominational school of the Missionary Baptist Convention of Georgia was established in 1899 under his leadership as president of the convention.

Among his other contributions, associate editor of **Augusta Sentinnel;** editor of **Baptist Truth;** author of **History of First African Baptist Church,** 1888.

On April 24, 1900, Emanuel King Love, pastor, preacher, educator, writer, organizer, Missionary, denominational leader, founder, evangelist, civil rights fighter, Servant of Jesus Christ was called from his earthly labors to his heavenly reward. Fifteen years pastor of First African Baptist Church, Savannah, Georgia; four years president of Missionary Baptist State Convention of Georgia; thirty-two years a preacher of the gospel of Jesus Christ.

"He gave some as apostles, and some as prophets, and some as evangelists, and some as pastors and teachers, for the equipping of the saints for the work of service, to the building up of the body of Christ;" Ephesians 4:11-12.

REV. JOHN HENRY MOORE

J.H. Moore pastored churches in Henry and Spalding Counties. He was the builder and pastor of the Eighth Street Baptist Church of Griffin, Georgia, and Moderator of Cabin Creek Association.

A number of years, he was Vice-President of the General Baptist State Convention. When W.G. Johnson died in 1914, he succeeded him as president, holding that position when the conventions were negotiating to reunite.

In 1901, he was host pastor of the General Baptist State Convention, and in 1906 preached the convention sermon in Darien, Georgia, using as a text, Romans 13:1.

He is listed among the gifted preachers of his day, carrying out to his utmost Paul's command, "Preach the word; be ready in season and out of season; reprove; rebuke, exhort, with great patience and instruction". II Timothy 4:2.

REV. JAMES MADISON NABRIT

James Madison Nabrit was born in Atlanta, Georgia. When a youth, he accepted Christ and was baptized in the Providence Baptist Church of Atlanta, Georgia. Becoming a spiritual and ecclesiastical heir to that church.

To be a productive Christian and citizen, he was aware of the  importance of a good education. Further realizing the value of being educated in a Baptist school, Morehouse College was chosen for his undergraduate work and the University of Chicago, for graduate school.

Although a native of Atlanta, an impressive metropolis, even of that day, he was initiated into the pastoral ministry in the smaller towns and cities of the state. The following churches were served by him: First Baptist Church, Forsyth; Bethesda Baptist Church, Americus; Springfield Baptist Church, Augusta; Mount Olive Baptist Church, Atlanta, and First Baptist Church, Memphis, Tennessee.

From 1922 to 1937, he provided faithful and capable leadership as president of the General Missionary Baptist Convention of Georgia. Retaining this position until departing the state to assume the presidentcy of American Baptist Theological Seminary in Nashville, Tennessee. From 1932 to 1946, he served as secretary of the National Baptist Convention, U.S.A., Inc. While residing in Atlanta, he was a professor at Morehouse College.

Every available opportunity that was presented him to serve fallen humanity, was accepted. He understood his purpose in life. To be felt, known, heard or seen - one must serve. He served joyfully. "Serve the Lord with gladness; come before Him with joyful singing." Psalms 100:2.

REV. LEANDER ASBURY PINKSTON

A native of Hancock County, Sparta, Georgia, whose early religious training came from the knee of a grandmother, who rocked in a chair singing many of the songs of the faith, including, "Ride on King Jesus".

After serving in Europe during World War I, L.A. Pinkston came

to Atlanta to enroll in Morehouse College. His oratorical skill was keenly developed during this time.

Among his early pastorates were the Bethlehem Baptist Church of Covington, Georgia, followed by a call to the Beulah Baptist Church, Atlanta; Tabernacle Baptist Church, Augusta. Returning to Atlanta as pastor of the Traveler's Rest Baptist Church.

From 1937 to 1959, President of the General Missionary Baptist Convention of Georgia, Inc., the longest ever held by anyone in the convention's one hundred and ten year life.

Pinkston was an impressive presider and a masterful parlimentarian. He gained high regard in presiding over the National Baptist Convention in 1941 in Cleveland, Ohio, when Dr. D.V. Jemison of Selma, Alabama was elected president by a commanding lead over the popular Chicago pastor, Dr. J.C. Austin.

L.A. Pinkston will always be remembered for his warmth and friendliness as long as those live that knew him.

"Now a certain Jew named Apollos, an Alexandrian by birth, an eloquent man, came to Ephesus; and he was mighty in the Scriptures." Acts 18:24.

REV. FRANK QUARLES

Reportedly to have been born in Thomasville, Thomas County, Georgia, a slave. He worked as a driver for his owner and, when freed was employed as a hack (taxi) driver. In both positions, he  was exposed to the cultured and listened to their conversations, thereby receiving his education.

From 1862 to 1881, he pastored Atlanta's Friendship Baptist Church, the Mother Church. He was among the founders of the Missionary Baptist Convention of Georgia in Augusta, 1870. Possibly because of his education, eloquence and respect, his peers chose him as the first president. A position he held until 1881.

Frank Quarles must be remembered for the convention foundation he laid during some of the most delicate years of our people in America. He like Phillip in Samaria adhered to the voice of God, "Arise and go south to the road that descents from Jerusalem to Gaza". Acts 8:26.

REV. MAJOR W. REDDICK

It would take an unusual man to be a friend of two conventions, so highly respected by all to be chosen by them upon reuniting to  serve as their president. Such was the person in M.W. Reddick, who has been acclaimed as a powerful person, of great determination.

He was well trained, esteemed by members and friends, as Pastor of Bethesda Baptist Church, Americus and Summerhill Baptist Church, Pelham, Georgia, President of Americus Baptist Institute. From 1915 to 1922, served courageously as President of the General Missionary Baptist Convention of Georgia, the first president after unification.

A well laid foundation was prepared by him upon which his successors could build upon. Our revered gratitude must be expressed to his solemn memory for the commendable job done.

"The wicked flee when no one is pursuing. But the righteous are bold as a lion." Proverbs 28:1.

REV. G.M. SPRATLING

Reverend G.M. Spratling pastored the Bryant Baptist Church of Brunswick, Georgia and served as president of the Missionary Baptist Convention, 1901 - 1903.

He had rendered faithful service to the Baptist cause for many years, prior to being selected by his denominational peers to lead their common objective.

For this juncture of the convention's life, a trustworthy man was needed. Spratling was chosen for the task.

"Many a man proclaims his own loyalty, But who can find a trustworthy man?" Proverbs 20:6.

REV. LEVI MAURICE TERRILL

Levi Maurice Terrill, who became known as a "Musical Preacher", was born in Moberly, Missouri, September 18, 1899. Moving to Kansas City, Kansas before his formative years, attending the Harriet Beecher Stowe Elementary School and Sumner High School. While at Sumner, he and three other students formed a quartet and became very popular around the two Kansas cities.

Impressed with pharmacy by his brother-in-law, Mr. Drew, who ran a pharmacy in Kansas City, Kansas for a number of years. He decided to study pharmacy, enrolling at the Bowen School of

 Pharmacy in Brunswick, Missouri. Became a licensed pharmacist in 1922. For three years, he practiced the profession of his training at Service Pharmacy (later becoming Yates and Milton) at Butler and Auburn Avenue in Atlanta, Wade Pharmacy, Washington Avenue and Hull in Athens, Georgia.

Levi accepted Christ as a youth and joined the Mount Pleasant Baptist Church (later to become Walnut Boulevard Baptist Church) in Kansas City, Kansas. He was baptized by Rev. J.R.

Richardson, the pastor of the church. Whose preaching further inspired him to enter the gospel ministry. He preached his first sermon, March 11, 1917 at Mount Pleasant.

Pastor Richardson further inspired him to prepare himself academically for the Christian ministry. Professor Curry of Sumner High School also saw great potentials in this student and encouraged him to go to Morehouse College, to receive good Baptist training. This, he did, receiving the A.B. Degree from there in May 1928. Later earning the Master of Arts Degree from Atlanta University.

In May 1925, Rev. Fambro, pastor of Hills Chapel Baptist Church in Athens, Georgia ordained him.

Tremount Temple Baptist Church of Macon, Georgia called him

as pastor in June 1928. Many significant accomplishments were made during this first pastorate.

Rev. L.M. Glenn, pastor of First Bryan Baptist Church of Savannah, Georgia died in 1935. His desire of L.M. Terrill succeeding him as pastor of the oldest Black Baptist Church in America was expressed to some of the leading members of the church, before his demise. In 1936, this church extended Terrill a call to pastor, of which, was accepted.

Continuing in like fashion at First Bryan as a Tremount Temple, many appreciable contributions were made for the church and community. The interior of the church was painted, windows reconditioned, roof painted, plans were initiated to erect a Sunday School building, and many spiritual additions were received.

His personality, academic preparation, ambition and ability to reach out and up caused him to be recognized for connectional responsibilities. In 1937, the General Missionary Baptist Convention of Georgia, elected him Vice President at large. This position included membership on the Executive Board.

Other honors were, member of the Board of Directors of the National Baptist Convention, U.S.A., Inc. In 1937 and 1939, preaching in the National Baptist Convention at Philadelphia and Los Angeles, respectively. Three times chosen to preach in the National Baptist Congress of Christian Education, in Memphis, Tennessee, Atlanta, Georgia, and Kansas City, Kansas.

On June 2, 1940, he was chosen to speak over the National broadcast radio program of Wings over Jordan, from Cleveland, Ohio. His subject was, "The Challenge of the Present Day Negro Church".

Throughout Georgia, he was sought as a baccalaureate and commencement speaker, for high schools and colleges. Many churches throughout America, called upon L.M. Terrill for evangelistic services.

An opportunity for this rising preacher came in 1943 to return to Atlanta, to pastor the Zion Hill Baptist Church, at 666 McDaniel Street. Accepting, because of the desire to offer his children, better educational opportunities and to further his education. For the next twenty-eight years, he put his all in making Zion Hill an effective beacon light, in her community, city, state, nation and world. It became known as the "Musical Church, with the Musical Pastor". To further portray the broadness of her scope, Dr. Terrill used the phrase, "The Church where scholarship and deep Spirituality work well together".

The 89th Annual Session of the General Missionary Baptist Convention of Georgia, Inc. met in Bainbridge, Georgia at the First African Baptist Church in 1959. L.M. Terrill was elected president.

As chieftan of the state's largest Black organized body, the Sunday School and B.T.U. Conventions were organized into a congress and accredited. The convention became financially sovereign, purchasing and paying for its first Baptist Headquarters at 244 Ashby Street. An opportunity to purchase a larger facility at 144 Ashby Street was offered the convention. The convention followed his leadership in this endeavor, purchased and payed for it.

When the National Baptist Convention was divided in Kansas City, Missouri in 1961, over re-electing Dr. Joseph Harrison Jackson as president or electing Dr. Gardner C. Taylor, Dr. Levi Maurice Terrill was chosen to make the seconding speech. He did so with the same kind of rhetorical splendor as the others, and led the largest group of Georgians in support of Dr. J.H. Jackson, that ensured him of re-election. Because of this support, he received patronage for Georgia, becoming an assistant secretary in 1962. Entertaining the 88th Annual Session of the National Baptist Convention in Atlanta in 1968. Preaching the convention sermon in Kansas City, Missouri in 1969. Elected as one of the Vice Presidents of this National Baptist body during the same session.

This preacher-scholar was recognized by Morris Brown College in Atlanta in 1968 and the honorary Doctor of Letters Degree was conferred upon him.

The Centennial of the convention was celebrated during his presidency in November, 1970. He was the host pastor, and Zion Hill Baptist Church was the host church.

For forty-one years, Jewell Evelyn Middlebrooks Terrill was his companion. To this union three children were born, Jewell, Levi, Jr., and Victoria. He lived to see all of his six grandchildren.

After a confining illness of three months, on the early morning of January 31, 1971, a fifth Sunday, the book of the earthly life of Levi Maurice Terrill, A.B.; M.A.; D.D.; L.L.D. was closed. His memories and contributions embedded so deeply in the sands of time and the rock of ages. So long as the Christian family remains, the Baptist denomination exists, history is written, humane deeds are done, scholarship is presented, his name must be included.

If a list of Christian patriots is ever drawn up and compiled alphabetically, look under the T's for Terrill. If such a list is compiled according to centuries, then look in the twentieth century. Or if it is done so by denomination, look under Baptist. If by chance the author decides the top one hundred, or two hundred, or thousand, Terrill's name will be somewhere in the number.

Levi Maurice Terrill, may have gained his determination and enthusiasm from this message to the Hebrew Christians, "And what more shall I say? For time will fail me if I tell of Gideon, Barak, Samson, Jephthah, of David and Samuel and the prophets, who by faith conquered kingdoms, performed acts of righteousness, obtained promises, shut the mouths of lions, quenched the power of fire, escaped the edge of the sword, from weakness were made strong, became mighty in war, put foreign armies to flight". Hebrews 11:32-34.

REV. WILLIAM JEFFERSON WHITE

The Georgia Baptist paper became the official organ of the Missionary Baptist Convention of Georgia, the forerunner of the General Missionary Baptist Convention of Georgia, Inc. in 1895. But it was founded by William Jefferson White in Augusta, October 28, 1880.

W.J. White was a pioneer in every way imaginable for his race, education, religion, journalism, and civic responsibilities. He possessed Christian ideals, an acute vision that penetrated far into

the future. His movements and footsteps were always directed toward the destination of rectitude.

He was in the first graduating class of Augusta Baptist College, Augusta, Georgia. He organized, built and pastored the Harmony Baptist Church of Augusta, until he died. His influence lent greatly to Augusta Baptist College (now Morehouse) being located in Augusta in 1865. He was a constant consultant with many noted Southerners, one of who was Dr. Joseph T. Roberts, President of Augusta Baptist College.

In 1879, when Augusta Baptist College closed to move to Atlanta, to become Atlanta Baptist College, there were a number of boys who had to return home. President Roberts sent for Dr. White. The next day there were more than a dozen passes brought to the school for those boys to return home.

Although **The Georgia Baptist** became the official organ of the State Convention in 1895, it was owned and edited by W.J. White until 1913.

This preacher-journalist-humanitarian saw the necessity and power of the printed page as being one of the most effective weapons to win the war of oppression for his people. He utilized this method, to keep them informed of current denominational occurrences. To tell the important facts that would not be told, other than through the Black press.

In 1876, the Missionary Baptist Convention of Georgia made him the Sunday School Missionary agent. He served through 1877. This same convention made him president from 1894 to 1895. He was the catalyst, felt best to be able to hold the convention together during the turmoil of the split. W.J. White is not a past memory. He is a living legend among pulpiteers, denominational leaders and journalists.

William Jefferson White is a part of that, "Great cloud of witnesses surrounding us, let us also lay aside every encumbrance, and sin which so easily entangles us, and let us run with endurance the race that is set before us". Hebrews 12:1.

REV. C.S. WILKINS

C.S. Wilkins of Columbus, Georgia was Vice-President of the Missionary Baptist Convention under Emanuel King Love. He served as President from the time of Love's death until the next convention year.

"Blessed are the merciful, for they shall receive mercy." Matthew 5:7.

Bibliography: Autobiographical interviews; **Black Baptist Trail Blazers,** 1977; **Lifted from the Minutes**, 1979, W.W. Weatherspool; **First African Baptist Church of North America,** E.G. Thomas, 1923; **Walker Baptist Association History, 1908,** Roman J. Johnson; Journals of the Missionary Baptist Convention of Georgia and General Missionary Baptist Convention of Georgia, Inc.

Chapter 10
WOMEN'S AUXILIARY
1901

In 1901, while they met at the Eighth Street Baptist church in Griffin, Georgia, the General Baptist State Convention of Georgia organized a Women's Auxiliary. If one was organized prior to that time, there are no substantial facts to prive its continued existence. This date has been accepted as the origin.

Mrs. Sylvia C.J. Bryant, wife of Dr. Peter James Bryant, who

pastored Atlanta's Wheat Street Baptist Church, was elected as first president. She was a leader in her own right. Owner and principal of the Sylvia Bryant Baptist Academy on Auburn Avenue in the city of her residence.

When the conventions consolidated in 1915, she retained the same position. The following ladies were elected with her at that time to help carry the torch:
Vice President, Mrs. S.J. Fluker, Argyle
Recording Secretary, Miss Hattie J. Forrest, Valdosta
Financial Secretary, Mrs. A.B. Murden, Athens
Corresponding Secretary, Mrs. B.A. Johnson, Washington
Treasurer, Mrs. D.M. Gadson, Rome
State Directress, Mrs. Mattie Williams, Madison
National B.M., Mrs. Rebecca Daniel, Columbus
National O.B.O., Mrs. H.E. Harris, Atlanta

President Bryant remained in this position until 1920, when she was succeeded by her Vice President, Mrs. S.J. Sluker, whose corps of officers were:
Vice President, Mrs. D.M. Gadson, Macon
Recording Secretary, Miss Hattie Forest, Valdosta
Financial Secretary, Mrs. D.A. Murden, Athens
Corresponding Secretary, Mrs. B.A. Johnson, Washington
Treasurer, Mrs. Julia Woodruff, Savannah
Pianist, Mrs. W.F. McKenney, Atlanta
Assistant Pianist, Mrs. R.E. Ponder, Americus
Musical Directress, Mrs. H.E. Harris, Atlanta
Organizer of Children's Bands, Mrs. Hattie E. Harris, Atlanta
National Board Member, Mrs. Bessie Foster, Savannah
National State Director, Mrs. S.F. Brown, Newnan

This section from Mrs. Fluker's annual address in 1922, tells what kind of leader of women she was in a completely dominated men's world.

What Is Expected Of Women Of This Age

In the early ages of the world's history, and in the middle ages,

women were not expected to play their part in the drama of life and on the stage of time like conditions now demand.

God took from man's side a rib out of which was formed, and knowing this as I do, I've been more deeply impressed than ever that God meant for women to work and act side by side of men in the great campaign of human uplifting and for the advancement of the Master's cause on earth.

To become honored wives is a great achievement (especially when we are not mismatched), to become legitimate and devoted mothers in that method of propogating the human family with which God is pleased, but there is much more land to be possessed by women of this age.

After years of heart ache, prayers, suffering and sacrificing on the part of women they were instrumental in helping the abolitionists to push forward the sentiment which ultimately terminated in liberating the Sable sons of Ham in the United States of America.

Susan B. Anthony agitated, pleaded and prayed for years, and the ultimate results of her contention are that, legally speaking, every woman in America has the right to vote.

In the school rooms, colleges and universities, yea in Church, State and on the lecture platform we are expected to play an equal part as is expected of men today.

We have worked untiringly in the home, schools, colleges and in churches in days of long ago, but now we are represented as Senators as Georgia being first to produce a woman Senator, it is creditable to make mention in passing.

. . . In conclusion, your devotion to the cause of Christ, loyalty to our church and its usage, and the confidence you have placed in me to be your president the last two years, have endeared me to you, to the effect that neither time nor eternity can finally erase. When the Black Angel Death shall have flocked his wings in our chambers, and the waters of the Atlantic Gulf shall have ceased to wash the restless feet of this republic and when the mountains shall have for the last time kissed the glad glance of the sun among the moving millions going up to be with God and the Savior we adore, I will meet you.

Your servant for Christ
S. Jewell Fluker
President of G.M.B.W.C. of Georgia
Box 58, Argyle, Georgia[1]

---

[1]General Missionary Baptist Convention of Georgia minutes, 1922.

For the next twenty-four years, she carried on in that same Spirit, leading the women, working cohesively with the men and in her feminine way, leading them. The die of the Women's work of Georgia was cast by her influence and molded by her spirit.

Her health began failing in 1946 and she was unable to attend the session held in Savannah, at First Bryan. Her faithful Vice

President, Mrs. M.J. Thomas presided, and the next year, 1947, became her successor. Supported by:

Vice President, Mrs. L.S. Weatherspool, Atlanta

Recording Secretary, Miss Hattie J. Forest, Valdosta

Assistant Secretary, Mrs. Flossie Sanders, Augusta

Financial Secretary, Mrs. I.F. Henderson, Atlanta

Corresponding Secretary, Mrs. L.E. Grier, Atlanta

Treasurer, Mrs. Carrie Cross, Albany

Historian, Mrs. Evie Thompson, Atlanta

Parliamentarian, Mrs. C.B. Reese, Newnan

Musical Directress, Mrs. Rose Ison, Monroe

Assistant Musical Directress, Mrs. Viola Oliver, Savannah

President Thomas served until 1956, then becoming President emeritus. Mrs. L.S. Weatherspool, who was Vice President, succeeded her, providing faithful service to the Convention and the cause of Christ.

MRS. L.S. WEATHERSPOOL

The true test of any character is the ability to rise above native circumstances, adverse conditions, inconveniences and to make the best out of less than normal conditions. Then after reaching life's goal, unashamedly remember the past and attribute it toward success.

Prior to World War II our nation was an agriculture society. The majority of her citizens were born and raised on the farm or in the very small hamlets and villages that were rural oriented. These

persons endured hardships throughout life and were unafraid of toil. Many went from their rural habitats into our nation's classrooms that molded the minds of today's and yesteryear's youth. Others into the legislative structure. There were the countless numbers led into the pulpit to be the pulse beat of our nation's conscious and to ensure her spiritual temperature. From the sons and daughters of tillers of the soil and hewers of wood we

142

have that class of people in all walks of our nation's life. Were it not for them the depression of the thirties would have swept us into oblivion. World War II would have been our Waterloo. The Korean War would have proved us to be traitorous and treasonness. The revolution of the late 50's and 60's would have torn us apart at the seams, had there not been the influence and presence of the sons and daughters of the soil and their influence among their heirs and proteges. The division over Vietnam, disloyalty and irresponsibility would have thrown us overboard into the sea of forgetfulness.

It is one of the daughters of the soil, of which our attention is focused upon. Well acquainted is she with the fresh aroma of new plowed ground, freshly mown hay, the earth's freshness after the air is cleaned of its dust by rain. Familiar is she with the melodious sonnets of the chorus of spring's first bird or the squeal of a baby pig, or a calf's first sound. There are some things of nature that only those who have lived close to nature can understand and appreciate.

Such a person is Mrs. Lillie Mae Sirmons Weatherspool, a product of the black dirt flatlands of Brooks County, Georgia, the joining county to Florida's north boundary. She was born in Dixie, located between Thomasville and the county seat of Quitman. The oldest of four children born to Elihue Kellog and Mahala Eva Spencer Sirmons. This family was ranked among the successful black farmers of their section of this county. Economic standards were not the only measures of success. Their maintaining a church for their spiritual needs, growth and development, was a measuring rod. A further measure was their determination to educate, mentally stimulate and challenge their youth. They would accept no less than the best for their dollar value.

From the time of birth, Mrs. Weatherspool was exposed to the dual guiding lights of spirituality and education. The Simmon Hill Baptist Church, pastored by Rev. Wiley F. Tarver, a resident of Quitman, was located near her home. Along with her three brothers, she began attending Sunday School there. During a revival conducted by Rev. H.F. Taylor, pastor of Macedonia Baptist Church in Valdosta, Georgia, she accepted Christ as her Savior, and later was baptized by Pastor Tarver. This pastor was a tremendous inspiration to the youth of his church.

Simmon Hill Elementary School was located within close proximity to her residence. Like the religious life of their children, her family equally valued their academic exposure. Therefore, the journey into the halls of knowledge was begun. Because the residents of this community refused the less than average teachers, the county provided for them with their tax money. They sought teachers themselves that met their standards. Consequently, Simmon Hill was better than the average black school in its era. Three teachers of such calibre, Mrs. Weatherspool vividly remembers is her first teacher, Professor J.T. Hancock of Atlanta, Professor Marion Campbell of Quitman, and Professor H.S. Dixon of Sylvester, Georgia.

Another her memory recorded pleasantly was a Mr. Salmon who taught there prior to her enrollment. Mr. Salmon planted a seed in both her mind and her parents that grew into reality. He said to the adult Sirmons, there is a school in Atlanta called Spelman Seminary, and when this little, bright girl is old enough, I want you to send her there. Mr. Salmon was from Atlanta, and years later returned to the community as an agent with the Standard Life Insurance Company. Again he reminded her of his wish for her to go to Spelman.

Upon finishing the eighth grade at Simmon Hill, she went to Spelman for high school and college where she earned the Bachelor of Arts Degree. From there to Atlanta University and received the Master of Arts Degree.

Like most people there are many people we are indebted to for helping to mold and shape our lives outside our family and teachers. One such person she warmly remembers is Miss Lily Gaines who served as Jeannes Supervisor in Brooks County. As a child out of affection she was prone to imitate "Miss Lily" and because of this life long influence she still finds herself doing things in the manner she feels "Miss Lily" would do them.

After leaving Brooks County she did not leave her Christianity and church membership behind. Neither did she find Christianity cumbersome, fogy or unattractive. One of her first Christian responsibilities was recording secretary of the Thomasville Association, of which she served for a number of years even after moving outside the bounds of that body and her husband was called to pastor the Metropolitan Baptist Church in Columbus, Georgia.

She began serving in the General Missionary Baptist Convention in the 1930's and served as instructor in the Sunday School and B.T.U. Congress. Faithful service has been rendered as a committee worker in the Women's Convention. Because of that faithfulness the ladies called upon her to serve them as their vice-president for nine years. After proving further faithfulness, they then asked her to serve as their president for nineteen years. This she did with flying colors. Since 1975, she has been equally faithful as President Emeritus and does whatever called upon to do. Presently, she is a member of the Executive Board of the Convention.

Mrs. Weatherspool has been affiliated with the National Baptist Convention U.S.A., Inc. since 1935 when it met in New York City. She attended then primarily as an auditor. But since that time has been a faithful and loyal worker. She has had many signal honors such as being programmed to introduce the President of the Women's Convention, Mrs. S. Willie Leyton, to present her annual address in Houston, Texas. Because of Mrs. Leyton's illness she did so in absentia.

Since that time she has received many appointments in the Women's Convention. Such as Co-chairman of the Joanna P. Moore Tract Committee, instructor of Stewardship in the Morning

Mission Study.

Her Christian testimony and influence has had an impact on the local scene as well. She is the wife of Dr. W.W. Weatherspool, who has successfully pastored Atlanta's Mount Olive Baptist Church for more than forty years. During his tenure as pastor, he has built a spiritual church as well as a physical church with educational facility.

This pastoral team has traveled extensively throughout the world. As recent as 1978, they toured the People's Republic of China and later the same year toured parts of Europe, Egypt, Africa, Jordan and Palestine. They are not the physical parents of any children, but are considered affectionately as "mamma and daddy" to many.

In addition to her Christian service, she has served equally well in secondary and college education. She has taught in the following schools: South Highland High School, Anniston, Alabama, in the area of mathematics, Douglas High School, Thomasville, Georgia, as a mathematics instructor, supply teacher, Spencer High School, Columbus, Georgia, and a graduate assistant in mathematics at her Alma Mater, Spelman, College.

In 1958 the Atlanta Chapter of the Iota Phi Lambda Sorority named her Woman of the Year in Religion. She holds life membership in the National Association for the Advancement of Colored People.

The following organizations of which she has served, one of which she is a life member have awarded her with Certificates of Appreciation, plaques and merits for service: the National Alumnae Association of her Alma Mater, Spelman College; the Atlanta Chapter of the National Council of Negro Women; the National Association of Ministers' Wives - lifetime member; Women's Department of General Missionary Baptist Convention of Georgia, Inc. - lifetime membership; Women's Department of the National Baptist Convention U.S.A., Inc. - lifetime member; Mount Olive Baptist Church, Atlanta, Georgia.

Her labors have taken her across the boundaries of race. The Georgia Baptist Convention utilized her services as a part-time worker to conduct Mission Study classes. This assignment took her into many parts of the state. Like her world travels have made her a multi-national person, her services across racial lines have made her a multi-racial person.

Mrs. Weatherspool has lived through two revolutionary periods for women during this century, the "Woman's Suffrage" and "Women's Liberation". While she has not been actively involved in either, nor a likely proponent for the later. She found liberation through the salvation of Jesus Christ, and thus her life has been given to Him and her services rendered in His name.

Solomon in the Holy Writ likewise has words to describe her, "Every wise woman buildeth her house; but the foolish plucketh it down with her hands". Proverbs 14:1.

As a Christian woman she has built her house upon a solid foundation, both as a Christian servant, wife and educator.

Mrs. Weatherspool gave nineteen years of good service. In 1975, Mrs. C.M. Pearson, Atlanta, was elected President of the Women's Auxiliary. Her current officers are:

President Emeritus, Mrs. L.S. Weatherspool, Atlanta
First Vice President, Mrs. W.N. Robinson, Savannah
Second Vice President, Mrs. Gertrude Dyar, Rome
Corresponding Secretary, Mrs. J.E. Terrill, Atlanta
Recording Secretary, Mrs. R.R. Mallard, Ludowici
Assistant Recording Secretary, Mrs. Grace Huff, Columbus
Treasurer, Mrs. Ollie Hardy, Pine Mountain
Music Director, Mrs. Mary Murray, Fort Valley
Assistant Music Director, Mrs. Elizabeth Golden, Augusta
Pianist, Mrs. Carrie Simmons, Brunswick
Organist, Mrs. Rubye Moss, Atlanta
Director of Young People, Mrs. Doris Jordan, Canton
Corresponding Secretary, Mrs. Ethel Henderson, Atlanta

MRS. C.M. PEARSON

Born Charlie Mae Littlejohn to Charles and Dixie Alexander Littlejohn, prior to the adulthood of the Twentieth Century. Father Littlejohn was a native South Carolinian. Mother Littlejohn was a native Georgian, who died when her youngest daughter was six months old. Leaving she and oldest sister, Mrs. Sarah Ruth Littlejohn White to be reared by their grandmother.

The comforting smile worn by this matriarch of Georgia Baptist women matches perfectly her dramatic life. When five years old she accepted Christ and was baptized at six years old by Rev. Cyrus Brown in the Macedonia Baptist Church in Atlanta, Georgia. Rev. Brown performed the marital ceremony that united her mother and father in Holy wedlock in Macedonia. It was also his distinct privilege to baptize her mother, father and grandmother in the same church. At fifteen years old she served as Superintendent of Sunday School of her church. She no longer belongs to Macedonia and the church has since moved. She lives across the street from it and works about two doors from it at Baptist Headquarters.

This unusual lady has touched many lives. The late Dr. L.M. Terrill used to tell how she fed him and other hungry students, struggling to finish Morehouse College, when she lived on Brown Street near the campus. Among those who could attest of her helpfulness are Dr. Martin Luther King, Sr., Dr. Sandy F. Ray, Dr. C.N. Ellis, Dr. Martin Luther King, Jr., and others.

For fourteen years she successfully operated the Savoy Hotel on Auburn Avenue, the mecca of Black Businesses during that era. She started on a shoe string by borrowing one thousand dollars from Mr. Jess Hanley, a Funeral Home entrepreneur. The leading Blacks Worldwide stayed at the Savoy. To name a few, Mary McLeod Bethune, Rev. Dr. Henry Boyd Allen, The Wings Over Jordan Choir, The Ink Spots, Louis Jordan's Band, Eddie Rochester Anderson, Officers in Training at Fort Benning and many, many other Prominent Blacks.

During Dr. C.N. Ellis' presidency of the Atlanta Baptist Minister's Union, this group had a Radio Broadcast called, "Chariot Wheels". Their rehearsal and broadcast each Sunday night was done from the hotel ballroom that seated five hundred comfortably. In addition to these religious services, there were others. Each Tuesday morning she held staff meetings that were always opened with scripture and prayer. Each Sunday morning she taught a Sunday School class for the guests who desired to attend.

Her success in the hotel business might well be attributed to her consistant interest in human need. When Dr. & Mrs. W.W. Weatherspool were being intimidated by the K.K.K., she provided them free hotel accommodations. This can be matched with many more similar incidents. Because of her all around business acumen the Chamber of Commerce, Negro Business League and Southern Railroad all gave her citations for distinguished service. During World War II she was the only Black Woman to serve as air warden in Atlanta.

When the National Baptist Convention met in Atlanta in 1946 the Women's Convention held a banquet in her hotel with linen, china and silver. On another occasion the Minister's wives sponsored a reception for Mrs. Ross in her hotel, with the minister's wives serving as hostesses.

The testimony of which she tells that brought about the transition from the motel business to a full time Christian Servant, also tells that her smile originates from her heart and radiates on her face.

While attending a State Convention in Pelham, Georgia she became seriously ill. Her doctor gave her six months to live. More meaningful than the doctors prediction the Lord spoke to her, telling her the need to give up the hotel. She then promised the Lord if He restored her health, that she would.

Mrs. Janice Singleton, Executive Secretary of the Women's Mission Union of the Georgia Baptist Convention offered her one hundred and forty dollars a month travel expenses. An offer was also made to purchase her hotel of which was refused. Another trip on the road brought a reoccurrence of illness. Upon returning to Atlanta her physician recommended her to a specialist. Examinations and test were made. Upon finding the results the specialist recommended that she go to another specialist in New York. But while she was deciding to go, her doctor told her if there were any changes, to call him, she left his office praying and continued throughout the night. Around 6:00 a.m. the following morning there was a very definite change. She called the specialist and was given an appointment for 9:00 a.m. His examination revealed her body had undergone a complete recovery since his examination the day before. That ailment has not occurred since.

Almost simultaneously with her physical recovery came the second offer from the same people to buy the hotel. This time she followed through.

Thus launching a career into fulltime Christian Service. Mrs. Singleton then offered her the opportunity to work for the Georgia Baptist Convention. She was reluctant because of hearing about the Executive Secretary, Dr. Searcy Garrison's, racial stance. A decision was made to talk with him, and after a very candid talk that gave her a better understanding of him, she accepted. Soon after making the decision she discovered her greatest opposition was not from the whites but the blacks.

On many occasions, especially during the early years while traveling throughout the state, she stayed in white homes. She reports in all of these years she never lost friendship with anyone and recalls only one disfavorable experience. One white lady in whose home she stayed wanted to call her by her first name. She reported the incident to Mrs. Singleton, her supervisor, who in turn wrote the lady a very nice letter. The next time she saw the lady and each time thereafter she very warmly called her, Mrs. Pearson.

Her teacher has been life and the world her school room. One of the formal school settings of which she matriculated was the Nannie Helen Burroughs National Trade School in Washington, D.C. While there she completed the curriculum offered, but received something far greater than the certificate offered upon completion. She established a friendship with Miss Burroughs that lasted the remainder of the later's lifetime. Equally as meaningful, Miss Burroughs became her mentor until she drew her final breath.

Miss Burroughs was the President of the Women's Convention of the National Baptist Convention. For six years Mrs. Pearson filed and compiled the records of the Women's Convention in Miss Burroughs office. This responsibility enabled her to travel throughout the nation and the world.

Her recognition among the Black Baptists of Georgia resulted because of her national recognition. Many of the women from Georgia who are recognized in the National Baptist arena now should give her expressions of thanks. Mrs. J.E. Terrill, Mrs. L.S. Weatherspool, Mrs. Arvella Turnipseed, and many others are holding positions because of her instrumentality.

Although she worked in a liaison capacity with the white Georgia Baptists and black Georgia Baptists, it carried her into more white churches than black. Many black ministers whom she had befriended while in the hotel business or when they were in school were the first to invite her to their churches. This opened doors for her and are still doing so.

Ridge Avenue, S.W. was once a very fashionable community. She owned a home on this street that would be an almost invaluable ante-bellum house today. These homes no longer exist because of the area becoming a commercial one. She has many fond memories of her home and neighborhood. In addition to its beauty and comfort many notables and friends were entertained there.

When Mrs. Pearson intimated her desire to become president of the Georgia Baptist Women, there were a few who uttered all she could do was travel for the white Baptists and talk about missions. There was another untold number who had not forgotten that she was the one who had discovered them hidden in the isolation of their rural church or unknown associations. She had both encouraged and helped them to come to the the State Convention. And for all the years they had been attending she was the only person of convention prominence who they knew and knew them. She had never forgotten them, and when the time came for her to accomplish her wish, they were not going to forget her, and they didn't.

On that rainy Wednesday morning of November 12, 1975 in the sanctuary of Atlanta's Friendship Baptist Church, in spite of the unethical, unchristian and unsavory efforts of some, she was chosen by a mammoth number of our states ladies to be their leader. Ever since that day, they have proven she is their leader, because they have followed her.

For three years now our offices have been adjacent on the same floor. We have traveled the length and breadth of this state together. For the past three years, she has been a part of the team that carries the convention to the people, for twelve days each year. To cover the twelve Districts of our Convention, five to six thousand miles are traveled. She has in every way been a part of the team and never lost her smile. Her smile is by no measure a sign of weakness or fear. She can be equally as stern when necessary as she is sweet and compassionate.

Although she has never been a mother by giving birth to a child, she has two daughters and one son, Mrs. Doris Lunday Fugua, Miss Freddie Bason, Mr. John Lunday. She has likewise become mother to their parents and countless others, throughout Georgia, America and the world.

I am sure every church, association, State and National Convention and denomination has a Madonna like Mrs. C.M. Pearson. If they haven't, there is a missing link. Mrs. Pearson is ours, we are thankful for her. We want her to know, not merely by words but actions and deeds.

The Holy Bible's Proverbist Solomon describes her well, "A worthy woman who can find, for her price is far above rubies... Strength and dignity are her clothing; and she laugheth at the time to come. She opened her mouth with wisdom; and the law of kindness is on her tongue. She looketh well to the ways of her household, and eateth not the bread of idleness". Proverbs 31:10, 25-27.

Today Baptist women in Georgia are serving in key roles of the Convention, as members of the executive board, in all facets of policy making. We are united in all of our meetings. Mrs. Pearson, as President of the Women's Convention, is in charge the first two days of the annual session, and the first day of the adjourned session. With the men being present in both, all sermons are delivered by pastors of the Convention. Likewise, women participate on the Convention's programs.

Mrs. Fluker's message in 1922 to the women also reached the men. We have come a long way together. There are many mountains ahead that must be scaled, threatening rivers to forge, blistering deserts to cross, low valleys to pass through. Just as we succeeded in surmounting all the obstacles that were before us in the past, they will not deter us in the future as we march onward together, side by side, to possess the lands ahead.

Bibliography: Minutes of the Georgia Missionary Baptist Convention of Georgia, Convention records, **The Georgia Baptist** paper and **Lifted from the Minutes**, W.W. Weatherspool, 1979.

Bibliographies of Mrs. Pearson and Mrs. Weatherspool by interview.

Chapter 11
NATIONAL BAPTIST CONVENTION, U.S.A., INC.
1880

What is now the largest and most powerful Black organization in the world had a very humble beginning with about one hundred and fifty persons present, with eleven states being represented, November 24, 1880.

This meeting was held in the heart of Confederacy, with the First Baptist Church, Montgomery, Alabama, Rev. W.H. McAlpine, Pastor.

Rev. W.W. Colley, a returned Missionary from Africa; having been appointed by the Southern Baptist Convention and served from 1875 to 1879, was instrumental in convening such a large aggregation of people from a vast circumference.

When Colley returned to America, he was employed by the Negro Baptists of Virginia to tour America to organize a general Convention among Negro Baptists. This need grew out of the constant turmoil that arose between Black and White Missionaries in Africa, regarding the cruel treatment often inflicted upon the natives by White Missionaries.

Colley's call was answered on the above mentioned date and place by the referred number, for the noble reason to organize a Convention whose emphasis would reach beyond the bounds of American soils for Christ.

Looking back on that day and its significant outcome, that meeting must be described as one of intense Spiritual and moral consquences. It has been reported to have been filled with such awe created by Colley, much weeping and shouting took place before the official opening by almost everyone present.

After about a thirty minute devotion, Colley served as temporary Chairman. Himself in tears, flowing into his long beard. The moments of silence that elapsed as he sought to gain his composure allowed the audience to observe his illuminated face. The gavel was lifted and sounded on the Holy desk, declaring the opening of the meeting and its purpose. Thus was born The Foreign Mission Convention on this beautiful sunlit fall day. With joy, all present were as radiant inside that church sanctuary as the Sun was upon the Alabama hills and valleys.

Rev. W.H. McAlpine was elected President, eleven others were elected Vice-Presidents, Rev. J.M. Armstead, Secretary, an Assistant Secretary was elected, also a Treasurer.

By organizing this Convention, Black Baptists in America were now given a new sense of national power, influence and responsibility. This thrust them into the vanguard of denominational recognition and input.

Their next step was to organize a Board of Directors, and establish a headquarters in Richmond, Virginia. This board was commissioned to reach unenlisted churches, associations, State Conventions and other bodies to raise funds for foreign mission endeavors in Africa and other areas.

A Foreign Mission Board of the Convention was established, electing Rev. A.Binga, Jr. of South Richmond, Virginia as first Chairman, W.W. Colley as first Corresponding Secretary or Executive Secretary and field agent with an annual salary of one thousand dollars. Colley is the patriarch of Black Baptist Foreign Missions, since through him the idea became alive and survived among our denomination. Its accomplishments and impact have been legion and innumerable.

The document that guided this group in the early years is best expressed in the Preamble of the Constitution of the Baptist Foreign Mission Convention of the United States of America, which reads,

"Whereas it becomes necessary and is our duty to extend our Christian influence to advance the Kingdom of Christ, and as African Missions claim our most profound attention and feeling that we are most sacredly called to do work in this field and elsewhere abroad; therefore, we, the representatives from the various Churches, Sunday Schools, and societies of the Baptist denomination in the United States, do hereby solemnly organize ourselves in a Convention for the above-named objects: We agree to the following Constitution: This Convention shall be styled and known as the Baptist Foreign Mission Convention of the United States of America."

Secretary Colley resigned in 1883, to become the Board's first missionary to Africa. He was accompanied by his wife, Rev. and Mrs. J.H. Presley, Brother J.J. Coles and Rev. H. McKinney. They established a mission station at Grand Cape Mount. Mrs. Presley's health failed, her child died and in less than a year, Rev. Presley returned a helpless invalid. Quite a cost to pay to share the love of Christ, but not near the price He paid for us to have that love.

The first session of the Foreign Mission Convention in 1880 reported their financial receipts as three hundred seventeen dollars and six cents. In its third session in 1883, before Colley or Presley departed for Africa, Presley and Coles reported from their contact with Virginia churches alone, Rev. J.H. Presley, four hundred forty-six dollars and fourteen cents, Brother J.J. Coles one hundred one dollars and fourteen cents, one hundred and twenty-two converts from three months work.

Another plateau of Black Baptists is dated 1886 when her horizons spread geographically and objectively.

AN OPEN LETTER FROM W.J. SIMMONS
Dear Brethren: April 5, 1886, an open letter to the Baptist clergy and laymen was issued by Rev. William J. Simmons, an American Baptist, asking if we should have a National Convention to discuss questions of interest to our beloved denominations. At that time the following reasons were given.

1. To promote personal piety, sociability, and a better knowledge of each other.

2. To be able to have an understanding as to the great ends to be reached by the denomination.
3. To encourage our literary men and women, and promote the interest of Baptist literature.
4. To discuss questions pertaining especially to the religious, educational, industrial, and social interests of our people.
5. To give an opportunity for the best thinkers and writers to be heard.
6. That, united, we may be more powerful for good and strengthen our pride in our denomination.

Having been solicited to write the Call by many whose names and endorsements are here unto affixed, the Call is hereby made by their advice and solicitations for said convention to meet in St. Louis, Mo., August 25, 1886, 10 o'clock a.m., in the First Baptist Church, and the pastor thereof is hereby requested to serve as a Committee of Arrangements, with power to select his associates.

Wm. H. Seward, Louisville, Ky., and Rev. R.H. Cole, 2609 Goode Avenue, St. Louis are hereby requested to serve as Committee of Transportation.

Wm. J. Simmons[1]

Being nationally known, Dr. Simmons got a tremendous response from his letter. Approximately six hundred people attended of all descriptions, graduates in law, medicine and theology; respected professors of Philosophy, German, Hebrew, Latin, French, Greek; Ex-State representatives, ex-senators; two ex-lieutenant governors; a number of Black editors and teachers; a senator from Mississippi, who was a Baptist, and a Baptist Missionary from London, England.

This array of Black aristocracy of that day participated in founding the American National Baptist Convention, then to elect the following officers:
W.J. Simmon, President
J.R. Young, Vice-President
J.L. Johnson, Vice-President
L.R. DeBaptiste, Corresponding Secretary
T.S. Clanton, Recording Secretary
W.H. Steward, Recording Secretary
D.A. Gaddie, Treasurer
Miss L.W. Smith, Historian
A Constitution was drawn up and adopted, permitting the group to embark upon their voyage into history. One of their main objectives was to unite all Negro Baptists in America for the work of Missions. It has been reported Vice-President J.L. Johnson said during this meeting, "Knox lifted Scotland, Luther lifted Germany,

---

[1]Minutes of the National Baptist Convention, U.S.A., Inc.

and it remains for us to lift up the heathen in the land of our fathers - Africa.".

We must be reminded of the enviable passion that existed among the founders of the National Baptist Cause for Missions, that began in 1880, when the Foreign Mission Convention was organized. The American National Baptist was organized five years and nine months later.

Seemingly for some time, the American Baptist Convention attempted to operate missions separately from the Foreign Mission Convention, who already had missionaries on the field three years prior to their other denominational counterparts organization. A resolution was adopted at the second meeting of the American Convention to send a committee to the Foreign Mission Baptist Convention to meet with them. This request met favorable reception.

This pact was not the solution for unification, for in 1893 another group was formed in Washington, D.C., whose horizons were to be national. It was named the Baptist National Educational Convention, composed of a group of erudite pastors.

In the same year, 1893, since much confusion existed among Black Baptist leaders, an effort was put forth to unite the three Conventions. The New England Convention, organized in 1875, African Foreign Mission Convention and the Foreign Mission Convention of America, organized in 1880. They attempted to unite their financial resources to send missionaries to the foreign field and expand their outreach. This attempt failed as they launched out to raise five thousand dollars between them to begin a new work in the Congo, for the missionaries to labor.

After fourteen years it seemed the work of the Foreign Mission Convention was at a very low ebb. Only one missionary remained on the field in Africa, R.A. Johnson, who was largely self-supported. All the others were either dead or at home.

It seems this dilemma was not precipitated from lethargy on the part of Black Baptists, neither the shortage of funds. But because of lack of confidence in the administrative credibility of L.M. Luke, Corresponding Secretary of the Board in Richmond. He was suspected of practicing poor business procedures.

S.E. Griggs, a student of Richmond Theological Seminary, was employed by the Board to answer the attacks against Luke. His approach to answer the question was scholarly and diplomatic, but it did not restore the lost confidence on the part of Board members and Convention constituents.

All groups were to meet in Montgomery in 1894. The Board was too embarrassed to come to Montgomery. The efforts of the "Triportite Convention" had failed. Had all the Conventions or their representatives come to Montgomery, there would have been five. The New England and The African Foreign Mission Conventions did not appear. Although all were vying for national attention, but failing because of poor administration and the lack of workable programs.

The Black Baptist population of 1890 and their assets prove where the weakness was in the connectional life.

1890 NATIONAL BLACK BAPTIST STATISTICS

1,071,092	Black Church Members
311	Associations
9,079	Churches
4,590	Ministers
2,603	Sunday Schools
143,832	Sunday School Students
$1,334,092.00	Church property value
$181,063.41	Contributed for religious and educational work
39,151	Baptisms

After all reports were in that picturized the true demeanor of the Board, and all were satisfied, sincere efforts had been put forth to unite all Black Baptist of America. A scholarly orator, a graduate of Bushnell University, named A.W. Pegues offered the following resolution that depicts his awareness of reaching the corrective measures of curing the ailment.

"Whereas, The interest and purposes of the three National Bodies, namely, the Foreign Mission Convention, the National and Educational Conventions, can be conserved and fostered under the auspices of one body; and whereas, the consolidation of the above-named bodies will economize both time and money; Therefore, be it resolved, that the Foreign Mission Convention appoint a Committee of nine, who shall enter immediately into consultation with executive boards of the National and Educational Conventions for the purpose of effecting a consolidation of the three bodies upon the following plan:

1. That there shall be one national organization of American Baptists.
2. Under this, there shall be a Foreign Mission Board, with authority to plan and execute the foreign mission work according to the spirit and purpose set forth by the Foreign Mission Convention of the United States of America.
3. That there shall be a Board of Education and a Board of Missions to carry into effect the spirit and purpose of the National and Education Conventions respectively."

Such a committee was appointed in Montgomery, Alabama, at the First Baptist Church in 1894, and was charged to bring their findings to Atlanta, Georgia in 1895. To report during the session that would convene at the Friendship Baptist Church, pastored by Dr. E.R. Carter.

The Committee members were:
W.H. McAlpine
A.W. Pegues
Joseph E. Jones
A.S. Jackson
J.H. Frank
A. Hobbs

Jacob Bennette
Wesley G. Parks
A.J. Stokes

A year was to lapse, before the session would convene in Atlanta and would allow time for the committee to arrive at the necessary findings. They were prepared when called for in 1895, having done the necessary studying . Their report was favorably received, and what took place thereafter is best told by the Constitution:

PREAMBLE

Whereas, It is the sense of the Colored Baptists of the United States of America, convened in the City of Atlanta, Ga., Sept. 28, 1895, in the several organizations as "The Baptist Foreign Mission Convention of the United States of America", hitherto engaged in mission work in the United States of America; and the "National Baptist Educational Convention", which has sought to look after the educational interest that the interest of the way of the Kingdom of God required that the several bodies named should, and do now, unite in one body. Therefore, we do now agree to and adopt the following Constitution:

ARTICLE I
NAME

This body shall become known and styled The National Baptist Convention of the United States of America.

ARTICLE II
THE OBJECT

The object of this Convention shall be to do mission work in the United States of America, in Africa, and elsewhere, and to foster the cause of education.

ARTICLE VI

The Convention shall elect at each annual meeting a Foreign Mission, a Home Mission, and an Education Board consisting of fifteen members each. Each Board shall have a President, Vice-President, Recording Secretary, Treasurer, and Corresponding Secretary with powers of general managers subject to rules and regulations of the Board. These officers and two others elected by the Board shall constitute the Executive Committee.

ARTICLE VII
Qualifications

All Agents, Missionaries, and Corresponding Secretaries employed by the Board of this Convention must be members of some regular Baptist Church, in union with the churches composing this Convention. They must, previous to their appointment, furnish satisfactory evidence of genuine piety, fervent zeal in the Master's cause, and talents which fit them for the service for which they are to be employed.

From descriptions specified in this Constitution, the Foreign Mission Convention became a board to operate as an agency of the National Baptist Convention, U.S.A.

Rev. E.C. Morris of Arkansas was elected President, sixteen others elected Vice-President, two from Texas and one each from the other fourteen states that were represented; three Secretaries and a Treasurer. The Foreign Mission Board, The Home Mission Board and the Educational Board were the three boards of the Convention.

The Foreign Mission Board's headquarters remained in Richmond, Virginia and L.M. Luke of Caddo Parish, Louisiana, was elected Corresponding Secretary. This move was a vote of confidence in him, irrespective of past sentiments against him. His tenure was short lived, lasting only until December 31, 1895, when he succumbed to death while preaching in the Old Fifth Street Baptist Church, Louisville, Kentucky.

L.G. Jordan, Pastor of Union Baptist Church of Philadelphia, succeeded Luke in October, 1896. Soon after assuming this secretariat, he moved the headquarters to Louisville, Kentucky. This move produced an unhealable wound. The support of churches of Richmond and vicinity was lost and their allegiance shifted to the Lott Cary Missionary Society, and remains there today.

Another area of dissatisfaction that occurred about this time was the constitution preamble's exclusion of the Convention operating its own Sunday School Publishing Board. Some felt having one would produce estrangement with the white Publishing Companies of whom many were or had been Colporteurs for. They further claimed these groups had made many contributions toward the denominational cause.

Emanuel King Love, Pastor of First African Baptist Church of Savannah, Georgia, President of the Missionary Baptist Convention of Georgia, who had once worked for the American Baptist Publication Society and the Home Mission Society of New York, an author in his own right, was a moving force behind the Convention publishing its own material. It was his message delivered in St. Louis, Missouri in the 1896 session of the Convention that gave much impetus toward their decision of initiating their own publishing house.

Love did not hide his relationship with the American Baptist Publication Society, but emphasized he could not be disloyal, nor rebellious against the National Baptist Convention's decision of establishing their publishing house. He further impressed upon them, he was a loyal Negro, and would always stand, live, fall or die with his race and denomination. Without a publishing house, the Negro Church, schools or families future is not near as bright and glorious as it will be with one. People minus enterprises exemplify they lack the spirit of progress; they will be unable to command the respect of the nation and gain world recognition. People are no more than their literature.

From St. Louis, Missouri, the Convention went to Boston, Massachusetts for its 1897 session. When the Publishing Board made its first report, many of the Lott Cary sympathizers and supporters who were already disenchanted over the Foreign Mission Board Headquarters being moved from Richmond, Virginia to Louisville, Kentucky, seceded.

This program of the Seventeenth Annual Session held in Boston reflects the emphasis the Convention was placing on missions.

"Go ye therefore, and teach all nations, baptizing them in the name of the Father, and of the Son, and of the Holy Ghost.

"Teaching them to observe all things whatsoever I have commanded you; and, lo, I am with you alway, even unto the end of the world." Amen.—St. Matthew 28: 19, 20.

"When well, I did my duty. Now I am sick, must leave you to others."—Solomon Cosby

"Tell the friends at home, don't forget to pray for us."—H. McKenney.

"The labor and victory is ours, the glory belongs to God "—J. J. Cole.

"How much owest thou my Lord?" (Last text of Dr. L. M. Luke.)

1880—Programme—1897

OF THE

17th Annual Session

OF THE

National Baptist Convention of America

REV E. C. MORRIS. D. D, PRESIDENT.

HELD WITH THE

Twelfth Baptist Church,

Phillip Street, near Garden,

REV. A. W. ADAMS, Pastor

BOSTON, MASS., SEPTEMBER 15th, to the 20th, 1897.

Compiled and arranged by

REV. L. G. JORDAN, Foreign Missionary Secretary,

547 Third Street, Louisville, Ky.

Printed by The Banner Publishing Co., 1842 Lombard St., Philadelphia, Pa.

The Christian Banner

REV. G. L. P. TALIAFERRO, EDITOR.

THE CHRISTIAN BANNER is our National Baptist paper. It is ably edited; wisely managed, and the matter that it contains each week is fresh and carefully selected by competent and able contributors representing all parts of the United States and Africa. Its columns are used by a large portion of the ablest men of the denomination, and it is the national medium of communication of the Baptists of this country and Africa. The accomplishments of this religious journal in the past three years have been many, and its influence for good is still on the increase. It is the paper for every home. No better investment was ever made with one dollar than that invested in a year's subscription for this journal is the testimony of thousands. Send one dollar at once to THE CHRISTIAN BANNER PUBLISHING COMPANY, 1842 Lombard Street, Philadelphia, and have this paper come to your home. You can order the Sunday School periodicals of the American Baptist Publication Society from the Christian Banner Publishing Company at the same price as you can from the Society. See price list in The Christian Banner. You can order your Hymn Books, Bibles, and all the books you need from us just as cheap as elsewhere. We do all kinds of Book and Job Printing.

The Christian Banner Publishing Co., 1842 Lombard Street, Philadelphia.

REV. J. J. COLES—Was born in Charlotte county, Va., April 25th, 1857.
Labored in Africa, 1883 to 1892.
Returned to America in 1893, and was elected Corresponding Secretary of the National Baptist Convention.
Died at Richmond, Va., Nov. 7th, 1893.

Evening.

7.30 p. m.	Devotional Services, J. E. Knox, A. M., Ark.
8.00 "	Paper—"Power of Organization," H. M. Raiford, Columbia, S. C.
8.30 "	Sermon—"Systematic Benevolence," D. A. Scott, of Marshall, Tex.
10.00 "	Adjournment.

Saturday, September 18th.

9.30 a. m.	Opening Address, J. Q. A. Willhite, Birmingham, Ala.
10.00 "	Address, Wm. H. Steward, A. M.
10.30 "	Address, Mrs M. A. Clark, Baltimore.
11.00 "	Address, Mr. John S. Trower, Philadelphia, Pa.
11.30 "	General Discussion.
12.00 "	Adjournment.

"All I can add in my loneliness, is, may Heaven's rich blessing come down on everyone—American, Englishman or Turk—who will help to heal the open sore of the world."—Livingstone.

Afternoon.

Patriotic Meeting.

Sunday, September 19th.

9.30 a. m.	Model Sunday-school in charge of Rev. R. J. Temple, Natchez, Miss.; Rev. G. H. Stevens, M.A., Syracuse, N.Y.
11.00 "	Denominational Sermon, Rev. C. H. Parrish, D. D., Louisville, Ky.
3.00 p. m.	Missionary Mass Meeting.
	Rev. C. T. Walker, D.D., Augusta, Ga. and Sec. Jordan.
7.30 p. m.	Sermon, Rev. W. L. Grant, Topeka, Kan.

REV. G. F. A. JOHNS—Born in Congo, Africa.
Came to America about 1878.
Returned to Africa, Jan. 26, 1897.
Died at Cape Town, June 26th, 1897.

iii

160

REV. J. O. HAYES—In Brewerville, West Africa, at work.

Has spent 12 years among our brethren in dark, dark Africa.

Born in North Carolina.

Monday, September 20th.

9.30 a. m. Devotional Services, A. Hamilton Monroe, La.
10 00   "   Address, Mrs. D. E. Harvey.
10.30   "   Sermon, Rev. C. S. Brown, A. M., North Carolina.
11 00   "   Business Meeting.
12 00   "   Adjournment.

"The true story of that nine months' march has never yet been written, and it will never be, for the full data cannot be supplied. But here is material waiting for some coming English Homer or Milton to crystalize into one of the world's noblest epics ; and it deserves the master-hand of a great poet-artist to do it justice. See these black men, whom your scientific philosophers would place at one remove from the gorilla, run all manner of risks, by day and night, for forty weeks ; now going round by a circuitous route to insure safe passage ; now compelled to resort to stratagem to get their precious burden through the country ; sometimes forced to fight their foes in order to carry out their holy mission. Follow them as they ford the rivers and traverse trackless deserts, daring perils from wild beasts and relentless wild men ; exposing themselves to the fatal fever, and burying several of their little band on the way ; yet, on they went, patient and persevering, never fainting or halting, until love and gratitude had done all that could be done, and they laid down at the feet of the British Consul on the 12th of March, 1874, all that was left of Scotland's great hero, save that buried heart."
—Tribute to the fidelity of the Black Men, who carried the body of Dr. David Livingstone, from the interior of Africa to the coast. From "The New Acts of the New Apostles.

Afternoon.

2.00 p. m. Devotional Services, Rev. J. H. Carter, D.D., Newark, N.J.
2.30   "   Report of B. Y. P. U. Work.
3 30   "   Address, J. L. Cochran, St. Louis, Mo.
4.00   "   Adjournment.

REV. R. A. JACKSON—In mission work in Cape Town, South Africa.

Now in America on business for the King.

Married ; has a wife and four children.

REV. R. L. STEWART —Born in Tennessee. At work in Liberia.

He has spent a number of years in Africa, and is now traveling in America in the interest of his work.

"My way has been to make collections for Foreign and Home Missions every Sunday morning in the year, and to keep the subject constantly on before the people. Then in April we make a special collection, which is always preceded by a week of daily prayer in which we meet together at 8 o'clock in the morning to pray for the one thing, that the people may have their hearts drawn out to give for the work of evangelizing the world. I preach on the subject on the Sunday before the collection is to be taken, and then put the responsibility of giving upon the people, refraining from all special solicitation or urging."—DR. A. J. GORDON.

"The spirit of missions is the Spirit of our Master; the very genius of our religion. A diffusive philanthropy is Christianity itself. It requires perpetual propagation to attest its genuineness."—Livingstone.

REV. H. McKENNEY—Born in Mississippi; died at Cape Mound, W. C. Africa in April, 1887, while serving as missionary of the National Baptist Convention.

His remains were laid to rest by the natives among whom he had labored.

v

Mrs. R. A. JACKSON—Standing faithfully by her husband in his work.
She is in charge while he is away.

RUM IN AFRICA—No part of Africa is exempt from the curse of the liquor traffic. Christian people are earnest in their efforts in sending missionaries, but the same vessel which bears the Word of Life, usually carries about 70,000 gallons of rum. If, here in our own land, amid so much that is noble and elevating, surrounded by churches and temperance societies, more money is spent for whiskey than for food, what can be expected from those in the darkness and ignorance of Africa? Thousands perish every year from rum ; "on a single Sunday afternoon, an English gentleman counted 317 natives dead drunk, while many others were partially so." "Gin is currency ; wages are paid in gin, and almost everything can be purchased with it." The crowning disgrace is

JOHN TULE—Born in Timbulon, South Africa.
Baptized by Bro. Jackson.
Ordained at Philadelphia.
Hopes to return in the fall.

that this traffic is protected and carried on by the so-called Christian nations of the world. For the greed of gain, the curse of darkness and death is forc d on those who so greatly need the gospel of light and life. The revenue from the traffic is immense, but it is "a revenue raised at the expense of the lives of the people, a revenue at the price of blood." What can we do to help our brethren in Africa? We can resolve that Africa shall be freed from this curse which is sapping her life. We can talk about it until all are familiar with the story of her wrongs. We can educate our people to use their influence in crushing out this great evil. We can call upon our God in full assurance of faith, knowing He will help us in our struggle to save those for whom Christ died.

REV. L. M. LUKE D.D·—Born at Caddo Parrish, La., July 12th, 1857.
Was made Financial Agent of our National Foreign Mission Convention in 1892, and Corresponding Secretary in 1895.
Died December 31, 1895, at Louisville, Ky.

vi

163

J. I. BUCHANAN—Born in Maryland, U.S.A.
Converted and baptized in Africa.
Ordained with brother Thomas by brethren Jackson and Johns. May 30th.
He is now pastoring in Middle Drift, S.A.

At Home.—13000 Negro Baptist Churches.

14000 Negro Baptist Bishops.

17,000,000 Negro Baptists in America.

Supplied 3000 Sunday-schools with literature for the quarter for '97.

Our Sunday-school and churches gave to the American Baptist Publishing Society on Children's Day and Bible Day, over $8000.

Publish about thirty journals.

Abroad.—Five churches in Africa, and a number of projective missions.

Thirteen workers and twelve native helpers,

Baptized during the Conventional year of 1897, eighty-two.

Present membership, 309.

Rev. Geo. M. THOMAS—Born in Cape Town South Africa.
Baptize d by Bro. Jackson.
Ordained by Rev. G. F. A. Johns and Rev. Jackson at Cape Town, May 30th, 1897.
Pastoring at Queenston, S. A.

Every missionary Baptist should consider it a privilege to be a co-worker with God in the salvation of a lost world.

Missions are of God and will succeed in spite of false religions conniving teachers and stingy people and prejudical leaders.

JOHN CHILEMBWE—Belongs to the Ajawa Tribe, East Central Africa.
Now in our country.
Will enter Virginia Seminary as the beneficiary of the Pennsylvania Baptists.

vii

SONS OF KING WILLIAM SHAW KAMA WHO ARE IN THIS COUNTRY FOR RELIGIOUS TRAINING.

ROLL CALL OF OUR MISSIONARIES.

1881 Rev. Solomon Crosby went to heaven from Legas, W.C. Africa,

1884 Rev. Henderson McKenny, took his flight from the summit of Cape Mound, W. C. Africa.

1893 Rev. J. J. Cole, laid by the implements of his warfare to enter his Master's joy from Richmond, Va.

Rev. J. O. Hayes with his wife and five children is at his post in Brewerville, Liberia, W. C. Africa.

Rev. R. A Jackson, wife and three children, Cape Town, South Africa, are holding five services on Sunday and one each evening in the week besides hand-to-hand contact daily with many who know not our Lord.

Rev. R. L. Stewart, wife and daughter are preaching and teaching in an industrial school near Monrovia, in Liberia, W. C. Africa. A letter addressed to any of those at work, as above, will be received. We ask that our readers write to and pray for them.

" The question now is not so much whether the heathen can be saved without the gospel, but whether we can be saved if we fail to send it to them."—C. H. SPURGEON.

Dr. Pierson mentions a missionary who when asked what led her to go to China replied " I had known Jesus as Saviour and Redeemer and Friend, but as soon as I knew Him as Master and Lord, he said to me "Am I thy Master ! Then go to China." Some of us are afraid to say to Christ with a whole heart "Master," lest he should say "Go to Africa." Yet can we never go so far for him as he went for us when he went to the cross.

The Negro Baptists of America during the past seventeen years, have raised $36,546.17 for African Missions. This does not include the money collected for 1894.

A GOOD MOTTO—"I am only one, but I am one. I cannot do everything, but I can do something. What I can do, I ought to do, and what I ought to do by the grace of God, I will do."

viii

Missionary Hymns.

No. 1. L.M.

Before Jehovah's awful throne,
Ye nations bow with sacred joy,
Know that the Lord is God alone,
He can create and He destroy.

We are His people, we His care,
Our souls and all our mortal frame,
What lasting honors, shall we rear,
Almighty Maker, to Thy name?

We'll crowd thy gates with thankful
songs,
High as the heavens our voices raise,
And earth with her ten thousand
tongues,
Shall fill thy courts with sounding
praise,

Wide as the world is thy command,
Vast as eternity thy love,
Firm as a rock thy truth shall stand,
When rolling years shall cease to
move.

No. 2. C.M.

When all thy mercies, O my God,
My rising soul surveys,
Transported with the view, I'm lost,
In wonder, love and praise.

Unnumbered comforts on my soul,
Thy tender care bestowed,
Before my infant heart conceived,
From whom those comforts flowed.

Ten thousand thousand precious gifts
My daily thanks employ ;
Nor is the least a cheerful heart,
That tastes those gifts with joy.

Through every period of my life
Thy goodness I'll pursue ;
And after death, in distant worlds,
The glorious theme renew.

No. 3. L.M.

Uplift the banner! Let it float
Skyward and seaward high and wide
The sun shall light its shining folds;
The cross on which the Savior died.

Uplift the banner ! Angels bend
In anxious silence o'er the sign,
And vainly seek to comprehend,
The wonder of the love divine.

Uplift the banner ! Heathen lands
Shall see from far the glorious sight
And nations gathering at the call,
Their spirits kindle in its light.

Uplift the banner ! Let it float,
Skyward and seaward high and wide
Our glory only in the cross
Our only hope the Crucified.

No. 4. L.M.

Arm of the Lord, awake, awake ;
Put on thy strength, the nations shake
Now let the world, adoring, see
Triumphs of mercy wrought by thee.

Say to the heathen from thy throne,
"I am Jehovah, God alone,"
Thy voice their idols shall confound,
And cast their altars to the ground.

Let Zion's time of favor some ;
O bring the tribes of Israel home!
Soon may our wandering eyes behold
Gentiles and Jews in Jesus' fold.

Almighty God, thy grace proclaim,
Through every clime, of every name ;
Let adverse powers before thee fall,
And crown the Saviour, Lord of all.

ix

No. 5. 7s, 6s. D.

From Greenland's icy mountains,
  From India's coral strand,
Where Afric's sunny fountains,
  Roll down their golden sand ;
From many an ancient river,
  From many a palmy plain,
They call us to deliver
  Their land from error's chain.

What though the spicy breezes,
  Blow soft o'er Ceylon's isle ;
Though every prospect pleases,
  And only man is vile ?
In vain with lavish kindness,
  The gifts of God are strown,
The heathen in his blindness,
  Bows down to wood and stone.

Can you whose souls are lighted
  By wisdom from on high,
Can we to men benighted,
  The lamp of life deny ?
Salvation ! O salvation !
  The joyful sound proclaim,
Till earth's remotest nation,
  Has learned Messiah's name.

Waft, waft ye winds his story,
  And you, ye waters roll,
Till, like a sea of glory,
  It spreads from pole to pole :
Till o'er our ransomed nature,
  The lamb, for sinners slain,
Redeemer, King, Creator,
  In bliss returns to reign.

No. 6, Gospel Hymns.

Hark ! the voice of Jesus crying—
  "Who will go and work to-day ?
Fields are white and harvest waiting,
  Who will bear the sheaves away?"
Loud and strong the Master calleth,
  Rich reward He offers thee :
Who will answer, gladly saying,
  "Here am I ; send me, send me !'

If you cannot cross the ocean,
  And the heathen lands explore,
You can find the heathen nearer,
  You can help them at your door.
If you cannot give your thousands,
  You can give the widow's mite ;
And the least you do for Jesus,
  Will be precious in his sight.

If you cannot speak like angels,
  If you cannot preach like Paul,
You can tell the love of Jesus,
  You can say He died for all,
If you cannot rouse the wicked,
  With the judgment's dread alarms,
You can lead the little children,
  To the Saviour's waiting arms.

Let none hear you idly saying—
  "There is nothing I can do,"
While the souls of men are dying,
  And the Master calls for you.
Take the task He gives you gladly
  Let His work your pleasure be ;
Answer quickly when he calleth,
  "Here am I ; send me, send me !"

No. 7. 6s, 4s.

Come, thou almighty King,
Help us thy name to sing,
  Help us to praise,
Father ! all-glorious,
O'er all victorious,
Come, and reign over us,
  Ancient of Days.

Come, thou incarnate Word,
Gird on thy mighty sword ;
  Our prayer attend ;
Come, and thy people bless,
And give thy word success,
Spirit of holiness,
  On us descend.

Come, Holy Comforter,
Thy sacred witness bear,
  In this glad hour :
Thou, who almighty art,
Now rule in every heart,
And ne'er from us depart,
  Spirit of power.

To the great One in Three
The highest praises be,
  Hence evermore ;
His sovereign majesty.
May we in glory see,
And to eternity,
  Love and adore.

, far away in heathen darkness dwelling,
Millions of souls for ever may be lost ;
Go, who will go, salvation's story telling,
Looking to Jesus, heeding not the cost?

Chorus :—

All power is given unto me,
  All power is given unto me,
Go ye into all the world and preach the gospel,
  and lo.
I am with you alway. '

See o'er the world, the open doors inviting,
  Soldiers of Christ, arise and enter in,
Brethren, awake ! our forces all uniting,
  Send forth, the gospel, break the chains of sin

'Why will ye die?" the voice of God is calling,
  "Why will ye die?" re-echo in His name ;
Jesus hath died, to save from death appalling,
  Life and salvation therefore go proclaim.

God speed the day when those of every nation,
  "Glory to God" triumphantly shall sing,
Ransomed, redeemed, rejoicing in salvation,
  Shout "Hallelujah for the Lord is King."

No. 9.   REV. JOHNSON OATMAN, Jr.

There's not a friend like the lowly
  Jesus,
  No, not one! no, not one!
None else could heal all our soul's
  diseases,
  No, not one! no, not one!

Jesus knows all about our struggles,
He will guide till the day is done,
There's not a friend like the lowly
  Jesus,
No, not one! no, not one!

No friend like him so high and holy,
  No, not one! no, not one!
And yet no friend is so meek and
  lowly,
  No, not one! no not one!

There's not an hour that he is not
  near us,
  No, not one! no not one!
No night so dark but his love can
  cheer us,
  No, not one! no not one!

Did ever saint find this friend for-
  sake him?
  No, not one! no not one!
Or sinners find that he would not
  take him?
  No, not one! no not one!

Was ever a gift like the Saviour
  given?
  No, not one! no not one!
Will he refuse us a home in heaven?
  No, not one! no not one!

REV. E. A. HOFFMAN.   No. 10.

What a fellowship,what a joy divine,
Leaning on the everlasting arms;
What a blessedness,What a peace is
  mine,
Leaning on the everlasting arms.

CHORUS.

Leaning, leaning,
Safe and secure from all alarms;
Leaning, leaning,
Leaning on the everlasting arms.

Oh, how sweet to walk in this pil-
  grim way,
Leaning on the everlasting arms;
Oh, how bright the path grows from
  day to day,
Leaning on the everlasting arms?

What have I to dread, what have I
  to fear,
Leaning on the everlasting arms;
I have blessed peace with my Lord
  so near,
Leaning on the everlasting arms.

Rev. J. J. Coles, Late Missionary and Corresponding Secretary ; Rev. D. N. Vassar D. D., Ex-Foreign Mission Treasurer and group of Veys, taken by Mrs. L. A. Coles at Mendoo Mission Station, W. C. Africa.

National Baptist Series
Sunday School Periodicals,

Published by the Home Board.

108½ Cedar St.,   Nashville, Tenn.

Rev. E. C. Morris, Editor.,

Rev. R. H. Boyd, D.D., Corresponding Secretary and Manager.

Publishers of Quarterlies, Lesson Cards, Hymnals, Hymn Books and all Church and Sunday School Supplies.

SEND FOR SAMPLES AND PRICE LIST.

The Baptist Magazine,

Published Quarterly at Washington, D.C.

$1.25 PER YEAR.

Rev. W. B. Johnson, D. D. Editor and Manager.

Afro=American Mission Herald,

PUBLISHED MONTHLY,

At 547 Third St., Louisville, Ky.

By Rev. L. G. Jordan, Cor. Sec'y.

For the Foreign Mission Board.

SUBSCRIPTION, 25 CENTS PER YEAR.

READ THIS, PLEASE.

We call your special attention to our periodicals. If you will compare them with the periodicals issued by other houses you will see that they are as cheap, or cheaper, in price, greatly superior in quality, and edited with an ability which cannot be surpassed.

Baptist People Should Take Baptist Periodicals.

Especially should this be the case when they can get a better article for the same or less money. There is now no possible excuse for Baptists using papers or quarterlies which do not teach Baptist doctrine.

By taking the periodicals of the American Baptist Publication Society

People Help Themselves

and the cause they profess to love. The profits accruing from their sale go into missionary and benevolent work. If Baptist people everywhere throughout the land gave the Society their patronage we could put colporters and Sunday-school missionaries in every State and books and tracts in every home.

Written and Prepared for the Whole World,

the periodicals of the Society are adapted to all sections of our own land and to other lands as well. They present the work of the denomination at large. No one who wishes to obtain a broad denominational outlook can afford to be without them.

The Best Writers,

North, South, East and West, at home and abroad, are engaged in their preparation.

Try our Periodicals for One Quarter,

if you have not already done so, and see the effect in your Sunday-school. We will make special terms for their introduction.

A. J. ROWLAND, Secretary.

⮜BAPTIST PERIODICALS⮞

The best GRADED, the best MADE, the best CIRCULATED, and the CHEAPEST denominational literature in the world.

HERE ARE THE PRESENT PRICES.

Note carefully, and compare with prices of other houses.

Club prices of five or more copies to one address for one quarter.

	Per Copy		Per copy
Baptist Superintendent	7 cts.	Our Little Ones (weekly)	6¼ cts.
Baptist Teacher	10 "	Reaper, (monthly)	2 "
Senior Quarterly	4 "	Reaper, (semi-monthly)	4 "
Advanced Quarterly	2 "	Our Boys and Girls,	8 "
Intermediate Quarterly	2 "	A New Juvenile Weekly.	
Primary Quarterly	2 "	Our Young People, in clubs of	
Picture Lessons	3 "	four or more (weekly)	13 "
Bible Lessons	1 "	Colporter, 5 cents a year in clubs of 20	
Bible Lesson Pictures	$1.00	or more.	

Your patronage will help the Bible, Colportage, Chapel Car, and Sunday School Work of the denomination.

AMERICAN BAPTIST PUBLICATION SOCIETY,
1420 Chestnut St., Philadelphia, Pa.

Some of the sessionists were, Calvin A. Brown, Albert W. Pegues and Samuel Vass of North Carolina; John W. Armstead, A. Binga, Jr., John W. Kirby, Phillip F. Morris and Richard Spiller of Virginia; W.S. Alexander and W.J. Howard of Maryland. Virginia Union and Shaw Universitites weighed heavy in the cause of this split. Centering around the Black faculty members, along with some of these men being employed by white publishing companies as colporteurs.

Thus the first division of the National Baptist Convention occurred in 1897. However the Lott Cary Convention was not really organized until 1899, with Rev. C.S. Brown becoming the first President.

The new Publishing Board was placed under the Home Mission Board, of which Rev. R.H. Boyd was Corresponding Secretary, and was administered by a committee of nine men. Its title when organized was "The National Baptist Convention Publishing Board", rather than "of the National Baptist Convention". It being placed under the Home Mission Board and the word "of" being omitted were two grave mistakes that caused years of trouble and almost destroyed the National Baptist Convention, U.S.A.

Boyd succeeded in building the Publishing Board, that its literature was being sought by all the membership churches and quite a publishing dynasty was built. In the nine years of its production, 1906 to 1915, its gross income was estimated as two million and four hundred thousand dollars.

CONVENTION CHRONOLOGY 1898 - 1915

Secretary L.G. Jordan of the Foreign Mission Board recommended to ask each church for a monthly donation, and each fifth Sunday a collection for foreign missions, this was accepted.

In 1899, the Baptist Young People's Union Board was organized. A responsibility to educate African converts was realized this same year. A plan was launched to bring them to America for education if they would return to their native land as Missionaries.

The Baptist Women's league was organized in 1900. Mrs. S.W. Leyton of Philadelphia, was first President. Her successors were Miss Nannie H. Burroughs and Mrs. Mary O. Ross. This is the predecessor of the Women's Auxiliary of the National Baptist Convention. To keep an accurate account of money to keep the Convention properly informed, an auditor was elected in 1901, and the Constitution was properly amended to provide for this. Birmingham was the host in 1902. This session was marred with tragedy when about one hundred people were killed in a stampede, someone screamed "fight" and was mistaken for "fire". The 1903 session authorized the Home Mission Board to provide financial help to bankrupt or needy churches. In 1904, an attempt was made to establish a home for aged ministers.

The Jamestown Exposition was held in 1905 and was endorsed

172

by the Convention, by sending forty delegates to the first Baptist World Alliance in London, England. Among whom was Miss Nannie Helen Burroughs, who was to become founder of the National Training School for Women and Girls, founded in Washington, D.C. in 1906, under the auspices of the Women's Auxiliary. Records reveal the Convention took an adamant stand against Jim Crow laws in coach travel in all states.

Twenty-five delegates were chosen in 1909 as representatives of the Convention at the Ecumenical Missionary Conference in Edinburgh, Scotland. By now, apparent difficulties were arising with the Publishing Board. A committee was appointed in 1910 to investigate the Publishing Board and certain propositions. Rev. E.J. Fisher of Chicago, Illinois, was appointed Chairman. It grew to be known as the "Fisher Investigative Committee". The winds of dissatisfaction continued to blow and howl in 1911 until in 1912 an ultimatum was given the Publishing Board. A committee was appointed in 1913 to research for written records and oral information to produce a history on the Negro race and Negro Baptists. The funds gained were used for foreign missions, expenses and compensation for committee members.

When the Convention emphasized its former position of full control of all boards, a devastating storm erupted. Convention leadership by now had lost respect for R.H. Boyd, the Publishing Board's secretary. Because of his refusal to give any information regarding ownership of properties, control and ownership of the Publishing Board. The Convention had no other choice but to sue for control.

The Tennessee Court ruled in favor of Boyd and his followers. The Convention accepted its defeat, lost the publishing board and some of its churches.

The second split occurred in 1915. This new group was named National Baptist Convention of America, commonly called Unincorporated or Boyd. Rev. E.P. Jones was elected first President. Rev. R.H. Boyd remained Corresponding Secretary of the Publishing Board.

Bibliography: Nation Baptist Journals, **Baptist Advance**, 1964, E.A. Freeman

Chapter 12
NATIONAL BAPTIST CONVENTION, U.S.A., INC.
1916 - 1953

A valuable lesson had been learned by the National Baptist Convention, U.S.A. They rallied to rebuild their loss, first by incorporating the Convention, and organizing a Sunday School Publishing Board of the National Baptist Convention. Both S.P. Harris and William Haynes served briefly as secretaries. In 1920, the Board elected A.M. Townsend, who served commendably until his death in 1959. He was succeeded by D.C. Washington, during

whose tenure the title Corresponding Secretary was changed to Executive Director. The administration was exceedingly fruitful until his death in 1974. Mrs. C.N. Adkins, a member of the distinguished Nabrit family, whose father once served as President of the American Baptist Theological Seminary and Secretary of the Convention, succeeded Dr. Washington. She became the first woman to hold this position, not because of any groups coercion, but because of her administrative acumen. The Publishing Board has been completely revolutionized under her guidance.

Much attention was being placed upon the Publishing Board during this era. The Convention had not forsaken its Foreign Mission's zeal, Secretary Jordan continued his tenacious efforts. His successor was J.E. East, who continued in a forthright way. By now missionary work is being carried out in five foreign countries. A total of sixty-one stations established, eighty-three out stations, forty-three churches organized, approximately fourteen thousand and seven hundred communicants, with forty-three native workers and four hundred and fifty-one assistants. In 1934, J.H. Jackson was elected by the Board as Corresponding Secretary. Immediately a program was initiated to liquidate the Board's indebtedness of twenty-three thousand dollars. Within four months, seven thousand dollars had been applied to it. His tenure must be accredited with the best business procedures applied during the Board's history. The debt was continuously decreased and receipts increased, permitting the Secretary to survey the foreign fields, to keep abreast of developments there. He was succeeded in 1941 by C.C. Adams, who served until 1961, William J. Harvey was to become the next Secretary in 1961. His most immediate predecessor, who had withdrawn from the Convention and was attempting to divert traditional supporting churches to his newly organized group. Harvey successfully overcame those invasions and has continued the Board's advancements with enviable effectiveness.

While the National Baptist Convention, U.S.A., Inc. was reconstructing, the National Baptist Convention of America was constructing. A view of their 1917 program will acquaint us with them in their early years.

Official

AND

Musical Program

OF THE

National Baptist Convention

(Unincorporated)

HELD IN

Atlanta, Georgia

September 5-11, 1917

NATIONAL BAPTIST PUBLISHING BOARD
NASHVILLE, TENN.

OFFICIAL PROGRAM

OF THE

37th Annual Session

OF THE

National Baptist

Convention

(Unincorporated)

HELD IN

Atlanta, Georgia

September 5-11,

1917

PROGRAM.

Wednesday—Morning Session.

10:00 A. M.—Convention called to order.
Devotional exercises by Rev. J. W. Wylder, Ga.; Rev.
R. J. Moore, Ala.; Rev. T. C. Phillips, S. C. Theme,
"The Gospel for the Whole World."
Addresses of Welcome.
Response, Rev. H. M. Williams, Texas.
11:30 A. M.—Appointment of Committees on Credentials and
Finance.
Recess for the purpose of enrollment.

Wednesday—Afternoon Session.

2:30 P. M.—Devotions: Rev. W. J. M. Price, Ky.; Rev. C. T.
Dorrah, Fla.; Rev. C. C. Caldwell, Miss.
3:30 P. M.—Report of Committee on Enrollment.
Recess.

Wednesday—Evening Session.

7:30 P. M.—Music by National Chorus.
Devotional: Revs. P. W. Dunavant, Mo.; J. C. Fields
Tenn.; W. H. Woods, Okla.
8:00 P. M.—Sermon, Rev. E. W. Bowen, S. C.; alternate,
Rev. E. H. Branch.
Collection. Adjournment.

Thursday—Morning Session.

9 00 A. M.—Devotional: Revs. C. H. Sharp, Ga.; P. T. Washington, La.; J. E. Haywood, Ill.
11:30 A. M.—Report of Foreign Mission Board. Introduction of speakers by Chairman of the Foreign Mission
Board, Rev. E. W. Moore, D. D., Columbus, O.
2)

Sermon or Address on Missions, Rev. D. W. Over, Denver, Colo.

Report of the Board by the Corresponding Secretary, R. Kemp, S. C. Appeal for contributions follows.

11:30—President's Annual Address.

Recess.

Thursday—Afternoon Session.

2:00 P. M.—Devotional, Revs. J. H. Earle, J. Wesley Carter, Ohio; J. H. Holder, Ind.

2:30—Report of Officers.

Report of Committee on Permanent Organization.

3:30 P. M.—Report of Home Mission Board. Report and Offering.

5:00—Recess.

Thursday—Evening Session.

7:30—Devotional, Revs. T. H. C. Messer, Pa.; G. II. Daniels, Mo.; J. A. Nelson, N. C.

8:00—Sermon, Rev. B. J. Prince, D. D., M. D.; alternate, Rev. C. J. Smith.

Friday—Morning Session.

9:00 A. M.—Devotional: Revs. Fannin, Ga.; J. C. Calhoun, Tex.; M. L. Porter, Ky.; Dr. L. V. Collins, La.; Wm. Clark, Texas.

9:30 A. M.—Reports of Committees.

10:00-11:00—Report of B. Y. P. U. Board.

11:00-12:00—Report of Publishing Board.

Offering.

Recess.

Friday—Afternoon Session.

2:00 P. M.—Devotional: Revs. L. H. Ingram, Ala.; P. H May, Fla.; A. Hubb, La.

2:30 P. M.—Introduction of Fraternal Representatives.

3:00 P. M.—Report of the Educational Board and Rally.

Recess.

Friday—Evening Session.

7:30 P. M.—Devotional: Revs. I. W. Crawford, Miss.; W. B.
Reed, Conn.; G. W. Woodbey, Cal.
8:00—

Saturday—Morning Session.

9:00 A. M.—Devotional: Revs. T. H. Fannings, Ga.; J. S.
Steele, Ark.; T. T. Timberlake, Ky.; A. J. Wimberly,
Ga.
9:30—Session of Laymen's Missionary League.
10:30—Report of Evangelical Board, Dr. B. J. Prince, Ill.,
Chairman, presiding. Remarks by Dr. E. W. White,
Texas. Reading of report by Jas. S. Anderson, Cor-
responding Secretary.
11:00—Report of Church Extension Board.
Recess.

Saturday—Evening Session.

7:30—Devotional: Revs. R. F. Friar, Ohio; B. F. Ferrell,
Ind.; T. W. Stephenson, Okla.
8:00—Sermon, Rev. R. H. Bowling, Va.; alternate, Rev. H.
A. Alfred, Tenn.

Sunday—Morning Session.

9:00—Sunday school.
11:00—Sermon, Dr. E. P. Jones; alternate, Dr. F. H. Cook.

Sunday—Afternoon Session.

Foreign Mission Mass Meeting. Ten thousand people are
expected to attend this meeting in the interst of Foreign Missions. Addresses will be delivered by Dr. C. P. Madison,
Norfolk, Va., and Mrs. G. M. DeBaptiste Ashburn, President
of the Women's National Baptist Convention Auxiliary and
returned missionary from Africa.

Sunday—Evening Session.

7:30—Devotional.
8:00—Sermon, Dr. J. W. Hurse, Mo.; alternate, Rev. Allen,
Kan.

Monday—Morning Session.

9:30—Devotionals: Drs. M. E. Robinson, Texas; H. W. Knight, Illinois; Chas. W. Lewis, Ind.

10:30—Report of Benefit Board.

11:30—Report of Woman's Auxiliary Convention. Final reports of all committees.

Bible study each morning from 8 to 9 o'clock. Drs. Johnson, of Virginia, and Wm. Hicks, Miss.

*REV. EDW. P. JONES, President.

REV. T. J. KING, Secretary.

OFFICIAL PROGRAM

OF THE

Seventeenth Annual Session

OF THE

WOMAN'S AUXILIARY CONVENTION
(*Unincorporated*)

HELD WITH

LIBERTY BAPTIST CHURCH

Atlanta, Georgia

SEPTEMBER 5-11,

1917

PROGRAM

Wednesday—Morning Session.

10:00—Opening Session, Union Meeting, Friendship Baptist Church.

12:00—Woman's Auxiliary Executive Board, Liberty Baptist Church.

Afternoon Session.

2:00—Song Service—Big convention choir, Mrs. E. P. Bushell, Chorister.

2:15—Devotional exercises, Miss I. J. Casen, Florida.
Topic, "Missionary Effort; What It Is."
"Any service that supplies the needs of men is Missionary. Efforts. Being of a triune nature, it has three classes of needs. Physical, Intellectual and Spiritual." (Matt. 25:36, 37; Matt. 6:33; 2 Tim. 2:45.)

3:00—Formal opening of the Convention by the President, Mrs. G. M. DeBaptist F. Ashburn.
Notice—Delegates who have not sent to the Corresponding Secretary their representation fee are requested to see the Enrollment and Finance Committees at once.

3:15—Music—Service of songs.

3:20—Addresses of Welcome and Greetings:
"On behalf of Liberty Baptist Missionary Society," Mrs. S. F. Pattman.
"On behalf of the Baptists of the City, Miss Lizzie Wynn.
"On behalf of the Baptists of Georgia," Mrs. E. M. Ballou.
"On behalf of W. B. M. U. of Georgia," Mrs. W. J. Neal, President, Cartersville, Ga.

3:50—Response to Addresses of Welcome and Greetings, Mrs. Mary Johnson, Pennsylvania.
Response to W. B. M. U. Greetings, Mrs. J. H. Winn, Texas.

(24)

183

4:00—Echoes from Field Workers (three minutes each)—
Vice Presidents.

5:00—Offering by States.

5:10—Music. Introduction of Visitors. Announcements.
Adjournment.

Evening Session.

7:00—Song Service.

7:15—Devotional Exercises, Miss Casen.
Topic: "A Requirement of a Successful Christian Life
—Faith." Mark 11:22; John 3:16; John 11:25, 26;
Acts 14:22; Rom. 1:17; Rom. 5:1; 1 Cor. 16:13;
Gal. 5:22; Heb. 6:12; Heb. 11:6; John 5:4.

7:45—Annual Sermon, Dr. E. W. Moore, Ohio.

8:45—Solo, Mrs. Annie Washington, Indiana.

8:55—Offering. Announcements. Adjournment.

Thursday—Morning Session.

5:30—Sunrise Prayer Meeting, led by Louisiana and Mississippi delegations.

9:00—Song Service.

9:10—Devotional Exercises, Miss Casen.
Topic, "Missionary Method—Go or Send." Ex. 3:10;
Ezra 1:2, 3; Jer. 1:17; Mal. 4:5; Matt. 3:1; John
1:41, 42; John 4:28, 29; Acts 3:26; Acts 8:4; Acts
11:22, 28, 30; Acts 13:3.

9:40—Report of Enrollment Committee.

9:50—Music.

10:00—Annual Address of the President, Mrs. G. M. De B. F.
Ashburn; Mrs. A. Washington, Vice President, presiding.

11:00—Music.

11:05—Address—"How the District Conventions Can Finance
Our National Baptist Training School, Located at
Nashville," Mrs. S. E. Atkinson, Texas.

11:15—Address—"The Part Our Local Societies Can Play in
Equipping the Training School," Mrs. M. B. Fortier,
Louisiana.

11:25—Address—"What the State Conventions Should Do in
Raising Finance for Our Training School," Mrs. E.
J. K. Hines, Indiana.

11:35—Address—"The Need of United Efforts on the Part of Christian Women," Mrs. Fannie Maderson, Arkansas.

11:45—Music. Introduction of Visitors. Offering. Announcements. Adjournment.

Afternoon Session.

2:00—Service of Songs.

2:10—Devotional Exercises, Miss Casen.
Topic: "Missionary Motive—Love." John 3:16; John 15:12, 13; Matt. 5:43-48; Lev. 19:18; Luke 10:27; 2 Cor. 5:14; 1 Cor. 13.

2:25—Music.

2:30—Report of the Corresponding Secretary, Mrs. M. A. B. Fuller.
Cash offering and pledges for the Woman's Baptist Training School.
Music.
Report of the Treasurer, Mrs. Emma Grimble.
Reading of Minutes. Announcements. Adjournment.

Home Field.

Evening Session.

7:00—Song Service.

7:10—Devotional Exercises, Miss Casen.
Topic: "Missionary Authority." Matt. 10:1, 5, 16; Matt. 28:19; Mark 16:15; Luke 10:1-3.

7:25—Address: "The Attitude of the Distressed Toward the Church and the Social Worker," Mrs. Helen Adams Moore, Ohio.

7:35—Address: "The Social Worker as an Aid to the Court," Mrs. Addie Clark, Tennessee.

7:45—Address: "Equipment for Service," Mrs. Daisy Russell, Illinois.

7:50—"Wielding Our Smaller Organic Units into Links of National Service," Mrs. Ella B. Woods, Kentucky.

8:00—Address: "Enlisting Unenlisted Women in Missionary Work," Mrs. Rufus Cage, Tennessee.

8:10—Address: "Sowing and Reaping," Mrs. J. W. Radford, Texas.

8:20—Address: "How to Make a Missionary Society Go," Mrs. Francis McFalls, North Carolina.

8 :30—Address: "The Spirit of Service," Mrs. S. B. Strickland, California.
8 :40—Address: "The Duty of Local Missionary Societies to the Denominational Program," Mrs. Bessie Whiteside, Indiana.
8 :50—Offering. Announcements. Adjournment.

Friday—Morning Session.

5 :30—Sunrise Prayer Meeting, led by Oklahoma and Arkansas delegations.
9 :00—Song Service.
9 :10—Devotional Services, Miss Casen.
　　　Topic: "Woman's Part." 1st, "Love Him," Matt. 22 :26-37; 2nd. "Follow," Mark 8 :34; 3rd. "Witness," Matt. 10 :32; 4th. "Shine," Matt. 5 :14-16; 5th. "Love Others," Gal. 5 :13.
9 :30—Address and Greetings from Our Foreign Mission Board, Rev. James Kelly, Texas.
　　　Pledges for the work.
10 :00—Address: "Visions and Tasks," Mrs. W. J. Neel, President W. B. M. U., Georgia.
　　　Vocal Solo—Mrs. E. P. Bushell, Texas.
10 :30—Address: "The Gospel of Co-operation," Mr. J. E. McCullough, General Secretary, Southern Sociological Congress, Washington, D. C.
11 :00—Address, Hon. William Harrison, Oklahoma.
　　　Vocal Solo—Miss Lulu Butler, Texas.
11 :30—Address: "Making the Best Use of Our State Organizations for World-Wide Evangelization," Mrs. D. A. E. Ferguson, Tennessee.
11 :40—Address: "The Cause of Southern Migration," Rev. W. J. Ballou, Georgia.
12 :00—Music. Announcements. Adjournment.

Afternoon Session.

2 :00—Song Service.
2 :10—Devotional Exercises, Miss Casen.
　　　Topic: "Reward." Matt. 25 :31-40; Mal. 3 :16-18; Matt. 13 :41-43; Dan. 12 :3.
2 :30—A Report and Address on Temperance and Nation-Wide Prohibition, Mrs. G. E. Adams, Texas.
2 :45—Address: Representative of the Anti-Saloon League of America.
3 :00—Address: "War Crisis as It Concerns My Race," Mrs. Agnes Ford, Florida.

3:15—Address: "How the Back Yard Garden Will Help Win the War," Mrs. J. H. Thompson, Oklahoma.
3:25—Address: "How to Enlist the Interest of Non-Interested Pastors in Women's Work," Mrs. S. A. Mimms, Mississippi.
3:35—Address: "Fireside School," Miss Ada Morgan, Tennessee.
3:45—Address: "How to Train Our Young People for Service Through the Y. W. A. Organization," Mrs. Eva M. White, Louisiana.
3:55—Address: "How to Denominationalize a Church," Mrs. J. S. Morton, Pennsylvania.
4:05—Address: "The Duty of the Church to the Denominational Programme," Mrs. F. B. Winfield, Illinois.
4:15—Address: "Woman as a Worker in the Kingdom," Mrs. G. B. Coates, Alabama.
Introduction of Visitors. Announcements. Adjournment.

EVENING.

Young People's Night—Mrs. Eva C. Hooper, Illinois, Presiding.

7:00—Song Service.
7:15—Devotional Services, Mrs. C. M. Smith, Kentucky. Topic: "Study." 2 Tim. 2:15; 1 Pet. 2:2; Psalm 119:11; Psalm 37:30, 31; Prov. 4:4.
7:30—Vocal Solo—Miss Helen Messer, Pennsylvania.
7:35—Address: "Woman's Mission and Its Fulfillment," Miss E. C. Wyatt, Alabama.
7:40—Instrumental Solo, Mrs. Vernetta J. Smith, Ohio.
7:45—Vocal Duet, Misses Carrie and Hazel Hubbs, Louisiana.
7:55—Address: "The Value of Christian Schools," Miss Irene Shepherd, Alabama.
8:00—Vocal Solo, Miss Hattie Evans, Louisiana.
8:05—Address: "The Value of Christian Education," Miss Pearl Jones, Indiana.
8:10—Vocal Solo, Mrs. J. B. Batson, Tennessee.
8:15—Address: "Our Part in Modern Sunday School Movements," Miss Julia Garnell Logan, South Carolina.
8:20—Vocal Solo, Mrs. F. H. Lewis, Louisiana.
8:25—Address: "Influence of Christian Young Women," Mrs. M. J. Lewter, Florida.
8:30—Instrumental Solo, Mrs. A. E. Booker, Ohio.
8:35—Address: "Financing Young Women's Missionary Circles for Effective Kingdom Work," Miss Mazie Ryan, South Carolina.

8:40—Address: "What America Owes the Heathen Girl," Miss Iola Carter, Georgia.

8:45—Instrumental Solo, Mrs. A. C. Williams, Alabama.

8:55—Address: "A Better Sabbath Observance," Mrs J. B. Beckham, Missouri.

9:05—Address: "Greater Efficiency in Local Work," Mrs. J. H. E. H. Nelson, South Carolina.

9:15—Vocal Solo, Miss Lula Butler, Texas.

9:25—Offering. Announcements.

9:35—Closing Chorus by the Convention Choir.

Saturday Morning—Children's Period.

5:00—Sunrise Prayer-meeting, led by Texas and Georgia delegations.

9:00—Devotional Services, Miss Casen.
> Topic: "Obedience." 1 Sam. 15:22; Matt. 7:21; Luke 6:46-48; John 14:21-23; Acts 5:29-32; Rom. 15; 1 John 2:3-5.

9:15—Music.
> (All Superintendents of Children's Bands are requested to occupy seats on the platform.)

9:20—Address: "The Latent Powers Hidden in a Boy," Mrs. E. M. Abner, Texas.

9:30—Address: "Amusements for Children," Mrs. G. L. Prince, Missouri.

9:40—Address: "The A. F. Cadet and Its Place in the Church," Mrs. B. J. Prince, Illinois.

9:50—Address: "Negro Doll Clubs—Their Racial Influence," Mrs. Ethel Tatedrake, Kentucky.

10:00—Address: "The Social Side of the 'Teen' Age of the Girl," Mrs. G. W. Raiford, South Carolina.

10:10—Address: "The Danger Period of the 'Teen' Age of the Girl," Mrs. K. M. Jones, Oklahoma.

10:20—Address: "The Boy and His Gang,', Mrs. M. J. Rucker, Mississippi.

10:30—Address: "How to Induce Children to Remain for the Preaching Service," Mrs. I. H. Kelly, Texas.

10:40—Election of Officers.
Reading Minutes. Committees' Reports. Miscellaneous Business. Announcements. Adjournment.

Afternoon Session.

2:30—Executive Board Meeting.

Evening Session.

7:00—Song Service by Big Convention Choir.

7:15—Devotional Exercises, Mrs. M. A. Taylor, Mississippi.
Topic: "The Fruit of the Spirit." Gal. 5:22.

7:30—Musical Programme, by Atlanta talent, assisted by Convention delegates.

8:00—Address: "How to Finance Baptist Schools," Prof. W. H. Fuller, Secretary General Baptist Convention, Education Board, Texas.

8:30—Address: "The Ideal Layman in Action," Prof. C. T. Hume, Tennessee.

8:50—Address: "Christ and the Plain People," Dr. R. H. Boyd, Tennessee.

9:10—Report of Executive Board. Presentation of Medals, Banners and Pennants. Announcements. Adjournment.

Sunday—Morning Session.

10:30—Song Service, Convention Choir.
Devotional Services, led by Rev. E. D. Hubbard, Mississippi.

11:00—Sermon, Dr. John H. Frank, Kentucky, Editor Union Review.
Offering. Announcements. Benediction.

Afternoon Session.

Union Missionary Mass Meeting, Friendship Baptist Church.

Evening Session.

7:30—Song Service, Convention Choir.
7:45—Devotional Services, led by Rev. F. F. Young, Indiana.
8:00—Sermon, Dr. H. M. Williams, Texas.
Music. Presentation of Officers. Offering.
Final Adjournment.

Ushers and Pages.

Misses Ella Taylor, Ella Baker, Carrie Taylor, Martha Willis, Iola Carter, Mamie Wimbish, Josephine Wynn, Rosa Gibson, Idella Hardin, Beatrice Murden, Lizzie Wynn, Mesdames Lizzie Corn, Idella F. Henderson, Lizzie McDuffie, Ada Goosby, S. F. Pattman, Julia D. Deal, R. M. Reddick, Matilda Goosby, Lucinda Holiday.

Committee on Courtesies.

Mesdames Lethia L. Craigg, Lucy Ware, Mattie Norris, Lucinda Holliday, Chaney Hughes, G. D. Howard, Mary J. Eberhardt, R. S. Dathon, E. R. Carter, Katie Stocks, Amanda Bowen, Ernest Hall, Hattie Green, M. L. Glenn, Maggie Cooper, Mark Bell, Maud Brown, Laura Houston, Ellen Mathis, Ada Roman, Minnie Banks, Hattie Garrison, B. J. Davis, Emma Sharp, Mary Grant, Marie Butler, Hattie Green, Clara Hopkins, Lucy Martin, A. L. Jackson.

Chairman and Secretary of Needle Work Booth.

Mrs. Eva C. Hooper, Illinois; Mrs. L. M. Jones, Texas.
Buy a piece and carry home to friends.

EVERY CHURCH NEEDS A GOOD COMMUNION SET

NY CONGREGATION can have its wants supplied by securing one of these Quadruple-Plated Silver Communion Sets at a moderate price and on reasonable terms. A set consists of one flagor two goblets and two bread plates. If the church wants more goblets or plates, they can be furnished at an additional cost. The commemoration of the Lord's Supper is a very sacred ordinance. The custom for centuries has been to have special vessels for this occasion. Thus a communion set becomes an important part of this service. Many churches have used the old-style communion set while others use an individual set. Both are appropriate and well-recommended. One is no reflection upon the other.

192

A Sunday School Congress of the National Baptist Convention was born in 1916 in Memphis, Tennessee as an outgrowth of establishing the Sunday School Publishing Board, and uniting the Baptist Young People's Union into the National Baptist Sunday School and B.Y.P.U. Congress. Dr. D.W. Cannon was elected first President, Dr. W.H. Jernigan was elected President, Dr. O. Clay Maxwell was elected Vice-President. In 1958, Dr. O. Clay Maxwell was elected President, Dr. Martin Luther King, Jr. was elected Vice-President. Dr. E.A. Freeman was elected President in 1969, Dr. James B. Cayce was elected Vice-President. After Dr. Cayce's death in 1972, Dr. T. Oscar Chappelle was elected Vice-President.

The administrative titles were changed, in 1975 by recommendation of Dr. J.H. Jackson, to Superintendent and Assistant Superintendent, in conformity to educational organizations. The organizational name has likewise been changed to National Baptist Congress of Christian Education.

An official organ was also needed, since **The National Baptist Union-Review,** formerly had served as the official organ to the Convention became a part of the split group. The official organ of the National Baptist Convention, U.S.A., Inc. became the **National Baptist Voice.**

Dr. E.C. Morris served as President of the Convention until 1922, a total of twenty-seven years. W.G. Parks was elected in 1923, serving for one year.

On May 6, 1924, the American Baptist Theological Seminary in Nashville, Tennessee was opened. In the 1913 session of the Convention, a committee was appointed of L.K. Williams, J.W. Bailey and others to communicate with the Southern Baptist Convention to help them in working out a solution to provide for highly qualified Black graduates, who were aspiring for the Gospel Ministry, a means of Seminary training. Their contact was O.L. Hailey of the Texas Baptist Convention. E.Y. Mullins introduced a resolution to that body in favor of their request, and it was adopted.

The outgrowth of which was the National Baptist and Southern Baptist Conventions, set up a special corporation to operate an interracial nonsectarian school. Both groups supply the financial resources. A curriculum has been developed that leads to the Bachelor of Arts, Bachelor of Theology, Bachelor of Divinity, and Master of Religious Education degrees.

Since its beginning, the following have served as Presidents, Sutton E. Griggs, 1924-1926; W.T. Amiger, 1927-1929; Roy A. Mayfield, 1932-1934; J.M. Nabrit, 1936-1944; Ralph Riley, 1944-1956; Victor T. Glass acting President, 1956-1957; Maynard P. Turner, 1957-1963; Charles E. Boddie, 1963-1980, after June 1, 1980, will become Chancellor. Odell McGlothian will assume the presidency on June 1, 1980.

Dr. L.K. Williams, a respected orator, persuasive preacher and knowledgeable administrator, became President of the Convention in 1924. These letters can better depict the organizational structure of the Convention, and the communication network during his administration.

L. K. WILLIAMS, D.D., LL.D.   J. M. NABRIT, D.D., Secretary
   President   Atlanta, Ga.

The National Baptist Convention, U. S. A.

Headquarters: 3101 SOUTH PARKWAY
CHICAGO, ILL.

January 12, 1932.

Rev. D. D. Crawford,
  239 Auburn Ave., N. E.,
  Atlanta, Ga.

My dear Brother Pastor:

    I am writing you in interest of the Foreign Mission Department of our National work. I wish to wholeheartily endorse the plan of our Foreign Mission Board, with headquarters at 7C1 S. 19th St., Philadelphia, Pa., whereby their finances will be put on a firmer basis. If this plan is successful the welfare of our missionaries who go to foreign lands will be happier, more secure, and our work better supported there. This will mean a larger degree of success in their missionary endeavors.

    Briefly stated, we have approximately 22,000 churches in some way affiliated with our National Baptist Convention. Our Foreign Mission Board is trying to get not less than 5,000 of these to give at least One Dollar per month, paid monthly, for the support of this work. They are endeavoring to get a similar number of church auxiliaries, such as Sunday Schools, Missionary Societies, and B. Y. P. Us., to give at least a like amount.

    I am writing to ask that you cooperate with our Foreign Mission Board fully in this plan by having your church send it a contribution each month. If you can augment such a contribution by having some of your auxiliaries also to contribute monthly, it will be greatly appreciated. I might say for your information that the Olivet Baptist Church, Chicago, with its auxiliaries, is supporting steadily the work of our Foreign Mission Board.

    With every good wish for a prosperous New Year,
I am

        Yours most sincerely,

        L. K. Williams

        L. K. Williams, President
LKW:EBB   National Baptist Convention.

THE FOREIGN MISSION BOARD

NATIONAL BAPTIST CONVENTION, Inc.

REV. J. E. EAST, *Corresponding Secretary*

701 South Nineteenth Street
PHILADELPHIA, PA.

March, 1932

Rev. D. D. Crawford,
Atlanta, Ga.

My dear Pastor:-

I had hoped to have written you much earlier in the
year, but we have been very busy in an effort to raise funds to
save our missions in Africa; thus the lateness of this communication.

Briefly, I am earnestly soliciting your cooperation in
our mission work, which is suffering gravely under the stress of
economic conditions. We cannot discharge our missionaries; we
haven't the means to bring them home, nor would they have employment if they were recalled from the field.

Many of the children in our missions have been given to
us. If we sent them away, they would be uncared for, since we do
not even know where some of their parents are. How, then, can we
send them back into the darkness after having given them a glimpse
of life and light?

An offering from your church once a month would help us
keep our missionaries on the field and our mission stations open.
We are asking for at least $1.00. If you can give more, we would
be grateful. If you cannot give $1.00, fifty cents or twenty-five
cents would be appreciated. Anyhow, do give us a MONTHLY OFFERING
for the support of our missionaries who are so heroically carrying
on under the current adverse conditions.

We look forward to your first offering and beg your
prayers.

Faithfully yours,

J. E. East
Cor. Sec'y.

The National Baptist Convention, U. S. A.

SECRETARY
J. M. NABRIT, A. M., D. D.
Georgia

TREASURER
R. B. ROBERTS, D. D.
Tennessee

AUDITOR
F. D. MORRIS, A. B.
Illinois

VICE PRESIDENT AT LARGE
D. V. JEMISON, D. D.
Alabama

1ST REGIONAL VICE PRESIDENT
A. L. BOONE, D. D.
Ohio

2ND REGIONAL VICE PRESIDENT
T. S. HARTEN, D. D.
New York

3RD REGIONAL VICE PRESIDENT
W. H. ROZIER, D. D.
California

ATTORNEY
WM. H. HAYNES
Illinois

STATISTICIAN
ROLAND SMITH, A. B.
Alabama

HISTORIOGRAPHER
L. G. JORDAN, D. D.
Tennessee

HAS A MEMBERSHIP OF 3,750,000

BOARDS OF THE CONVENTION

SUNDAY SCHOOL PUBLISHING BOARD
A. M. Townsend, D. D., Secretary
Tennessee

FOREIGN MISSION BOARD
J. E. East, D. D., Secretary
Pennsylvania

HOME MISSIONS AND EVANGELISM
T. T. Lovelace, Secretary
Illinois

B. Y. P. U. BOARD
E. W. D. Isaac, Jr., Secretary
Tennessee

BENEFIT BOARD
J. B. Greene, D. D., Secretary
Florida

EDUCATIONAL BOARD
E. L. Twine, D. D., Secretary
Mississippi

NATIONAL BAPTIST VOICE
R. C. Barbour, A. M., Editor
Tennessee

WOMAN'S AUXILIARY
Mrs. S. W. Layten, President
Pennsylvania
Miss N. H. Burroughs, Secretary
District of Columbia

ROLAND SMITH, A. B.
Statistician

P. O. Box 733

TUSCALOOSA, ALABAMA

July 3, 1933

Dr.D.D.Crawford
Atlanta,Georgia

Dear Brother:

I am now obtaining the Religious Statistics
for our Denomination.I am urging that you
fill out the Enclosed Questennaire fully,
and forward the same to me not later than
July 15,1933.

Your cooperation in this matter will be
greatly appreciated by me.The Statistical
facts of Negro Baptist must be obtained
before an accurate standing of Negro Baptist can be given in our report.

With best wishes to you for health and
success in your work.I am

Sincerely yours,
Roland Smith
Roland Smith,Statistician.

NEXT SESSION MEMPHIS, TENN., SEPT. 6 - 11, 1933

NATIONAL BAPTIST VOICE

R. C. BARBOUR, EDITOR

SAVE THE PUBLISHING HOUSE CAMPAIGN

Rev L D Crawford, D L
1S5 Auburn Ave
Atlanta Ga

Nashville, Tennessee
February 10, 1933

My dear Co-worker:

We are facing a very serious situation. We are fighting to save the
Morris Memorial Building, the home of our Publishing House. The closing of
the Nashville People's Bank and Trust Company precipitated a serious
crisis. Our National Baptist Convention and the Sunday School Publishing
Board owed the closed bank more than $42,000.

To make a long story short, our leaders have succeeded in compromising this
debt for $25,000. They had to raise $7,500 immediately, and then made the
promise to pay $5,000 in the next sixty days. In the meantime the Douglass
National Bank closed in Chicago, and our leaders had to raise an additional $4,000.

We must raise five thousand ($5,000) dollars by the third week in March.
Five hundred of us can do this by giving ten dollars each. We cannot de-
pend upon our millions. If you fail us, we are going to fail. Write in your
pledge at once.

Our denomination has proven itself a great constructive, enterprising group.
It is too late in the day to fail now. Each one of us must take this appeal
seriously. Should we fail it would be the basest ingratitude to God in view
of the bounteous blessings to us. It would amount to the repudiation of our
leaders who have lead us through these trying times.

Remember: THE THIRD SUNDAY IN MARCH IS SUNDAY SCHOOL PUBLISHING BOARD DAY.

Sincerely,

R. C. Barbour

ORGANIZED 1880   INCORPORATED 1915

The National Baptist Convention, U. S. A.

HAS A MEMBERSHIP OF 3,750,000

J. M. NABRIT, Secretary

PHONE: WALNUT 5138
254 HARRIS STREET, N. E.

ATLANTA, GEORGIA

May 22, 1933

Dear Brother:

You are hereby notified of the meeting of the sub-Committee on Program for the National Baptist Convention to be held at 10 A. M., Thursday, June 8, in Memphis, Tennessee.

The Committee will complete the program for the regular session.

Dr. W. H. Jernagin, president of the Congress, Dr. A. M. Townsend, director of the Congress, and Professor E. W. D. Isaac, assistant director, and their committee, are also requested to meet to perfect their program so as to avoid duplication of speakers. If you cannot be present and have names to submit from your state or suggestions to offer, please send same to Secretary Nabrit, in care of Dr. T. O. Fuller, assistant secretary, Howe College, Memphis, Tennessee, by the 8th of June.

The meeting will last one day, only.

Yours very truly,

L. K. Williams, president
J. M. Nabrit, secretary

The president extends you a special invitation to this meeting, hoping that you will find it possible to be present in person. Thank you.

NEXT SESSION—MEMPHIS, TENN., SEPT. 6-11, 1933

SUNDAY SCHOOL PUBLISHING BOARD

OF THE NATIONAL BAPTIST CONVENTION, U. S. A.

PRINTERS : PUBLISHERS : BINDERS

CHURCH AND SUNDAY SCHOOL SPECIALTIES

A. M. TOWNSEND, D. D., Secretary

Fourth Ave. and Cedar St.

Phone 6-6656

NASHVILLE, TENNESSEE

MORRIS MEMORIAL
HOME OF SUNDAY SCHOOL PUBLISHING BOARD

July 16, 1932

Rev. D.D .Crawford, B.D.
239 Auburn Ave. N.E.,
Atlanta, Ga.

My dear Dr. Crawford:

Your letter of July 15, received and contents carefully noted. It is true
that the reduction in prices of literature is a problem with us now, and we
are giving the same our careful consideration. You will recall that at the
Kansas City Convention, the Convention itself endorsed and approved the
Sunday School Publishing Board's recommendation that the prices in our literature be increased and that the constituency be appealed to to support this
increase. the hope was that this might afford an opportunity to the Sunday
schools in this way, to make additional contribution to increase the income
of the Sunday School Publishing Board to help to pay the indebtedness on
the Publishing House.

We found that our prices at that time were far below the prices of other publishers - even the National Baptist Publishing Board, and so when we did increase our prices, we were yet only on an average with prices of literature
of other publishers. This increase of prices on our literature was met and
accepted universally with the Sunday schools. It has only been within the
past year that we have had any complaints whatever on the prices of our
literature. We have had a few complaints and even then, when the situation
was explained, our patrons seemed to be satisfied. We made the explanation
that if comparisons were made, it would be found that our prices were on the
average of all other publishers and that whatever increase of prices there
was on our literature, that it was a means by which the Sunday schools could
make a contribution to help pay the debt on our Publishing House, and that
a small amount coming from each Sunday school in this way, would go far toward helping us to meet the heavy obligations and payments on the Publishing House debt. Other publishers reported to us that there was no complaint
coming from their constituents and that there was no demand that the prices
be reduced. We note that just this year, that it seems that the publishers
have taken into consideration in reducing the prices of their publications.

So in keeping with the conditions of times, and also that some publishers
have considered reduction in prices on literature, and our desiring to help
our Sunday schools that are trying to help us, we have already cut the prices
of our literature which went into affect this quarter. Perhaps you have not
had this called to your attention, so that our prices now are on a par with
other publishers of Sunday school literature. We realize that this is going
to affect our income, and it seems to me that instead of a suggestion being
made that we would further reduce our prices, that we should continue to
appeal to our constituency to patronize their own Publishing House, for this
is our only source from which we can in any degree count on to get money to

July 16, 1932
#2....Rev. D.D. Crawford

pay on the debt of the Publishing House.

In addition to our income being affected by the reduction of our
prices of literature, as you know now, there is an increase in pos-
tage rate - even on publications, and this together with the fact,
that there has been no reduction in the cost of printing materials,
stock, inks, etc., is going to make our task even more burdensome,
and if the Convention does not work out some plan by which there may
be some moneys coming in to us to supplement what we are able to
make by way of profits, we do not see our way through.

I think the less agitation we can make with reference to the prices
of literature, that it will be better for us. Of course, if we
did not have the burdensome debt of the Publishing House, we could
reduce prices of our literature within a very small margin of profit
to the interest of the Sunday schools, but since the burden of the
debt is upon us, we cannot afford to reduce the prices of our literature below the prices as set by all other publsihers, at least.
And then on the other hand, we are compelled to attempt to keep our
literature up both as to quality and as to standard, or else we will
lose on another hand.

These are problems that we have been working with and trying to solve
for the past few months both in our own interest and in the interest
of our patrons. We hope we shall have your continued cooperation
and support in our desperate struggles right through here.

                              Sincerely yours,

                              A. M. Townsend
                              SECRETARY

AMT:MM

Woman's Convention, Auxiliary to the National Bapt. Convention

(ORGANIZED SEPTEMBER, 1900)
OWNS AND CONTROLS THE NATIONAL TRAINING SCHOOL FOR WOMEN AND GIRLS

OFFICIAL ROSTER

Mrs. S. W. Layten, Pennsylvania, President
Mrs. Edna Strickland, Texas, Vice-President
Mrs. Mary R. McDowell, Mo., 2nd Vice-Pres.
Mrs. M. V. Parrish, Kentucky, Treasurer
Mrs. V. W. Broughton, Tenn., Rec. Secretary
Mrs. M. E. Goins, Missouri, Ass't Secretary
Mrs. E. Arlington Wilson, Texas, Historian
Mrs. C. B. Carter, Calif., Parliamentarian
Miss N. H. Burroughs, Wash., D. C., Cor. Sec.

FIELD FORCE

Mrs. E. E. Whitfield, Field Secretary
In Pennsylvania

MRS. S. W. LAYTEN, PRESIDENT
764 South 23rd Street
Philadelphia, Pa.
January 7, 1932.

OBJECTS

1—To engage in world wide Missions, by Praying, Giving and Working.

2—To stimulate and enlist the women of all Missionary Baptist Churches in Missionary and Educational work at home and abroad.

3—To labor for the Highest Development of Christian Womanhood.

Rev. D. D. Crawford, D. D.,
239 Auburn Avenue, N. E.,
Atlanta, Ga.

My dear Dr. Crawford:

I read in some paper a few days ago that you had been ill. By this time that you will be restored to health, and also that the New Year may bring you along with the rest of the church people prosperity.

I am again asking that you will kindly intercede and secure my Southeastern Clergy Permit?

Thanking you sincerely, I am

Yours truly,

President Woman's Convention,
Auxiliary National Baptist
Convention.

National S. S. and B. Y. P. U. Congress

AUXILIARY TO THE

National Baptist Convention, U. S. A.

DIRECTED BY

The Sunday School Publishing Board

A. M. TOWNSEND, D. D., Secretary

AND

The National B. Y. P. U. Board

E. W. D. ISAAC, Secretary

A Veritable School of Methods in Sunday School and B.Y.P.U. Work

OFFICE

A. M. TOWNSEND, Director General

412 Fourth Avenue, North

Nashville, Tennessee

December 31, 1932

Dr. D.D. Crawford, D.D.
195 Auburn Ave
Atlanta, Ga.

My dear Sir:

Please find enclosed copy of the outline of the Five Year Program for the National S.S. and B.Y.P.U. Congress. As a Religious Education Leader and Worker, we are inviting and requesting you to give this outline a close and critical review, and make whatever suggestions you may think will improve it.

Kindly note your suggestions on this copy and return to me by January 15th. Your criticisms and suggestions will be presented and will be of great help to the Program Committee in its further canvass and perfection of this program in its meeting on January 24, at the Green St Baptist church, Rev. M.W. Jones, Pastor, Louisville, Ky.

Appreciating your helpfulness and cooperation in this undertaking to the end that the Congress may have a constructive program, we remain

Sincerely yours,

a. m. Townsend

DIRECTOR GENERAL

AMT:MM

203

SUNDAY SCHOOL PUBLISHING BOARD

OF THE NATIONAL BAPTIST CONVENTION, U. S. A.

PRINTERS : PUBLISHERS : BINDERS

CHURCH AND SUNDAY SCHOOL SPECIALTIES

A. M. TOWNSEND, D. D., Secretary

Fourth Ave. and Cedar St.

Phone 6-6656

NASHVILLE, TENNESSEE

MORRIS MEMORIAL
HOME OF SUNDAY SCHOOL PUBLISHING BOARD

March 18, 1932

Rev. D. D. Crawford, D.D.
239 Auburn Ave. N.E.
Atlanta, Ga.

My dear Dr. Crawford:

Your letter of March 17th received. I have been confined to my bed and
room for more than five weeks and have not as yet been released by my
physician. I have had an attack of Bronchitis that has held me and
I have had to use extra precaution on account of this changeable weather
to avert possible serious complications. We are hoping that the weather
will open up soon and I will be able to be about my active duties.

I was not able to attend the Board meeting at Hot Springs where I intended to have a conference with President Jernagin and Mr. Isaac, on
the Congress program etc. The fact is that I have not taken up the
matter of the Congress program with anyone as yet, and I have not written to Rev. Thompson as yet. I will take up the matter with him, and
will write him in plenty of time for we do not know just now what we
are going to expect of him. This is a part of the program that was expected to be worked out in our conference.

We are glad to note that we are to have the full cooperation of Georgia
toward making the Congress at Chattanooga a success. With all good
wishes, we remain

Sincerely yours,

A. M. Townsend

SECRETARY

AMT:LL

204

The Cannon Memorial Foundation

IN MEMORIAM

For the Promotion of

RELIGIOUS EDUCATION

Morris Memorial Building

Fourth Ave. and Cedar St.

Nashville, Tenn.

MEMBERS OF THE COMMISSION

S. N. Vass, D. D., Litt. D., Director General
J. H. Creed, Secretary, Gadsden, Ala.
Jno. L. Webb, Treasurer, Hot Springs, Ark.
J. B. Adams, Brooklyn, New York
Byrd Prillerman, College, W. Va.
D. D. Crawford, Atlanta, Ga.
L. T. Clay, Detroit, Mich.
J. T. Brown, Nashville, Tenn.
Miss Lucy E. Campbell, Memphis, Tenn.
Mrs. O. C. Maxwell, St. Louis, Mo.
Mrs. C. D. Trice, Chicago, Illinois
Mrs. Hattie E. Harris, Atlanta, Ga.
Mrs. H. K. Hill, Orlando, Fla.
Mrs. Olivia Ford, New Orleans
Mrs. Beulah Johnson, Los Angeles, Calif.

September 1, 1933

Dr. D. D. Crawford
253 Chestnut Street
Atlanta, Ga

Dear Brother:

As Chariman of the Cannon Memorial Foundation I
am calling a meeting of the Commission to
convene on the second day of the Congress at
Memphis.

You are requested to come up to the rostrum
immediately after the morning session of the
second day of the Congress, and if it is not
secluded enough to hold a meeting we will secure
a room in the same building where we can have our
meeting.

Business of importance is to be transacted and it
is earnestly hoped that you will be present at this
meeting by all means.

Yours truly,

S. N. Vass

CHAIRMAN

SNV:JMJ

SUNDAY SCHOOL PUBLISHING BOARD

OF THE NATIONAL BAPTIST CONVENTION, U. S. A.

PRINTERS : PUBLISHERS : BINDERS
CHURCH AND SUNDAY SCHOOL SPECIALTIES

A. M. TOWNSEND, D. D., Secretary

Fourth Ave. and Cedar St.

Phone 6-6656

NASHVILLE, TENNESSEE

MORRIS MEMORIAL
HOME OF SUNDAY SCHOOL PUBLISHING BOARD

April 4, 1932.

DEPARTMENT RELIGIOUS EDUCATION
S. N. VASS, D. D., LITT. D., SECRETARY

Dr. D. D. Crawford
239 Auburn Avenue N.E.
Herndon Bldg.
Atlanta, Ga.

Dear Dr. Crawford:

I am hastening to reply to your letter of the 2nd to say that the matter of teacher training is not receiving the attention to which it is entitled, for all the denominations are making great progress in this direction. While it is true that our original purpose was to first get together at least $1000.00 and to use the interest on that amount in such a way as to arouse increased activities in teacher training throughout the country with the Congress as a center, we have made such poor progress in collecting this sum of money that we feel that we are not justified to wait longer, but that we ought to make some use of a small part of this money to stimulate teacher training that is being carried on in the field of the Congress and also under the separate state conventions. Last year we exhibited a banner in the Congress that is to be offered this year to the State Convention that makes the best showing in teacher training.

Now some of us think that we would still further stimulate the work by awarding medals at the different State Conventions that are carrying on teacher training work for the best showing made by any state in a way that I shall hereafter outline. I have had favorable letters from Dr. Jernagin Prof. Creed, Dr. Adams, Dr. Brown and Mr. John L Webb. If you favor this proposition I would very much appreciate it if you would drop me a line immediately so that we can proceed to have these medals made.

I judge that you are preparing to attend the meeting here of the Board of Directors of the Congress this week. But we have called no meeting of the Cannon Foundation for this week and therefore it very necessary for us to have your vote in writing for record. I would greatly appreciate it if you would let me hear from you at your earliest convenience.

Yours very truly,

S. N. V.

SNV:JMJ   SECRETARY OF RELIGIOUS EDUCATION.

Manufactures Everything Used by B. Y. P. U. Societies and Junior Unions.
Prints Everything Used by B. Y. P. U. Societies and Junior Unions.

THE NATIONAL  B.Y.P.U. BOARD

E. W. D. ISAAC, D. D. Corresponding Secretary
409 Gay Street, Nashville, Tennessee.

June 6, 1931.

Rev. D. D. Crawford,
141 Auburn Ave. N.E.,
Atlanta, Ga.

Dear Brother:

We have your letter requesting us to send you fifty (50)
Railroad Identification Certificates. Beg to advise that we
are enclosing the same herewith. May we ask that when you
give out the Certificates that you take the serial number of
each Certificate; also the name and address of the persons to
whom they are given. Should these not be enough to meet your
demand we shall be very glad to furnish you more.

With best wishes.

Yours respectfully,

E. W. D. Isaac
SECRETARY

EWDI,Jr/CJC

The following are the 1940 National Baptist Convention, U.S.A., Inc. statistics, given by Statistician Roland Smith. The Convention is now sixty years old. Compare with the 1890 statistics given in the previous chapter:

STATE CONVENTIONS AFFILIATED WITH THE NATIONAL BAPTIST CONVENTION

Alabama - Alabama Baptist State Convention
President - Dr. D.V. Jemison
Secretary - Rev. U.J. Robinson
Arkansas - Regular Arkansas Missionary Baptist Convention
President - Rev. J.R. Jamison
Secretary - Rev. W.L. Purifoy
- Arkansas Baptist State Convention, Consolidated
President - Rev. J.F. Clark
Secretary - Rev. N. Nichols
California - Western Baptist State Convention of California
President - Rev. Chas. H. Hampton
Secretary - Rev. W.P. Carter
Connecticut - Connecticut Baptist Missionary Union
President - Dr. F.W. Jacobs
Secretary - Rev. John B. Pharr
District of Columbia - Baptist Convention of District of Columbia and Vicinity
President - Dr. C.T. Murray
Secretary - Mr. W.P. Opey
Florida - General State Baptist Convention
President - Rev. J.N. Stokes
Secretary - Rev. R.H. Whitaker
Georgia - General Missionary Baptist Convention of Georgia
President - Dr. L.A. Pinkston
Secretary - Dr. D.D. Crawford
Illinois - Baptist General State Convention of Illinois
President - Dr. J.L. Horace
Secretary - Dr. M.D. Dickson
Indiana - General Baptist State Convention
President - Rev. S.S. Reed
Secretary - Rev. J.A. Hall
Iowa - Minnesota, South Dakota and Nebraska General Association
President - Rev. G.W. Robinson
Secretary - Rev. J.H. Reynolds
Kansas - Kansas Missionary Baptist State Convention
President - Dr. Wm. H. Ballew
Secretary - Rev. Geo. A Hampton
Louisiana - Louisiana Baptist State Convention
President - Rev. Thos. A. Levy
Secretary - Rev. H.C. Ross

Maryland - United Baptist Missionary Convention of Maryland
President - Rev. Geo. A. Crawley
Secretary - Rev. Ward Yerby
Michigan - Wolverine State Baptist Convention
President - Rev. E.L. Todd
Secretary - Rev. F.A. Williams
Mississippi - General Baptist State Convention
President - Rev. A.A. Cosey
Secretary - Rev. W.M. Walton
Missouri - Missouri Baptist State Convention
President - Rev. S.C. Doyle
Secretay - Rev. C.B. Johnson
Nebraska - New Era Baptist State Convention
President - Rev. F.P. Jones
Secretary - Rev. F.C. Williams
New Jersey - Afro-American Baptist Convention
President - Dr. D.L. Aiken
Secretary - Rev. Wm. B. Scott
New York - New York Colored Baptist State Convention
President - Rev. T.H. Sims
Secretary - Rev. J.O. Jones
Ohio - Ohio Baptist State Convention, Inc.
President - Rev. J. Franklin Walker, D.D.
Secretary - Rev. N.L. Show
- Ohio Baptist General Association
President - Rev. Chas. Crable
Secretary - Rev. A.W. Jackson
Oklahoma - Oklahoma Baptist State Convention
President - Rev. E.W. Perry
Secretary - Rev. S.A. Clark
South Carolina - Baptist Education and Missionary Convention
of South Carolina
President - Rev. H.H. Butler
Secretary - Rev. L.C. Jenkins
Tennessee - Tennessee Baptist Missionary and Educational
Convention
President - Rev. S.A. Owen
Secretary - Rev. D. Albert Jackson
Texas - Texas Baptist Convention
President - Rev. A.W. Pryor
Secretary - Rev. W.M. Butler
- Baptist Missionary and Educational Convention of Texas
President - Rev. J.R. Burdette
Secretary - Rev. M.E. Butler
Virginia - Goodwill Baptist Convention of Virginia
President - Dr. C.C. Scott
Secretary - Dr. W.L. Ransome
West Virginia - West Virginia Baptist State Convention
President - Rev. J. Carl Mitchell
Secretary - Rev. H.R. Williams

SUMMARY OF DENOMINATIONAL STATISTICS 1940-41

STATES	CHURCH MEMBERSHIP						SUNDAY SCHOOL			
	Churches	Number of Preachers	Total Membership	Total Gain	Total Loss	Baptisms	Schools	Enrollment	Teachers and Officers	Value of Church Property
Alabama	2,371	2,000	254,398	9,902	3,684	6,392	2,100	86,918	7,728	$ 7,603,681
Arizona	18	9	914	46	13	32	5	298	45	40,106
Arkansas	1,158	1,300	154,584	3,078	1,707	2,964	1,250	52,511	4,636	3,777,433
California	97	200	34,160	1,000	533	292	150	11,600	104	1,230,270
Colorado	17	18	3,688	106	34	53	9	1,353	121	110,300
Connecticut	26	35	6,416	136	102	69	11	2,216	199	1,230,270
Delaware	15	9	1,364	82	32	43	10	457	41	742,000
District of Columbia	177	375	44,817	764	417	176	85	15,293	1,366	3,068,458
Florida	921	900	139,576	2,803	1,650	1,114	1,000	48,389	4,355	3,485,974
Georgia	3,963	5,308	536,829	22,043	9,479	12,263	2,800	184,833	16,634	12,500,000
Illinois	325	418	134,354	5,559	3,977	691	327	86,930	7,823	3,880,540
Indiana	174	365	35,184	1,002	542	362	165	11,686	1,053	1,734,664
Iowa	46	38	4,980	177	77	86	40	1,886	167	237,150
Kansas	126	138	16,994	534	260	173	150	5,842	525	1,852,850
Kentucky	474	800	91,790	2,991	1,431	1,020	600	31,474	2,832	3,570,184
Louisiana	1,483	976	143,739	5,479	2,067	2,112	1,200	48,342	4,350	3,275,174
Maryland	99	140	81,864	1,757	1,322	183	115	28,486	2,562	1,502,045
Michigan	119	160	45,794	950	830	292	125	15,887	1,429	1,743,755

SUMMARY OF DENOMINATIONAL STATISTICS—1940-41

STATES	Churches	Number of Preachers	CHURCH MEMBERSHIP Total Membership	Total Gain	Total Loss	Baptisms	Schools	SUNDAY SCHOOL Enrollment	Teachers and Officers	Value of Church Property
Mississippi	2,389	2,000	338,705	11,643	5,260	5,608	2,200	114,695	10,322	3,641,884
Missouri	276	300	47,932	1,316	711	386	250	16,326	1,496	2,373,919
Minnesota	7	10	1,385	54	26	32	4	560	40	
New Jersey	223	250	50,003	1,524	734	473	186	17,028	532	3,473,222
New Mexico	9	8	383	27	6	18	2	90	8	16,000
New York	165	250	55,993	1,887	839	534	550	18,929	1,706	4,868,435
North Carolina	1,700	1,434	280,169	10,738	6,145	4,165	1,300	96,352	8,671	4,920,298
Ohio	383	692	126,069	2,075	1,205	379	281	57,782	5,200	4,244,636
Oklahoma	595	650	50,616	1,486	871	393	550	31,272	2,814	1,385,419
Pennsylvania	436	450	58,216	2,931	2,679	461	300	75,000	4,200	7,411,419
South Carolina	1,364	1,695	319,162	8,824	5,033	3,963	1,010	109,960	9,846	4,615,947
South Dakota	3	5	182	14	4	9	9	158	15	157,000
Tennessee	898	975	144,366	1,054	2,378	5,782	900	52,357	4,712	3,845,979
Texas	2,222	2,500	327,201	11,454	5,257	1,347	2,150	111,540	10,038	5,965,272
Virginia	1,610	1,700	327,790	8,555	5,222	3,539	1,590	10,210	918	10,491,321
West Virginia	324	443	30,141	827	203	283	500	10,211	918	1,516,281
Other States	36	75	5,020	262	59	168	35	1,523	137	1,273,900
Total	24,575	27,212	3,946,821	131,441	67,145	55,205	21,392	2,090,819	118,593	$110,116,655

NUMBER AND CLASSIFICATION OF B. T. U.'s*
BY STATES

States	Senior Unions	Inter-mediate Unions	Junior Unions	Total Unions	Est. Enrollment
United States	2,191	630	368	4,341	253,699
Alabama	232	24	105	425	12,942
Arkansas	214	90	85	389	13,041
Arizona	18	2	7	27	1,689
Colorado	3	2	1	6	258
Connecticut	2	2	2	6	318
D. C.	19	9	4	37	2,757
Florida	200	43	107	350	16,470
Georgia	188	89	37	314	16,212
Illinois	39	22	26	87	16,600
Iowa	7	2	2	11	429
Kansas	42	6	21	69	3,159
Kentucky	18	6	8	32	1,275
Louisiana	135	35	70	240	17,157
Massachusetts	1			1	21
Michigan	13	9	10	32	5,871
Minnesota	1	1	1	3	198
Mississippi	375	83	148	606	19,158
Missouri	131	27	48	216	12,708
Nebraska	9	5	5	19	1,371
New Jersey	25	12	14	51	2,583
New Mexico	3	1	2	6	258
New York	28	17	13	58	4,555
North Carolina	22	19	17	58	2,332
Ohio	107	16	56	178	8,886
South Carolina				50	71,398
Pennsylvania	38			38	1,102
Tennessee	98	17	63	177	17,901
Texas	144	61	98	301	10,446
Virginia	17	10	5	32	1,446
West Virginia	11	6	9	26	930
Wisconsin	3	1	2	6	594

*1939 Report.

SUMMARY OF NEGRO BAPTISTS

Summary A—

Total church membership	3,946,824
Net gain in membership	63,296
Total number of churches	24,575
Total number of preachers	27,242
Total number of Sunday Schools	21,392
Total number enrolled in Sunday Schools	2,090,819
Total number of W. M. S.	7,852
Total number enrolled in the W. M. S.	65,320
Total number B. Y. P. U.'s	4,541
Total number of members enrolled	26,359

Summary B—

Total value church property, including parsonages	$110,116,566.00
Average value of church property per church	4,552.19
The average number of members per church	169
The average number of members per preacher	148

*1939 Report.

DIRECTORY OF BAPTIST INSTITUTIONS—THE EDUCATIONAL INSTITUTIONS

COLLEGES

Name	Location	Faculty	Students	Value of Property	Amount of Endowment	Total Income Last Year
Benedict College	Columbia, S. C.	32	274	$ 543,000	$ 136,317	$ 59,255
Va. Union University	Richmond, Va.	36	1222	1,000,000	872,014	145,677
Morris College	Sumter, S. C.	25	530	275,000	....	30,000
Butler College	Tyler, Tex.	14	255	7,500	....	15,000
Western College	Kansas City, Mo.	9	216	300,000	....	15,000
Bishop College	Marshall, Tex.	21	382	389,350	13,846	96,626
Arkansas Baptist College	Little Rock, Ark.	14	128	100,000	6,000	6,000
Shaw University	Raleigh, N. C.	40	467	644,287	356,026	148,237
Morehouse College	Atlanta, Ga.	20	417	700,000	1,139,782	125,899
Spelman College	Atlanta, Ga.	36	373	902,830	3,114,436	205,932
Storer College	Harper's Ferry, W. Va.	17	177	400,000	110,525	55,312
Leland College	Baker, La.	18	545	246,495	110,000	40,267
Totals	....	282	4986	5,508,462	5,858,946	943,205

213

JUNIOR COLLEGES

Name	Location	Faculty	Students	Value of Property	Amount of Endowment	Total Income Last Year
Seneca Jr. College	Seneca, S. C.	10	145	$ 90,000		$ 3,600
Florida Memorial	Live Oak, Fla.	10	189	6,800		20,000
Selma University	Selma, Ala.	23	505	178,798		24,325
Conree N. & I. College	Conree, Tex.	12	151	90,000		5,000
Florida N. & I. Institute	St. Augustine, Fla.	20	578	500,000		50,000
Coleman College	Gibland, La.	8	105			
Natchez College	Natchez, Miss.	11	92	250,000		20,000
Morris Booker Mem. College	Dermoott, Ark.	11	147			1,500
Friendship College	Rockhill, S. C.	11	284	120,000		27,638
Mather School	Beauford, S. C.	10	135	250,000		27,000
Georgia Baptist College	Macon, Ga.	8	115	100,000		11,000
Guadalupe College	Seguin, Tex.	4	25	200,000	10,000	20,000
Totals		138	2,471	$1,785,598	$ 10,000	$190,063

THEOLOGICAL SCHOOLS

Name	Location	Faculty	Students	Value of Property	Amount of Endowment	Total Income Last Year
Simmons University	Louisville, Ky.	13	82	11,650	3,000	7,394
Amer. Bapt. Theological Seminary	Nashville, Tenn.	11	161	75,000		24,000
Totals		24	243	$ 86,650	$ 3,000	$ 31,394

HIGH SCHOOLS

Name	Location	Faculty	Students	Value of Property	Amount of Endowment	Total Income Last Year
Marion Baptist Academy	Marion, Ala.	4	240	$ 12,000		$ 2,500
Bethlehem Ind. Academy	Monroeville, Ala.	11	197	7,000		1,000
Northern Neck Ind. Academy	Chatham, Va.	3	130	40,000		5,587
Bluestone Harmony	Keysville, Va.	7	142	50,000		3,647
Tidewater Inst.	Cape Charles, Va.	4	171	16,500		
Thomaston N. & I. School	Thomaston, Ala.	6	150	30,000		
Union Baptist Institute	Athens, Ga.	7				
Totals		42	1030	$ 155,500		$ 12,734

215

DIRECTORY OF DENOMINATIONAL PAPERS

Name	Location	Editor	Denominational Control	Circulation (copies)	Business Manager	Established
Baptist Leader	Alabama	W. H. Smith	Yes	2,000	H. B. Lanier	1890
Baptist Vanguard	Arkansas	Ulysses S. Parr	Yes	8,000	S. J. Quincy	1888
Union	S. Carolina	W. M. Howard	No	1,000	W. H. Howard	1928
Union Reformer	N. Carolina		Yes	4,000	A. B. Johnson	1892
American Baptist	Kentucky	T. H. Woolfolk	Yes	20,000	W. H. Ballew	1879
The Negro Star	Kansas	H. T. Sims	No	3,400	H. T. Sims	1908
Advance Disp.	Mississippi	A. A. Cosey	Yes	2,600	A. A. Cosey	1914
National Baptist Voice	Tennessee	R. C. Barbour	Yes		R. C. Barbour	1916
The Mission Herald	Pennsylvania	J. H. Jackson	Yes	6,000	J. H. Jackson	1896
Christian Review	Pennsylvania	C. M. Smith	Yes	20,000	Florence Johnson	1913
Western Star	Texas	T. M. Chambers	Yes	5,000	T. M. Chambers	1906
Georgia Baptist	Georgia	D. D. Crawford	Yes	1,100	D. D. Crawford	1880
Florida Baptist	Florida	E. G. Thomas	No	500	Floyd King	1941

NOTE: The "Directory of Denominational Papers" shows that there are thirteen (13) active papers, of which three have no denominational control. According to the number of Negro Baptists in the United States of America, the circulation of the denominational papers is very small. These papers have a circulation of 72,100 out of a total membership of 4,046,840 Negro Baptists.

NATIONAL BAPTIST CONVENTION, U. S. A., INC.

Condensed Balance Sheet*

June 30, 1944

ASSETS

CURRENT ASSETS:

Cash	21,867.61	
Accounts Receivable	47,889.71	
Inventories	33,778.57	
Marketable Securities		
Prepaid Expenses	1,363.73	
		$ 121,240.11

FIXED ASSETS:

Land and Building (Net)	$901,182.09	
Furniture & Fixtures (Net)	14,142.02	
Machinery (Net)	45,964.76	
Other Fixed Assets	1,467.75	
		962,756.62

OTHER ASSETS:

Investment in N.B.C. Bonds	$126,000.00	
Special Funds	1,578.34	
		$ 127,568.34

TOTAL ASSETS $1,316,464.69

LIABILITIES

CURRENT LIABILITIES:

Accounts and Notes Payable	$ 17,939.89	$ 71,939.89

FUNDED DEBT:

First Mortgage Bonds	None	
Second Mortgage Bonds	$126,000.00	
Refunding 55 134	48,800.00	
Notes Payable (Due after 1 Year)	60,000.00	
		234,800.00

TOTAL LIABILITIES .... $ 306,739.89

SURPLUS:

Excess of Assets over Liabilities		$1,009,724.80

TOTAL LIABILITIES AND SURPLUS ... $1,316,464.69

ASSOCIATIONS AND MODERATORS

ALABAMA

Salem Enterprise District........Rev. T. H. Hill
Box 11, Andalusia
Shelby Spring District.............Rev. R. C. Mixon
Shelby, Ala.
Snow Creek District.................   Rev. S. N. Reid
232 Woodruff
Anniston, Ala.
South East District.................Rev. E. M. Graham
South West District.................Rev. W. M. Banks
Rt. 1, Box 57, Goshen
Shady Grove District.................Rev. J. S. Smith
89 Chilton St.
Montgomery, Ala.
Selma Good Samaritan.............Rev. Whitney Greene
Rt. 1, Box 237, Selma, Ala.
Second Mt. Pleasant.................Rev. W. M. Morton
Uniontown, Ala.
St. Mary District.................Rev. I. H. Alford
1201 E. Adam St., Dothan, Ala.
Rushing Spring District.............Dr. N. C. Shepard
P. O. Box 202
Sylacauga, Ala.
Rural District.................Rev. A. Searcy
Elmore Rehoboth District........Rev. G. W. Bradford
Rt. 1, Box 176   Mr. Henry Nelson
Elmore, Ala.   Wetumpka, Ala.
Peace Baptist District.............Rev. W. A. Davis   Mrs. W. H. Thomas
1606 First Ave.   Ensley, Ala.
Ensley, Ala.
Old Pine Grove District...........Rev. M. Davie   Alto Lee
Union Springs, Ala.   Union Springs
North Dallas District.................Rev. W. S. Smith
1205 Lawrence St., Selma, Ala.
North Bound Bethlehem...........Rev. E. Pruitt
Rt. 1, Panola, Ala.
New Shady Grove District........Rev. E. G. Lesure
Rt. 3, Box 19, Selma, Ala.
New Pine Grove District...........Rev. S. W. Penn
Union Springs, Ala.
Needham Creek District.............Rev. Thomas Jackson
New Antioch District.................Rev. W. J. Long
P. O. Box 932, Tuscaloosa, Ala.
Star of Hope District.................Rev. J. R. Rich   Mr. W. R. Stanley
Rt. 2, Box 117, Camden
Star Progressive District........Rev. J. T. Latham
Rt. 6, Box 91, Birmingham
Union Mission District.............
Town Creek District.................Rev. S. D. Johnson
Mt. Meigs, Ala.

STATE	ASSOCIATIONS	MODERATORS	SECRETARIES

ALABAMA

Village Spring Manly Dist......
North Mt. Carmel Dist............Rev. W. H. Thomas
    1220 Coosa St., Birmingham
Mt. Calvary District............Rev. F. C. Jones
    1307 Avenue M, Ensley, Ala.
Mt. Moriah Liberty............Rev. M. L. Dixon
Will's Creek District............Rev. William Mallory
    192 E. Broad St., Gadsden, Ala.
Spring Hill Dist. No. 2............Rev. L. J. Green
    220 C. Alabama, Florence, Ala.
New Era District No. 2............Rev. M. J. Adams
    315 Cherry St., Dothan, Ala.
St. Paul District............Rev. G. W. Fredd Rev. C. H. Jeffries
    Sawyersville
Hopewell District............Rev. W. M. Crews
    319 Graham St., Marion, Ala.
Mt. Pilgrim District............Rev. W. M. Atmore
    1116 9th St., W. Birmingham
Uniontown District............Rev. W. L. Rhone
    Uniontown, Ala.
New Cahaba District............Dr. D. V. Jemison   Rev. Ed Jones
    1605 Lapsley St.   515 Manter Ave.
    Selma, Ala.   Selma, Ala.
Dallas County District............Rev. T. B. Brown   Rev. J. S. Shorts
    Rehoboth, Ala.   Orrville, Ala.
Colored Bethlehem Dist............Rev. W. T. Brown, Monroeville, Ala.
Colored Bethlehem ....Rev. M. C. Cleveland
    9 Davison St., Montgomery
Canaan Grove District............Rev. G. W. Wright, Florala
Canaan Pickensville............Rev. A. J. Johnson, Northport, Ala.
Bladon Springs District............Rev. J. E. Raine   Prof. J. E. Raine
    1628 Duke St.   Womack Hill, Ala.
    Selma, Ala.
Bethlehem Blount Spring   Rev. C. H. George
  District ....141 4th St., Birmingham, Ala.
Bethlehem District............
Alabama District............Rev. John McIntosh
    4 St. Clair St., Montgomery, Ala.
Alabama Middling Dist............Rev. G. W. Williams, Hope Hull, Ala.
Chilton County District............Rev. J. P. Cooper, Verbena, Ala.
Bowen East District............Rev. C. L. Williams
    Box 166, Lafayette, Ala.
Bibb County District............Rev. D. H. Jones
    1126 Escambia St., Birmingham, Ala.
Autauga District............Rev. B. T. Taylor
    Rt. 1, Box 34, Autaugaville, Ala.
Auburn District............
Hope Hill District............Rev. H. P. Richardson, Demopolis

STATE	ASSOCIATIONS	MODERATORS	SECRETARIES

ALABAMA (Continued)

Gilfield District................................

Geneva District................................Rev. R. J. Jones   Mr. C. D. Cole

     Geneva, Ala.   Slocomb, Alla.

First Mt. Pleasant Dist.............Rev. M. E. Jones, Demopolis, Ala.

First Colored Union Dist.........Rev. D. M. James

     Rt. 1, Box 15, Snow Hill, Ala.

Ebenezer District...........................Rev. W. D. David

     Box 388, Opelika, Ala.

Eastern Shore District.............Rev. B. F. Dudley

     1312 Basil St., Mobile, Ala.

East Perry District.......................Rev. E. B. Radden

     445 Washington St., Marion, Ala.

East Alabama District.............Rev. O. P. Paige   Mr. B. O. Magby

     Rt. 2, Box 259   Buffalo, Ala.

     Roanoke, Ala.

Early Rose District......................Rev. W. H. Harrison, Sylacauga, Ala.

East Alabama District.............Rev. J. C. Cook

     Rt. 2, Box 218A, Phoenix City, Ala.

Muscle Shoals District.............Rev. W. M. Ford

     408 Circle St., Florence, Ala.

Mt. Zion District...........................Rev. W. M. Gaines, Browns, Ala.

Mt. Hebron District......................Rev. H. Harris   Rev. I. H. Robins

     Union Springs, Ala.   Midway, Ala.

Kintibish District...........................Rev. J. H. Kirkland

Lillie Star District..........................Rev. A. P. Parker

     Rt. 1, Box 36, Centerville, Ala.

Lownes County District.............Rev. B. H. Harris   Mr. A. D. Reiss

     P. O. Box 238   Whitehall, Ala.

     Selma, Ala.

Mobile Sunlight District.............Rev. E. A. Palmer   James Washington

     Box 297, Prichard, Ala.

Morning Star District.............S. P. Goggans

Mt. Carmel District.......................Rev. G. S. Jarrett

     106 Garrett St., Montgomery, Ala.

Mt. Herman District.....................Rev. G. D. Finley   T. Y. Rogers

     Rt. 1, Box 70, York, Ala.   Cootapa

Mt. Olive Clebume County   Rev. R. T. Terrell
District ....

Mt. Olive Green County   Rev. F. Jowers, Mt. Hebron, Ala.
District ....

Mulberry District...........................Rev. C. I. Hewitt   A. A. Lacey,

Davis Creek and Holly   Covin, Ala.   Rt. 3, Vernon, Ala.

Spring District...........................Rev. P. H. Brown

     520 First Ave., Selma, Ala.

East Dallas District.....................Rev. S. D. McElroy, Eufaula

     Rev. R. B. Ford

Eufaula District...........................Tuskegee Institute, Ala.

Hardaway District...........................

     Rev. J. B. Briant   Mrs. Pearl Rodgers

Evergreen District.....................Rt. 2, Box 382   Evergreen, Ala.

     Brewton, Ala.

ASSOCIATIONS AND MODERATORS (Continued)

STATE	ASSOCIATIONS	MODERATORS	SECRETARIES

ALABAMA (Continued)
Free Mission District..............
Jefferson County District...........Rev. C. H. White
                                2006 Exter Ave., Bessemer, Ala.
Mt. Calvary District................Rev. F. T. Noland
Montgomery-Antioch Dist.......Box 76, Kellerman, Ala.
                                Rev. John McIntosh
Little River District..............4 St. Clair St., Montgomery, Ala.
Lebanon District..................Rev. Ross Bush
                                Rev. M. J. Williams
Union District......................Rt. 2, Box 33, Prairie Point, Miss.
                                Rev. E. H. Richard
Helicon District....................Rt. 1, Box 144, Garland, Ala.
Union Middle River...............Rev. James Palmer, Evergreen, Ala.
                                Rev. W. H. Perry, 2301 9th Ave.,
Flint River Miss. Bapt.   Birmingham, Ala.
Association ....Rev. W. A. Wilhite   Mrs. O. Fletcher
                                Rt. 2, Box 280   238 Va. St.
Spring Creek Dist. Bapt.   Decatur   Huntsville, Ala.
Association ....Rev. J. S. Dudley   Mr. J. W. Price
                                Gadsden, Ala.   Gaylesville, Ala.

ARKANSAS

Antioch ....Rev. Wm. Erby
                                1010 N. 10th St., Ft. Smith, Ark.
General Union......................Rev. M. V. Hudson
                                1418 Pulaski St., Little Rock, Ark.
Jefferson Springs..................Rev. A. Anderson, Hensley, Ark.
St. Marion ....Rev. T. M. Lacy, Gould, Ark.
Bradley ....Rev. J. E. Tidwell, Fordyce, Ark.
Ouchta ....Rev. M. W. Russ, Fordyce, Ark.
Greater P. L. M. & D............Rev. J. E. Shepherd, Marianna, Ark.
Columbia ....Rev. J. F. Russ, Magnolia, Ark.
Lafayette and Miller..............Rev. J. H. Wyart, Rt. 1, Hope, Ark.
Valley ....Rev. M. S. Peals, Brickey, Ark.
Great Western ....Rev. J. A. Johnson, Texarkana, Ark.
C. W. R............................Rev. W. S. Hayes, Brinkley, Ark.
Christian Liberty..................Rev. R. J. Johnson, RFD, Parkin, Ark.
East Arkansas......................Rev. M. Williams, Earl, Ark.
Mt. O. and P......................Rev. M. L. Scott, Marion, Ark.
                                John Lindsey, Marked Tree, Ark.
M. V. B. U........................Rev. R. G. Gates, Blytheville, Ark.
Southwest ....Dr. A. J. Jackson, 1103 Laurel St.,
                                Texarkana, Ark.
                                Rev. J. A. Johnson, Texarkana, Ark.
South Arkansas ....Rev. W. M. Chester   L. B. Alson
Tyronza ....Earl Ark.   Earl, Ark.
North Ark. District...............Rev. G. W. Dudley, Forest City, Ark.
Ozan District......................
Southeast District ....Rev. H. S. Newton, Montrose, Ark.
P. L. M. & D. District...........Rev. H. R. Stevenson, Helena, Ark.
                                Rev. T. M. Garrison   Rev. S. H. Hearns
                                Fordyce, Ark.   Fordyce, Ark.

STATE	ASSOCIATIONS	MODERATORS	SECRETARIES

ARKANSAS (Continued)

Bradley District................Rev. T. M. Garrison, Fordyce, Ark.
Little River District...............Rev. A. W. Williams, Ashdown, Ark.
Greater St. Marion.............Rev. M. V. Ferguson, Pine Bluff, Ark.
Cypress Creek District...........Rev. P. B. Knox   Mr. J. C. Thornton
        Conway, Ark.   Menifee, Ark.
Central District ....Rev. J. H. Neasley, Altheimer, Ark.
C. W. R. District...............Rev. B. W. Woody, Wynne, Ark.
Chicot District.............Rev. E. L. Carter, Eudora, Ark.
Watson District...............Rev. J. H. Mitchell, Dumas, Ark.
White River District.............Rev. E. W. Taylor, Earl, Ark.
Antioch District ....Rev. C. A. Bean, Fort Smith, Ark.
North Eastern District...........Rev. L. Calcote, A & B College,
        Little Rock, Ark.
St. Marion District.............Rev. W. E. Watson
        Pine Bluff, Ark.
M. C. B. F. District...........Rev. J. H. Pugh
        Memphis, Tenn.
Big Creek and Reedville............Rev. N. C. Hope, Dumas, Ark.
E. H. F. M. Association............Rev. I. H. Harvey, Luxora, Ark.
Nazarite District.............Rev. I. Robinson
Bethlehem District...............Rev. J. I. Bell, Postelle, Ark.
Ed. H. and F. Miss.............Rev. I. H. Harvey   Rev. E. Pitts
        Box 303, Luxora, Ark.   Dell, Ark.

CALIFORNIA

Los Angeles ....Rev. Geo. Miller, 1186 E. 42nd Place
        Los Angeles, Calif.
Tri-County District ....Rev. L. M. Curtis
        2035 E. 117th St., Compton, Calif.
Southwest District...............Rev. Wm. Reed, Brawley, Calif.
Providence ....Rev. B. W. Wade
        386 E. 43rd Pl., Los Angeles, Calif.

FLORIDA

Second Bethlehem ....Rev. T. M. Magwood
        215 E. Street, Leesburg, Fla.
Florida East Coast...............Rev. J. W. Drake   Rev. J. C. Coleman
        3rd Ave., Miami, Fla.   2057 N.W. 6th
First Bethlehem...............Rev. W. M. Burns, Tallahassee, Fla.
Union St. James...............Rev. L. M. Mathis
        318 10th St. Palatka, Fla.
Jerusalem ....Rev. R. M. Latimore
        804 S. Porter St., Gainesville, Fla.
First Central ....Rev. F. W. Williams, Branford, Fla.
Suwanee River Progressive......Rev. A. L. Jordan
        920 Columbia Lane, Gainesville, Fla.

First West Florida................

ASSOCIATIONS AND MODERATORS (Continued)

FLORIDA (Continued)

Second Central .... Rev. E. Tinsley
Rt. 2, Box 1, Greenville, Fla.

Emanuel .... Rev. B. W. Williams
915 W. 22nd St., Jacksonville, Fla.

Atlantic Coast .... Rev. S. A. Sampson
1425 N. W. 1st Ct., Miami, Fla.

Bethel ....
Mt. Zion N. E. Coast............... Rev. Jas. Massey, Ormond, Fla.
New Light .... Rev. J. B. Byrd
First South .... Rev. I. C. Nimmons
Seaboard .... Rev. John I. Ross
1475 N. W. 5th Place, Miami, Fla.

St. John River............... Rev. M. B. Britton
St. Augustine, Fla.

West Coast .... Rev. A. C. Crooms
P. O. Box 4103, Sta. A, Orlando, Fla.

GEORGIA

Antioch .... Rev. D. S. Scott
Rt. 1, Leesburg, Ga.

Atlanta .... Rev. M. L. King
193 Boulevard, N.E.   Rev. R. A. Graves
Atlanta, Ga.   Atlanta, Ga.

Benevolence .... Rev. S. F. Smith, Edison, Ga.
Bethesda .... Rev. S. M. Holton, Andersonville, Ga.
Berean .... Rev. E. D. Davis
931 37th St., Savannah, Ga.

Blue Springs .... Rev. S. H. Jordan, East Albany, Ga.
Buckeye .... Rev. W. P. Parker, Putney, Ga.
Building Union .... Rev. C. H. Dumas, Vidalia, Ga.
Cabin Creek .... Rev. A. S. Shaw, Cordele, Ga.
Camilla .... Rev. O. J. Moore   I. S. Mack
Griffin, Ga.   1023 Ashley Grove, S.W.
Atlanta, Ga.

Carrollton Union .... Rev. R. C. Crouch, Moultrie, Ga.
Cane Creek .... Rev. F. M. Hutchinson
111 Ozone St., Atlanta, Ga.

Central .... Rev. E. M. Johnson
250 Burbank Dr., Atlanta, Ga.

Central Ga. .... Rev. W. M. Thomas, Smithville, Ga.
Chattahoochee River .... Rev. J. H. Bankston   C. M. Montgomery
Ft. Gaines, Ga.   Coleman, Ga.

Columbus .... Rev. W. A. Reid
622 2nd Ave., Columbus, Ga.

Covenant .... Rev. J. J. Johnson, Buena Vista, Ga.
Educational ....
Eureka .... Rev. R. B. Brown
107 Poplar St., Savannah, Ga.

First North Ga............... Rev. S. M. Ferguson
Summerville, Ga.

Flint River .... Rev. J. L. Hoffman
Donaldsonville, Ga.

STATE	ASSOCIATIONS	MODERATORS	SECRETARIES

GEORGIA (Continued)

Frank Cooper...

Fowltown ....

Freewill Aid ....Rev. G. A. Turman, Lincolnton, Ga.

Friendship ....Rev. B. E. Vicks, Cuthbert, Ga.

Friendship ....Rev. L. W. Whipple, Hawkinsville, Ga.

Georgia Union...Rev. B. Gordon   Mr. A. W. Glover
Unadilla, Ga.   Pineview, Ga.

Georgia Baptist...Rev. E. D. White, Atlanta, Ga.

Great Eastern...Rev. J. L. Lowe, Leesburg, Ga.

Gethsemane ....Rev. M. J. Harris, Woodbine, Ga.

Gum Creek ....Rev. G. P. Haynes   Mr. D. W. Brown
801 River Rd.   Route 4
Albany, Ga.   Cordele, Ga.

Georgia Central ....

Harrison Union-Hancock...Rev. W. Reese, Tennille, Ga.

Home Mission ....Rev. W. M. Dominie, Camilla, Ga.

Home Mission Union...Rev. W. M. Printer
Rt. 1, Leary, Ga.

Hopewell ....Rev. W. B. Bell   D. G. Ebster
76 Brown Avenue   239 White St.
Atlanta, Ga.   Decatur, Ga.

Jeruel ....Rev. J. R. Barnett
945 Palmetto Ave., Atlanta, Ga.

Kiokee ....Rev. E. R. Riley, Albany, Ga.

Hopewell ....

Kennesaw ....Rev. W. H. Ferrell   Pro. B. F. Graves
48 Ross St.,   Atlanta, Ga.
Rome, Ga.

Little River ....Rev. Wm. Miller, Sparks, Ga.

Madison ....Rev. R. G. Cash, Madison, Ga.

Middle Ga. ....Rev. G. G. Taylor, Perry, Ga.

Middle Ga. Orthodox...Rev. J. T. Saxon
220 Norris St., Macon, Ga.

Montgomery ....Rev. Z. O. Gray, Glenwood, Ga.

Mt. Calvary ....Rev. J. H. Carter   Mr. W. F. Rivers
2311 Buena Vista Rd., Columbus, Ga.

Mt. Calvary Prog...

Mt. Calvary ....Rev. A. W. Vincent, Martinez, Ga.

Mt. Herman ....

Mt. Carmel ....Rev. W. W. Walker, Woodbury, Ga.

Mt. Moriah ....M. L. George   Mr. C. A. Dozier
Omaha, Ga.   Lumpkin, Ga.

Mt. Olive ....P. C. Daniel, Savannah, Ga.

Mt. Olive ....Rev. D. C. Clark, Sylvester, Ga.

Mt. Pleasant ....Rev. J. J. King, Forsyth, Ga.

Mt. Pleasant Calvary...Rev. J. L. Henley, Vidalia, Ga.

Mt. Tabor ....Rev. A. R. Curry   W. C. Shipman
Townsend, Ga.   McIntosh, Ga.

Mt. Zion ....Rev. J. H. Baines   Mr. C. W. Willis
Thomasville, Ga.   Cairo, Ga.

STATE	ASSOCIATIONS	MODERATORS	SECRETARIES

GEORGIA (Continued)

Mt. Zion Western	Rev. C. J. Gore, Richland, Ga.	
Nashville	Rev. J. C. Chatman	Mr. L. Sherman
	Adel, Ga.	Sparks, Ga.
New Grady	Rev. R. D. Wynn	
New Home	Rev. D. E. Jennings	
	1516 Holly St., Augusta, Ga.	
New Hope	Rev. A. Bell	81 Howell St.
	80 Randolph St., Atlanta, Ga.	
	Atlanta, Ga.	Mr. W. M. Lewis
New Hope	Rev. W. E. Atkins	
	Rt. 2, Colquitt, Ga.	
New Macedonia	Rev. R. B. Thompson	
	970 Smith St., S.W., Atlanta, Ga.	
New Proviso		
New Zion	Rev. J. H. Lockett	J. S. Dickerson
	529 Dunbar St., Atlanta, Ga.	
New Towaliga	Rev. J. H. Kurt	
	501 Center St., Monroe, Ga.	
Newton	Rev. C. F. Neals, Pelham, Ga.	
Noah's Ebenezer	Rev. M. R. Frye, Midville, Ga.	
No. Carolina-Georgia	Rev. Andy Wiley, Murphy, N. C.	
N. Georgia Central	Rev. L. J. Vaughn	Mr. A. P. Perry
	228 Pennington St.	Calhoun, Ga.
	Rome, Ga.	
Western Union	Rev. W. C. Adams	C. H. Kelly
	Hogansville, Ga.	LaGrange, Ga.
North Western No. 2	Rev. H. Vincent	J. S. L. Morrow
	Statham, Ga.	Bethlehem, Ga.
North Western No. 1		
Ocmulgee	Rev. C. N. Campbell	Mr. W. L. King
	Mystic, Ga.	Fitzgerald, Ga.
Oconee-Zion	Rev. H. A. McCloud, Vidalia, Ga.	
Nilgram	Rev. J. W. Thomas, Guyton, Ga.	
Progressive	Rev. G. W. Pollhill, Cordele, Ga.	
Pleasant Hope	Rev. W. A. Atkins, Colquitt, Ga.	
Quarterman		
Queen Victory	Rev. W. M. Hall	
	529 Clinton St., Macon, Ga.	
Rehoboth	Rev. J. G. Thomas	
	472 Broad Street	Rev. T. C. Kinchen
	Macon, Ga.	Dublin, Ga.
Rosemont	Rev. G. W. Jones	
	1109 8th St., Augusta, Ga.	
St. John	Rev. E. Z. Rozelle, Macon, Ga.	
St. Luke	Rev. W. M. Phillips	
St. Mary	Rev. Larkin Walker, Albany, Ga.	
St. Paul	Rev. C. T. Anderson	
	Bridgeboro, Ga.	
Second Flint River	Rev. William Stanback	
	Junction City, Ga.	

ASSOCIATIONS AND MODERATORS (Continued)'

STATE	ASSOCIATIONS	MODERATORS	SECRETARIES

GEORGIA (Continued)

Second Middle Ga. ....Rev. H. Hunter, Washington, Ga.
Second Mt. Zion............................Rev. G. H. Taylor, Girard, Ga.
Second Rehoboth ....Rev. J. M. Benton, Waycross, Ga.
Second Shiloh ....
Shiloh ....Rev. W. M. Jackson   Mr. R. G. Cash
                                    Atlanta, Ga.   Madison, Ga.
Shiloh Union ....Rev. W. D. Sparks, Shiloh, Ga.
South Georgia ....Rev. S. C. Coachman, Nashville, Ga.
Southwestern Union ....Rev. A. H. Turner, Glenn, Ga.
Southwestern ....Rev. A. J. Allen, Cuthbert, Ga.
Spring Creek ....Rev. C. H. Holmes, Colquitt
Star Light ....Rev. B. H. Driskell, Dublin, Ga.
Tatnall ....Rev. T. J. Lynch, Daisy, Ga.
Third Shiloh ....Rev. E. R. McLendon   Mr. L. S. Pelott
                                    Washington, Ga.   Rayle, Ga.
Thomasville ....Rev. S. S. Broadnax
                                    Thomasville, Ga.
Union ....Rev. G. G. Taylor, Perry, Ga.
Union ....Rev. W. M. Dansby   Mr. R. C. Wilson
                                    Lavonia, Ga.   Toccoa, Ga.
Union Grove ....Rev. T. Patterson, Americua, Ga.
Union Mid. River ....Rev. W. H. Perry
                                    2301 9th Ave. S.O.   Mr. C. S. Anderson
                                    Birmingham, Ala.   Dahlonega, Ga.
Walker ....Rev. S. Campbell, Midville, Ga.
Waycross-Satilla ....Rev. W. B. Golden   Mr. W. H. Bradley
                                    1409 Thomas St.   Box 328
                                    Waycross, Ga.   Brunswick, Ga.
Western Union............................Mr. W. H. Bradley, Brunswick, Ga.
Willochoochee ....
Young Men Hopewell............................Rev. G. W. Jackson, Albany, Ga.
Yellow River ....Rev. A. J. Clark
                                    Rt., Covington, Ga.
Zion ....Rev. A. R. Curry, Townsend, Ga.
Zion Hope ....Rev. John Howard, Abbeville, Ga.
Builders Union ....Rev. A. S. Shaw, Cordele, Ga.
Friendship ....Rev. M. Hooks   Mr. A. Lowery
                                    Fitzgerald, Ga.   P. O. Box 43
                                                          De Soto, Ga.
Friendship ....Rev. P. H. Head, East Point, Ga.

ILLINOIS

New Era ....Rev. J. H. Gibson
                                    4728 Forestville Ave., Chicago, Ill.
Bethlehem ....Rev. I. A. Thomas
                                    Box 248, Evanston, Ill.

ASSOCIATIONS AND MODERATORS (Continued)

STATE	ASSOCIATIONS	MODERATORS	SECRETARIES

ILLINOIS (Continued)

Zion ....Rev. L. Thompson, Mounds, Ill.

New Salem ....Rev. J. A. Lampley   Rev. L. A. Brown
                                        1854 Tudor Ave.   1926 Bond Ave.
                                        East St. Louis, Ill.   E. St. Louis, Ill.

Shiloh ....Rev. B. F. Laden
                                        3708 State St., Chicago, Ill.

INDIANA

Union ....Rev. J. A. Hall
                                        219 W. North St., Indianapolis, Ind.

Northern District ....Rev. T. S. Saunders
                                        4901 McCook St., East Chicago, Ind.

KANSAS

Kaw Valley District.................Rev. J. A. Moore   Rev M. J. Smith
                                        1964 Thompson St.   1960 Thompson St.
                                        Kansas City, Kan.   Kansas City, Kan.

Smokey Hill ....Rev. G. T. Rainey
                                        920 N. Clay St., Junction City, Kan.

Neosho District ....Rev. J. A. Rucker, Paola, Kan.

Northeastern District ....Rev. W. F. Beatty
                                        901 Division St., Atchison, Kan.

KENTUCKY

Central District ....

Howard Creek District.............Rev. T. H. Smith   Rev. J. E. Bowens
                                        571 Maryland St., Lexington, Ky.

First District ....Rev. J. R. Hunt
                                        304 E. th St., Hopkinsville 4, Ky.

South District ....Rev. G. R. Redd, Elizabethtown, Ky.

Mt. Calvary District................Rev. J. M. Watkins, Hardinsburg, Ky.

London District ....Rev. H. F. Mays, Straight Creek, Ky.

Zion District ....Rev. C. C. Willis, Columbia, Ky.

Consolidated ....Rev. G. K. Offutt, Ashland, Ky.

Mt. Pleasant District ....Rev. W. D. Thompson
                                        Linden St., Richmond, Ky.

Little River and Cumber-   Rev. D. W. Crenshaw
land District ....Cadiz, Ky.

Elkhorn and Sandy Valley   Rev. R. A. Beal
District ....Fleming, Ky.

Liberty District ....Rev. Alonzo, Webb
                                        Rt. 6, Glasgow, Ky.

Green River Valley...................Rev. A. J. Cunningham
                                        Central City, Ky.

STATE	ASSOCIATIONS	MODERATORS	SECRETARIES

KENTUCKY (Continued)

West Kentuckey Green Valley District .... Rev. O. O. Reynolds Wickliffe, Ky.

First District Baptist............... Rev. E. Pullin, 844 Clay St., Henderson, Ky.

LOUISIANA

Louisiana Greedman............... Rev. Wm. Jackson
2109 Jackson Ave., New Orleans, La.

Southern Bapist .... Rev. Ben Joseph
2107 St. Ann St., New Orleans, La.

Ideal Miss. Baptist............... Rev. S. A. Duncan
1412 S. Rampart St., N. Orleans, La.

Purelight Baptist .... Rev. C. S. Delonde
3302 Third St., New Orleans, La.

Westside Baptist .... Rev. Geo. Williams, Marrero, La.

Universal Baptist Biss............... Rev. F. F. Franklin
4120 General Ogden St. New Orleans, La.

Louisiana Freedman Baptist No. 2............... Rev. J. A. Scypion
Jackson and Claiborne Avenues New Orleans, La.

Fourth District .... Rev. T. A. Levy   Rev. E. D. Billup
Rosedale, La.   Box 1252
        Baton Rouge, La.

Fifth District .... Rev. T. A. Collins
Box 107, Houma, La.

Sixth District .... Rev. R. M. Boley, New Iberia, La.

Seventh District .... Rev. H. C. Ross   Dr. L. C. Simon
629 Avenue "C"   Opelousas, La.
Crowley, La.

Eighth District .... Rev. J. W. White
Box 65, Bunkie, La.

Ninth District .... Rev. S. L. Douglas, Newllton, La.

Calcasieu District .... Rev. Wm. Roquemore
1506 Callagher St., Lake Charles, La.

Concordia District .... Rev. E. Pettiway
Box 238, Ferriday, La.

Madison District Baptist............... Rev. Coggs, Tallulah, Ga.

E. Carroll District............... Rev. G. W. Owens
Box 1642, Lake Providence, La.

Tenth District Baptist............... Rev. E. E. Hollins
Box 202, Bastrop, La.

Little River Baptist............... Rev. G. L. Washington
Box 73, Vidalia, La.

Franklin Baptist .... Rev. L. H. Holmes, Monroe, La.

STATE	ASSOCIATIONS	MODERATORS	SECRETARIES

LOUISIANA (Continued)

Eleventh District	Rev. E. B. Morgan, Gibsland, La.	
Union County Baptist	Rev. W. B. Willis, Litroe, La.	
Union Determined Baptist	Rev. J. J. Fox, Jonesville, La.	
New Hope Baptist	Rev. W. M. Wyatt, Chatham, La.	
North Louisiana	Rev. C. W. White Box 24, Arcadia, La.	Rev. S. L. Harris Simsboro, La.
Liberty Hill Baptist	Rev. P. B. Lewis Box 158, Rouston, La.	E. H. Harris Arcadia, La.
Gum Springs Baptist	Rev. L. B. Braggs Rt. 2, Framerville, La.	
New Beulah Baptist	Rev. A. M. Brown, Bermuda, La.	
13th District	Prof. R. P. Players (Sect'y.) 1422 Murph St., Shreveport, La.	
Union District	Rev. S. Teamer Rt. 7, Box 181 Rodeisa, La.	Mr. J. E. Payne Box 105 Marshall, Texas
Second District	Rev. A. L. Smith	

MISSISSIPPI

Adams County Missionary Association	Rev. C. R. Anderson 10 Keim Ave., Natchez, Miss.	
African Miss. Baptist of Wilkinson Cty.	Rev. G. L. Davis Woodville, Miss.	
Claiborn County	Rev. A. E. Davis, Port Gibson, Miss.	
Coahoma County	Rev. R. C. Gallion Clarksdale, Miss.	Rev. Z. P. Pittman
First Enterprise Missionarary Baptist Assn.	Rev. J. M. Barlow Shubta, Miss.	
Hinds County	Rev. R. W. West Rt. 3, Box 34, Bolton	
Holmes County	Rev. C. C. Crafton Box 214, Tchula, Miss.	
Humphrey's County	Rev. J. A. G. Johnson Belzoni, Miss.	
Jackson Missionary Baptist Association	Rev. W. P. Whitfield Box 2261 Jackson, Miss.	Mr. W. D. Burns Rt. 3, Box 75 Jackson, Miss.
Lebanon District	Rev. J. W. Gayden Box 371, Belzoni, Miss.	
Jefferson County	Rev. W. N. Tyler	
Leflore County	Rev. A. W. Moore 107 E. Percy St., Greenwood, Miss.	
Madison County District	Rev. W. L. Jones RFD 2, Canton, Miss.	

STATE	ASSOCIATIONS	MODERATORS	SECRETARIES

MISSISSIPPI (Continued)

Missionary Baptist Association of Warren Cty. .... Rev. E. D. Straughter
2012 Ford St., Vicksburg, Miss.

Mt. Moriah Baptist .... Rev. Wm. H. Turner
RFD 2, Bov 69, Sardis, Miss.

Palo Alto Missionary .... Rev. D. S. Taylor, Greenville, Miss.

Pleasant Green .... Rev. G. P. Phillips
Rolling Fork, Miss.

Quitman County .... Rev. T. W. Laundrew, Marks, Miss.

Rankin County .... Rev. M. H. Calhoun, Ludlow, Miss.

St. John District .... hev. J. W. Terrell, Greenwood, Miss.

Cardis Missionary Baptist .... Rev. J. R. Pearson
Looxahoma, Miss.

Second Dist. Educational Association .... Rev. S. M. Harts   W. H. Wallace
Tutwiler, Miss.   Tutwiler, Miss.

Shiloh Miss. Baptist .... Rev. i.. Johnson, Biloxi, Miss.

Spring Hill Baptist .... Rev. O. W. Lenoir
Box 23, Tupelo, Miss.

Sunflower County Baptist Association .... Rev. N. A. Brantley
Rev. I. R. Chandler   Box 134
Inverness, Miss.   Indianola, Miss.

Sunflower County General Association .... Rev. W. H. Sanders
Box 537   Rev. E. L. Drew
Itta Bena, Miss.   Shaw, Miss.

Third New Hope .... Rev. R. B. Ooten, Rt. 1, Box 59,
Lawrence, Miss.

Washington County .... Rev. W. M. Walton, Greenville, Miss.

Yazoo County M. B. A. .... Rev. G. R. Session
Rt. 2, Box 41, Yazoo City, Miss.

Boliver County Educational Association .... Rev. S. M. Jones
Box 52, Chambers, Miss.

Washington County .... Rev. R. S. Buckner, Winterville, Miss.

Bethel Harmony .... Rev. E. H. Haynes
Rt. 4, Box 68, Louisville, Miss.

Center Mount Olivet .... Rev. J. E. Ferrow
Rt. 0, Box 252, Columbus, Miss.

Gethsemane Mount Moriah District Association .... Rev. P. H. Greene, Artesia, Miss.

Pontotoc District .... Rev. S. Watson   Prof. W. P. Woods
Holly Springs, Miss.   Ecru, Miss.

Mount Olive Mission Baptist Association .... Rev. C. N. Eiland
Box 85, Louisville, Miss.

Third Enterprise M. B. A. .... Rev. S. A. Tullos, Hickory, Miss.

Whitfield District ....

Antioch District .... Rev. C. R. Anderson   Mr. E. W. Rhone
Natchez, Miss.   Natchez, Miss.

MISSOURI

Berean District .... Rev. S. Morgan Miller
4565 Cottage Ave., St. Louis, Mo.

Central District .... Rev. L. D. Hardiman
412 N. Osage St.   A. H. Smith
Sedalia, Mo.   Bunceton, Mo.

STATE	ASSOCIATIONS	MODERATORS	SECRETARIES

MISSOURI (Continued)

New Era District........Rev. R. E. Holland
615. E. 14th St., Kansas City, Co.
Union District ....Rev. E. B. Phillips
2911 Dickson St., St. Louis, Mo.
Springhill District ....Rev. G. W. Mack
·Box 125, Pascola, Mo.
Pemiscott ....Rev. E. C. Keeble, Poplar Bluff, Ark.
Third District ....Rev. G. W. Broughton Mr. J. Jackson
922 Alive St., Poplar Bluff, Ark.
Mt. Zion District........Rev. T. R. Sayles
223 W. Robald, Brookfield, Mo.

East End ....
Guiding Star ....Rev. H. P. Phillips
2221 Carr St., St. Louis, Mo.

North Jersey ....Rev. C. T. Wilcher
534 N. Fifth St., Newark, N. J.
Seacoast ....Rev. E. D. Crawley
20 Dewitt Ave., Asbury Park
Middlesex Central ....Rev. Geo. L. Harris
1053 Williams St., Elizabethtown, N. J.
Bethany ....Rev. Victor S. Griggs
Church St., Moorestown, N. J.

NEW YORK

North Jersey ....Rev. Geo. Sims
131 W. 131st St., New York, N. Y.
Manhattan, Westchester, Rey L. Kay
  Bronx & Staten Island........18 Wood St., Yonkers, N. Y.
Eastern Baptist ....Rev. James R. Moore D. C. L. Franklin
164-19 108th Ave., Jamaica, N. Y.
Central Hudson ....Rev. H. D. Morris
120 Brookfield St., White Plains, N. Y.
Mohawk & Upper Hudson........Rev. M. S. Hunter
159 Quil St., Albany, N. Y.
Central District ....Rev. R. L. Weaver
150 Union St., Kingston, N. Y.
Western New York ....Rev. A. B. Washington
521 Erie Ave., Niagara Falls, N. Y.

ASSOCIATIONS AND MODERATORS (Continued)

STATE	ASSOCIATIONS	MODERATORS	SECRETARIES

NORTH CAROLINA

New Era Miss. Baptist............Rev. N. Hamer   Daniel Flowers
Neuse River Miss. Baptist........Box 72 Hairbluff, N. C. Chalborn, N. C.
     Rev. T. V. Foster Rev. F. L. Bullock
     Rocky Mount, N. C. B. J. Johnson
     Halifax, N. C.
Wake Baptist Association........Rev. G. S. Stokes
     Box 5, Middlesex, N. C.
Middle District Association......Rev. H. Peterson, Kelly, N. C.
Middle Baptist Association........Rev. J. W. Burdwell
     RFD 1, Henderson, N. C.
Brunswick-Waccansaw Assn....Rev. D. C. Gore   G. A. Best
     Whiteville, N. C. Whiteville, N. C.
New Era Baptist Assn..............Rev. N. H. Homer, Fair Bluff, N. S.
Reedy Creek Missionary   Rev. J. H. Clanton
  Baptist Association ....P. O. Box 883, Raleigh, N. C.
Middle Baptist Association......Rev. J. M. Burchette Mr. J. D. Morrow
     Ridgeway, N. C. Rt. 5, Henderson
County Line.............................Rev. D. P. Lewis, Lewisburg, N. C.
East Cedar Grove...................Rev. G. W. Thomas Mr. E. C. McLester
     Rt. 2, Roxboro, N. C.
Cedar Grove Baptist................Rev. W. M. Warner
     Star Route   Mr. James Swan
     Danville, Va.   Pelham, N. C.
Ebenezer Baptist Assn..............   Rev. Dwight Costney
     Rev. F. L. Howell 104 Tracy St.
     Rt. 2, Cherryville King Mt., N. C.
Deep River Miss. Assn..............Rev. O. P. Foster Mr. H. L. Womack
     Box 671, Burlington Rt. 2, Sanford
Zion Miss. Baptist Assn..........Rev. J. W. Diggs
     Rt. 1, Pee Dee, N. C.
Shiloh Missionary Baptist........Rev. H. I. Quick
     Rockingham, N. C.
Johnstan County ....Rev. J. W. Jones   A. B. Johnson
     818 E. Martin St. South St.
     Raleigh, N. C.   Raleigh, N. C.
Eastern Pamlico River.............Rev. Alonzo Moore Rev. F. A. Moore
     Rt. 2,
     Blount Creek, N. C. Bonnerton, N. C.
Mountain and Catawba.............Rev. W. S. Sherrill James Parker
     Rt. 2, Troutman Stony Point
Union Baptist Association........Rev. S. W. Smith Mr. J. R. Brewing
     Rt. 1, Box 113 Council, N. C.
     Council, N. C.
Kenansville Eastern M. B.........Rev. J. M. McNewkirk
     Rose Holl, N. C.
Rowan Baptist Association.....Dr. J. T. Hairston Dr. J. W. Hairston
     Austin St.
     Greensboro, N. C.
Mud Creek M. B. A...................Rev. E. W. Dixon
     44 Clingman Ave., Asheville, N. C.
St. John Association.................Rev. C. J. Cooper, Red Springs, N. C.

STATE	ASSOCIATIONS	MODERATORS	SECRETARIES

OHIO

Bethlehem District ....Rev. C. R. Worthy, Cleveland, Ohio

Toledo District ....Rev. E. Benton
216 John R. Street, Toledo, Ohio

Jerusalem District............Rev. B. F. Colvin
6504 Woodland Ave., Cleveland, Ohio

Progressive District ....Rev. J. W. Ribbins
2344 E. 30th St., Cleveland, Ohio

Eastern Ohio District ....Rev. I. R. Hall
2002 Wilson Ave., Youngstown, Ohio

Western Union ....Rev. Mitchell Coleman
325 N. Wayne Ave., Lockland, Ohio

Eastern Union ....Rev. J. A. Ashburn, Jr.
178 S. Oakley Ave., Columbus, Ohio

Northern ....Rev. J. C. Walker
2252 E. 86th St., Cleveland, Ohio

Providence ....Rev. J. T. Crable, Rendville, Ohio

Northwestern ....Rev. J. T. Dotson
704 Collingwood Ave., Toledo, Ohio

Logan County ....Rev. S. M. Edwards

OKLAHOMA

Central Wayland District............Rev. J. L. Hawkins   Rev. A. C. Lomax
Spiro, Okla.   Rt. 2, Spiro

North West Creek Dist.............Rev. A. C. Chinn   Rev. B. Moore
Pawhuska, Okla. 1702 N. Muslisn St.
Tulsa, Okla.

South Eastern District............Rev. J. Dean Caldwell, Harris, Okla.

South West Creek-Land   Rev. E. S. Scobey
Mark ....218 N. Hitchita, Wewoka, Okla.

East Zion District............Rev. J. P. Patterson
Box 96   Mr. S. S. Farley
Ponca City, Okla.   Oklahoma City

Oklahoma District............Rev. K. B. Davis, Rt. 6, Guthrie, Okla.

Collate District ....Rev. J. U. Green
10th & Grand, McAlester, Okla.

Creek District............Rev. A. L. Branch Mrs. Vassie Marsh
509 E. King St.   Greenwood Station
Tulsa, Okla.

Union District ....Rev. E. W. White
Box 141, Rentiesville, Okla.

PENNSYLVANIA

Allegheny General............Rev. H. H. Rucker
143 E. Chestnut St., Washington, Pa.

STATE	ASSOCIATIONS	MODERATORS	SECRETARIES

PENNSYLVANIA (Continued)

Union ....Rev. D. B. Russell
    7209 Monticello St., Pittsburgh, Pa.
Pennsylvania ....Rev. E. T. Lewis, 1724 D. Montgomery
    Avenue, Philadelphia, Pa.
Eastern Keystone ....Rev. A. Hobbs,
    559 Coulter St., Philadelphia, Pa.
Antioch Baptist Assn..............Rev. J. H. Patten
    1024 Christian St., Philadelphia, Pa.
Salem ....Rev. A. Alexander
    Coatsville, Pa.
Central ....Rev. R. F. Spraggins
    3 Chestnut St., Mt. Union, Pa.
Youghiogheny W. ....Rev. Maxie Smith
Bethany ....
Suburban ....Rev. G. G. McGee, Pinllyn, Pa.

SOUTH CAROLINA

Beaver Creek ....Rev. W. B. Coleman
    North Augusta, S. C.
Cooper Branch ....
Cedar Branch ....Rev. W. H. Vaughn, Aiken, S. C.
Holly Hill ....Rev. D. J. Dinkins, Holly Hill, S. C.
Mt. Olive ....Rev. W. B. Coleman
    North Augusta, S. C.
Macedonia ....Rev. H. B. Bush, Dunbarton, S. C.
Mt. Sinai ....Rev. S. C. Warren, Clover, S. C.
Mt. Hope ....Rev. L. B. Payton, Orangeburg, S. C.
New Enoree River.................Rev. Wm. Lipscomb
    Greenville, S. C.
New Zion..................................Rev. E. A. Johnson
    Varnersville, S. C.
Richland County ....Rev. C. B. Freeman   Rev. J. T. Watson
    Cayce, S. C.   Ridge Spring
Ridge Hill ....Rev. John Davis, Ridge Spring, S. C.
Savannah Valley ....Rev. A. Ware, Calhoun Falls, S. C.
Spring Grove ....Rev. A. C. Johnson, Augusta, Ga.
St. Paul ....Rev. Wm. Redfern, Cheraw, S. C.
St. Matthew ....
St. Matthew ....Rev. R. Rannell
Silver Spring ....Rev. M. S. Mosely, Aiken, S. C.
North Augusta ....
Charleston County ....Rev. W. Raven
    92 Hanover St., Charleston, S. C.
Calhoun ....Rev. J. W. Denmore
Fairfield County ....Rev. W. A. Adamson
    Star Route, Winsboro, S. C.
Four Mile ....Rev. Wm. Phinzy, Dunbarton, S. C.
Gethsemane ....Rev. N. Smith, Box 64, Ridgeway,S.C.
Jerusalem ....Rev. G. D. Daniels

STATE	ASSOCIATIONS	MODERATORS	SECRETARIES

SOUTH CAROLINA (Cont.)

Kingston Lake .... Rev. G. G. Daniels
Little River .... Rev. J. S. Donalds
Lovely Hill .... Rev. S. D. Rickenbacker
    Box 545   Rev. W. M.
    Bamberg, S. C.   Primus
                       St. George
Little Pee Dee .... Rev. W. B. Washington
    Rt. 1, Box 121, Yemasee, S. C.
Mt. Calvary .... Rev. R. B. Bush, Dunbarton, S. C.
Macedonia .... Rev. R. B. Bush, Dunbarton, S. C.
Wateree (Lower Division) .... Rev. J. A. Mack   J. P. Garrick
    Bishopville, S. C.   Sumter, S. C.
Mt. Canaan .... Rev. G. W. Blocker Trenton, S. C.
Mt. Carmel .... Rev. P. R. Washington
    Rt. 1, Box 121   Rev. Samuel
    Yemasee, S. C.   Graham
                    Pineland, S. C.
Mt. Hebron .... Rev. C. Anderson Mr. B. D. Jones
    2558 Calhoun St.   Pelion, S. C.
    Columbia, S. C.
Mt. Moriah .... Rev. J. W. Boykin Rev. R. E. Boykin
    Camden, S. C.   Rembert, S. C.
Nazarene .... Rev. E. A. Johnson, Varnesville, S. C.
New Enoree .... Rev. W. R. Reeder, Newberry, S. C.
Union Bright Light .... Rev. J. W. Blackmon
    Rt. 2, Lancaster, S. C.
                    Mr. M. M. Fant
                    Whitmire, S. C.
Waterree (U. D.) .... Rev. J. B. Barber, Hopkins, S. C.
Antioch .... Rev. S. Butler
    Rt. 2, Box 45, Cross, S. C.
Berea .... Rev. J. A. Alsobrook
    Adkins St., Bennettsville, S. C.
Bethlehem .... Rev. G. A. Ziegler Rev. J. P. Garrick
    Bamberg, S. C.   Sumter, S. C.
Black River ....
New Zion .... Rev. J. W. Shaw
Ooloney .... Rev. E. D. Watkins Ora F. Hollin
    Central, S. C.   Pickens, S. C.
Old Ashley .... Rev. P. H. Thompson
    Box 17, Estill, S. C.
Orangeburg County .... Rev. E. N. Felder Rev. A. A. McKisick
    Eloree, S. C.   Jonesville, S. C.
Pacolet River .... Rev. A. D. Duncan, Union, S. C.
Pee Dee .... Rev. F. W. Prince, Cheraw, S. C.
Reedy River .... Rev. P. J. Barton
    Box 316, Fountain Inn, S. C.
Rocky River .... Rev. J. C. Cowan
    237 Cleveland St., Anderson, S. C.
St. Paul .... Rev. S. W. Wilder

ASSOCIATIONS AND MODERATORS (Continued)

STATE	ASSOCIATIONS	MODERATORS	SECRETARIES

SOUTH CAROLINA (Contd.)

St. Vaughnville ....Rev. J. P. Robinson   Mayer Reeder
   Silver Street, S. C.   Silver Street
Sandy River ....Rev. L. A. Barber
   Allen Street, Rock Hill, S. C.
Simmon Ridge ....Rev. M. D. Mobley
   Rt. 1, Box 142, Saluda, S. C.
Spartanburg County ....Rev. B. F. Stewart
   Box 181, Spartanburg, S. C.
Spring Grove ....Rev. A. C. Johnson
Storm Branch ....Rev. R. B. Mabry
   1012 York St., Aiken, S. C.
Thickety Mt. ....Rev. W. S. Smith, Rt.4, Gaffney
Tumbling Shoals ....Rev. W. R. Martin, Greenville, S. C.

TENNESSEE

Bethel ....Rev. G. A. Nance, Jefferson City
Brown Creek ....Rev. A. L. Thens, Rt. 4, Jackson
Elk River Baptists..........................Rev. D. J. Tate   Mr. M. D. Battle
   418 W. Lane St.
   Shelbyville, Tenn.
Friendship ....Rev. J. L. Campbell
   512 N. 3rd St., Memphis, Tenn.
General ....Rev. A. D. Bell
   815 Alma St., Memphis, Tenn.
Hickory Grove ....Rev. E. A. Campbell
   452 Eastern Ave.   E. McClin
   Jackson, Tenn.   Jackson
Loudon ....Rev. Van J. Malone
   3215 Line St., Cleveland, Tenn.
Knoxville ....Rev. M. C. M. Harris
   1716 Bethel Ave., Knoxville, Tenn.
Memphis ....Rev. M. C. Durham
   1320 McLinmore St., Memphis
Mississippi Valley ....Rev. W. B. Shannon
   311 Hale St., aJckson, Tenn.
New Era ....Rev. E. L. Blair
   1336 Texas St., Memphis, Tenn.
N. Chickamauga and Chat-   Rev. W. W. Taylor
  tanooga ....1001 W. 10th St., Chattanooga, Tenn.
Obion River ....Rev. J. J. Bills   J. B. Spratlin
   Union City, Tenn.   Union City, Tenn.
Pilgrim Joy......................................Rev. A. R. Barnett
   1306 W. 46th St., Chattanooga
Pleasant Grove ....Rev. H. Myers, Memphis, Tenn.
Tennessee River District ....Rev. M. A. Lewis   Rev. J. C. Lewis
   Box 112, Ripley   Savannah, Tenn.
Riverside B. Union ....Rev. H. B. Brunson
   274 S. Orleans St., Memphis, Tenn.
West Tennessee ....Rev. T. Grimes
   130 Mobile St.   G. W. Wells
   Jackson, Tenn   Bolivar, Tenn.

ASSOCIATIONS AND MODERATORS (Continued)'

STATE ASSOCIATIONS	MODERATORS	SECRETARIES

TENNESSEE (Continued)

West Tennessee .... Rev. S. A. Owens Prof. W. L. Pullia
593 Wicks Ave., Memphis, Tenn.
White Haven .... Rev. W. H. Mosby
1434 Azolia St., Memphis
Zion .... Rev. L. D. Cheers D. H. Hall
1342 Barbour St., Collinsville,
Memphis, Tenn. Tenn.
West Tennessee .... Rev. J. E. Clark
1793 Bismark St., Memphis, Tenn.

TEXAS

Zion .... Rev. A. B. Lenox, Detroit, Texas
Friendship .... Rex. D. E. Johnson, Terrell, Texas
Trinity Valley .... Rev. F. K. Kirkwood
3604 Airline, Houston, Texas
Lincoln Southern .... Rev. J. H. Tobin
802 Ruthven, Houston, Texas
Lagrange .... Rev. G. T. Burley, Rockdale, Texas
Lagrange Missionary .... Rev. J. S. Simmons
Box 432, Lagrange, Texas
Central .... Rev. J. R. McPherson Miss Nancy
Box 405 Terrell
Fostoria, Texas Anderson, Texas
New Home .... Rev. N. N. E. Perkins, Jewett, Texas
Cypress .... Rev. James I. Gilmore H. M. Johnson
Wolf City, Texas Quitman, Texas
Lone Star .... Rev. H. Peacock, Jamestown, Texas
Unity .... Rev. G. R. King
Box 365, Texarkana, Texas
Sabine Valley .... Rev. J. P. Cannon
St. Augustine, Texas
East Texas Mt. Zion .... Rev. T. R. Harris, Marshall, Texas
East Texas Mt. Olive .... Rev. L. R. Taylor
High St., Longview, Texas
Texas Louisiana .... Rev. S. H. Howard, Marshall, Texas
West Texas .... Rev. Z. N. Hickson
411 E. 6th St., Mineral Wells, Texas

EAST TEXAS

Union Progressive .... Rev. A. W. Whetstone
Rev. J. H. Choice
Henderson, Texas Henderson, Texas
East Texas No. 2 .... Rev. J. G. Upshaw Rt. 5
•Rt. 1, Douglas, Ga.
Original W. T. .... Rev. M. P. Timms
P. O. Box 61J0, Big Springs, Texas
Willow Grove .... Rev. J. G. Jackson, Morgan, Texas
East Texas .... Rev. L. S. Cameron, Henderson, Tex.
Gallilee Griggs .... Rev. G. A. Sparks, Fort Worth, Tex.
Old Land Mark .... Rev. U. S. Keeling
Box 2266, Beaumont, Texas

ASSOCIATIONS AND MODERATORS (Continued)'

EAST TEXAS (Cont.)

Harmony	Rev. A. L. Moore, Corsicana, Texas	
Zion Hill		
North Texas	Rev. T. E. George, Pittsburg, Texas	
Palestine Baptist		
Zion Rest	Rev. J. W. Spelman, Henderson, Tex.	
Oak Grove	Rev. J. I. Gilmore, Wolf City, Texas	
Bethel Union	Rev. S. H. Howard, Marshall, Texas	

VIRGINIA

Bannister	Rev. P. L. Barksdale, Halifax, Va.	
Harmony	Rev. J. H. Bagley, Chase City, Va.	
Northern Neck	Rev. P. C. Young	Rev. J. J. Nicken
	Hehabalch, Va.	Ottawa, Va.
Cherrystone	Rev. J. J. Davis	Rev. D. M. Witcher
Pamunkey	Rev. S. B. Holmes	
	King William C. H. Va.	
Northampton	Rev. W. B. Carrington, Cheriton, Va.	
Northern Virginia	Rev. Frank Hearn	Rev. J. M. Baucum
	Washington, D. C.	Naanassas, Va.
Shiloh	Rev. W. T. Johnson	
	2504 Brook Rd., Richmond, Va.	
South Side Rappahannock	Rev. B. H. Gayles, Saluda, Va.	
Sunnyside	Rev. S. E. Ragland	Mr. A. J. Cun
	So. Boston, Va.	ningham
		Paces, Va.
Tuckahoe	Rev. J. E. Fountain	
	809 Clay St., Richmond, Va.	
Schaffer Memorial	Rev. C. J. Smith	
	236 S. Broad St., Salem, Va.	
Bluestone	Rev. M. G. Rux, Keysville, Va.	
Slate River Baptist	Rev. W. J. Jones, Bleinheim, Va.	
Tidewater Peninsula	Rev. C. E. Jones, Newport News, Va.	
Northern Virginia Baptists	Rev. S. B. Ross	
	1018 Oronoca St., Alexandria, Va.	
Valley Baptist	Rev. W. M. Gilbert	
	22 Gregory Ave.	Rev. W. L. Johns
	Roanoke, Va.	Bedford, Va.
Wayland Blueridge Baptist	Rev. W. J. Madden	Mr. C. B. Coleman
	Culpepper, Va.	Culpper, Va.

Amelia-Nottoway Baptist	Rev. L. W. Bass	S. C. Tlyyy
Protestant	Farmville, Va.	Richmond, Va.
Valley Baptist	Rev. C. W. Ingram, Staunton, Va.	
Bethany	Rev. E. D. Shands, North Emporia	
Clinch River Baptist Miss.	Rev. E. D. Long	O. King
	Appalachia, Va.	Clinch, W. Va.
James River Dist. Baptist	Rev. G. W. Haden, Gum Springs, Va.	
Mattipona Baptist	Rev. E. L. R. Guss	Rev. R. L. Taylor
	Guinea, Va.	807 N. 26th St.
		Richmond, Va.
Rockfish Baptist	Rev. Wm. Bailey, Wimgina, Va.	
Sharon Baptist	Rev. W. P. Jones	
	Rt. 2, Box 116, Norfolk, Va.	

ASSOCIATIONS AND MODERATORS (Continued)

STATE	ASSOCIATIONS	MODERATORS	SECRETARIES

VIRGINIA (Continued)

Lebanon Baptist ....Rev. Wm. Lamb   J. A. Bank
                       Claremont, Va.   Rushmore, Va.
Mattaponi Baptist ....E. L. R. Guss, Guinea, Va.
Chickahominy ....Rev. William L. Godsey

WEST VIRGINIA

Guyan Valley   Rev. D. E. Hopkins   Holden, W. Va.
Flat Top ....Rev. J. W. Crockett   Rev. J. C. Hen-
                       Box 224, Omar, W. Vo.   der,
                                       Bluefield, W. Va.
Mt. Olivet ....Rev. H. C. Head
                       N. Rand St., Charleston, W. Va.
Tygart Valley ....Rev. N. N. Parker
                       518 Water St., Clarksburg, W. Va.
Mt. Zion ....Rev. J. H. Younger   Rev. C. V. Gordon
                       546 Water St.   Box 1181
                       Claraksbury   Parkersburg
Winding Gulf ....Rev. W. M. Carter   Rev. J. A. Jackson
                       Sullivan, W. Va.   Box 562
                                   Beckley, W. Va.
Coal River Valley............................Rev. P. A. Saunders
                       Montgomery, W. Va.

After sixteen years of service as President of the Convention and one year as Vice-President of the Baptist World Alliance, the inimitable L.K. Williams met death in a plane crash, October 29, 1940.

Dr. D.V. Jemison of Selma, Alabama, who had served as Vice-President, was elected President. Rev. A.L. Boone of Cleveland, Ohio was elected Vice-President, in Cleveland, Ohio, September 1941. This leader would be charged with the responsibility of providing strong Baptist leadership during World War II. He would be remembered for fanning the dying spiritual embers of Black Baptists into glowing flames.

A noticeable increase of total church giving during this era was noticed, of which is reflected in Statistician Roland Smith's, 1944 report. Followed by the Associations and Moderators.

Hot Springs, Arkansas, had been the place of the Mid-Winter Board Meeting for years. In 1950, the Convention purchased a Bath House in that city for three hundred thousand dollars.

Bibliography: National Baptist Journals, **Baptist Advance,** 1964, E.A. Freeman, **The National Baptist Bulletin,** Roland Smith.

Chapter 13
NATIONAL BAPTIST CONVENTION, U.S.A., INC.
J.H. JACKSON ERA 1953 - 1980

Dr. Jemison's reign ended in 1953. Dr. Joseph Harrison Jackson, Pastor of Olivet Institutional Baptist Church of Chicago, Illinois, was his successor. Dr. Theodore Judson Jemison, youngest son of the past President and pastor of the Mount Zion First Baptist Church of Baton Rouge, Louisiana, was elected General Secretary. It may be noted, the same year Dr. Jemison led the Blacks of his city to the first successful bus boycott, ever launched in the south. The architects of the Montgomery Bus Boycott, two years later, were to borrow many of the ideas from Baton Rouge's blueprints.

No other President in the Convention's seventy-three year history ascended the throne so well prepared and conditioned for the job as J.H. Jackson, His attributes to lead what is now the World's largest Black organization is multifaceted, a uniquely gifted preacher, scholar, theologian, revered thinker, alert politician, and shrewd businessman.

Surely he came to the Kingdom for such a time, and for the days that lay ahead. The Korean War had just ended. In just a matter of time another war would be declared in full force, the Civil Rights War. There would be two powerfully effective Generals, both from the Baptist Camp. Their strategies would be different, both would be misunderstood and criticized, yet both would be effective and victorious. One would march in the streets and often go to jail. The other would refuse to march and go to jail, but would advocate financial sovereignty and strength through financial resources.

History in fairness and truth cannot overlook the impact made by the efforts of Jackson and King toward destroying the walls of racial injustice.

Records will substantiate J.H. Jackson's contribution toward human dignity. In 1959, the Bath House in Hot Springs was paid for. All other Convention indebtedness had been paid during this administration. A self-help program instituted, whereby member churches can borrow money for building or liquidating indebtedness. Convention agencies, rather than borrowing from commercial institutions, can borrow from the Convention.

Another split occurred in 1961. A fair election was held during the session in Kansas City, Missouri, Jackson won commandingly over Gardner C. Taylor. In a concession speech, Taylor declared the Baptists have given their mandate, we must now close ranks and march forward. In a matter of weeks, a letter was issued to many who were in opposition to Jackson. They met and organized the Progressive National Baptist Convention, elected Dr. T.M. Chambers, Sr. as their President. Dr. Marshall Shepherd, who was Chairman of the Foreign Mission Board, also joined them. There was no permanent damage done to the Convention or the Board with their withdrawal.

National Baptist Convention harmony, growth financially, Spiritually and numerically, soared after their departure.

FROM PROTEST TO PRODUCTIO[N]

Baptist Freedom Farm

(COURTESY TIMES HERALD)

Rev. Jasper Williams, Pastor Lane Avenue Baptist Church, Trustee of "Freedom Farm."

Dr. Joseph H. Jackson, President National Baptist Convention, USA, who initiated plan for "Freedom Farm."

Dr. A. E. Campbell, Chairman of the Freedom Farm Commission, and Vice President of the National Baptist Convention, USA.

Prominent visitors to Freedom Farm, located near Mason during dedicatory ceremonies included these prominent 'Memphians: Rev. A. L. Campbell Pastoring in Fayette County and farm commission chairman; Rev. Hooker, of nearby Arlington; and Rev. H. H. H[ ] pastor of St. Matthews Baptist Church and popular radio minist[ ]

NATIONAL BAPTIST FREEDOM FARM NEAR MASON, TENNESSEE DEDICATED

Using the bed of a farm truck, bedecked with U. S. Flags, as his platform, Dr. Joseph H. Jackson, president of the National Baptist Convention, U. S. A., Inc., last Wednesday morning, March 22nd, dedicated a 404-acre tract of West Tennessee land near Mason as the "National Baptist Convention Freedom Farm."

The dynamic churchman under whose direction this farm project was initiated to offer a program of self-help to tenants of "Tent City" and other under-privileged families who desire to raise their economic level without leaving the farm.

ROCKEFELLER TAKES NOTE OF BAPTIST FREEDOM FARM

Governor Nelson Rockefeller, of New York wired a message of congratulations to Dr. Joseph H. Jackson, of Chicago, extending congratulations upon his launching of a farm-aid program under direction of the National Baptist Convention, U. S. A., Inc. A life-long Baptist himself, New York's multimillionaire governor sent the telegram in care of Mr. C. A. Rawls, of Brownsville, Tennessee, coordinator of the "National Baptist Convention Freedom Farm," and well known insurance executive:

"It is a pleasure to send cordial greetings to the National Baptist Convention on the occasion of the dedication of the 401-acre farm it has purchased to provide homes of the families now living in "Tent City." The Convention is to be commended heartily for this thoughtful and benevolent act. My best wishes to you.

Signed
Nelson A. Rockefeller,
Albany, New York

PRIMED FOR ACTION—Dr. Joseph H. Jackson, president National Baptist Convention, Inc., is primed for action with a at the dedication of a new housing development to aid sharec[ ] in Fayette and Haywood Counties, Tenn.

ull Text of Dr. J. H. Jackson's Address At
Dedication of Baptist Freedom Farm

ie Honorable Governor of the State of Tennessee, The Officials of
ette County, Officers and Fellow Members of the National Baptist
vention, U. S. A., Inc.:

e have come today to dedicate this farm of four hundred and four
s representing a cash investment of $60,000.00; $15,450.00 of which
already been paid, leaving a balance of $45,150.00. We hope this
unt will soon be paid by the gifts and subscription of the churches
ie National Baptist Convention, U. S. A., Inc.

iis program today represents a new emphasis on the part of our
t convention. As a church we wish to be identified with our people
very walk of life; in the rural areas as well as in our towns and
s. For the people on the countryside are just as precious in the
t of God as those who live on the paved streets of our cities.
church must be identified with the people in their struggles and
ations, their needs, their defeats and their hopes.

church that does not indentify itself with the people is a church
will finally be deserted by the people. In the great Russian Revolu-
of 1917 the church was found on the side of the imperial powers
ie Czar, and she had invested more in gold and in material
essions than in those things which served the best interest of the
le. Because of this condition many of the people deserted the
ch and turned to the way of godless communism. In the struggle
nst communism religion is our first line of defense, for it reache:
gnity of man that godless materialism can never support.

iis investment today demonstrates our faith in ourselves as a race.
believe we have the talent, the vision and the strength to work
ig ourselves for the promotion of our own people and for the
incement of our state and nation. This tract of land with its fertile
is, beautiful lakes and this rolling hill reveal what we can do
n we bring together our little resources for a definite and con-
:tive purpose. We have just scratched the surface in this type of
eration. The American Negro can still rise to unprecedented heights
e will pool his money, invest it in worthwhile projects and work
her for self-development and self-improvement. The economic
of a people is essential, basic and most important if they are to go
ard in other fields of endeavor. We must not be ashamed to begin
. the soil and to toil with our hands to produce those things which
essential to human life and well-being.

FAITH IN THE SOUTH

ie fact that we have purchased this tract of land here in Fayette
ity in the fair southland, is open and undisputed testimony as to
faith in the southland. We believe there are enough people of
will in this county and in this state to encourage and to help men
women who wish to earn a decent and independent living by the
of their hands, their brains and all of the resources of their being.

we are exercising faith in our white neighbors, we beg of them
ive faith in us as sincere and devoted citizens of this great Republic.
irically the American Negro has been the most trusted friend of his
e neighbors. He has been patient when he did not quite under-

stand, and has been long-suffering under the most trying circumstances.
Fellowship and understanding between the races in the United State:
will do far more to strengthen the faith of the nations of the world in
American democracy than all the diplomats and all the peace corp
messengers among the nations of the world. Remember that we seek
to rear our families, to educate our children and to take our rightful
part in helping to make our nation greater and stronger. When we
make mistakes we are willing to be corrected according to the law.

FAITH IN AMERICA

We are here today dedicating this tract of land because we have
faith in our nation. America is more than the territories of the East
and the states of the south. America is more than the states of the
North. America is more than the territories of the East and the West.
America is the sum total of all of these. America is that democratic
community which has promised to every American citizen equal opportunity to enjoy the good things of life and to make their contribution to the nation's security and growth. We know now that wherever
we are the long arm of the federal law is over us and the protective
promises of the Federal Constitution are round about us, and we will
not seek the way of freedom in vain.

In committing ourselves to the task of helping to solve our own
economic problems, we believe that we help to lift the burden of tax
payers, and to reduce the expense and the number on relief rolls.

We believe in the laws of our land. We believe that freedom may
be found on the dusty roads and in fertile fields as well as in our
towns and cities. We believe the laws of justice are with us and
righteousness and truth stand in the defense of those who seek to
come to the full stature of manhood and womanhood. We believe
that God has ordained that all men shall eat freely of the fruit of
justice and freedom, and that no individual citizen in this great Republic can be truly safe and secure until the blessings of freedom
are extended to all peoples irrespective of class or creed.

We have faith in President John F. Kennedy and believe that what
we are doing here today will help him to carry forward his great
program of building a greater America for a greater task in the gravest
hour of our history.

And now to those of you who have come from "Tent City," we
beg of you, feel at home on this farm. Seize the tools at your disposal
and make full use of your opportunities, plow deeply into the bosom
of the soil and wring from mother earth the values that you desire,
and use this land as your land and these houses as your homes. Remember not in bitterness those who have wronged you in the past,
and labor not to wound the enemies of your progress; but go forward
in joy, exercising every right given to you by the Federal Constitution
under the stars and stripes and help make Fayette County a county
more rich with sacred personalities, more replete with the bounties of
freedom, and cause the land to bloom like a rose and the hillsides to
sing their songs of praise to the greatness of this nation and to the
glory of American democracy.

Dr. T.J. Jemison

- - EDITORIALS - -

STATESMANSHIP IN THE PULPIT

recent years we have become so accustomed to political agitation
demagoguery in too many pulpits, that it came as a pleasant sur-
when Dr. Joseph H. Jackson, president of the National Baptist
ention, and his group did something constructive.

en those who agitated the Negro tenant farmers and sharecroppers
challenging the dominant white powers of Fayette and Haywood
ties, Tennessee, and got them dispossessed to park alongside the
with their families in destitution, only Dr. Jackson's Baptists had
realistic remedy.

s remedy was to buy 600 acres of farm land on which these desti-
families could live and farm, and be free to vote as they chose
ut fear of reprisal; and the land has been bought, and the dis-
ssed Negro families are occupying and working it.

e National Baptist Convention, however, has gone to the root of
roblem (which is what radicalism means) and arranged with the
rian government to resettle such Negroes on 5,000 acres of prove farm land in Liberia.

w, who else is so coming to grips with the Negro farm problem?

—PITTSBURGH COURIER

EDITORIALS

is only a short distance of seven miles from "Tent City" near
rville, to the "National Baptist Convention Freedom Farm" on
outskirts of Mason but when these two points are viewed in
s of their respective meaning to the Negro they are as far apart
e proverbial poles. For Tent City symbolizes the shame and ugly
acle of second-class citizenship. The outgrowth of economic re-
ls, physical violence and exploitation of a hapless people by those
would deny them even the rudiments of democracy.

e other point, however, is a 404-acre tract of rich farmland where
the tent dwellers may go and take a new lease on life in an
sphere conducive to their all-round development, and generally
eir best interest as well as that of the nation at large.

e family of six, Earl Anderson, his wife, and four children, had
dy signed up as the first tenant on the farm by the time the
ists gathered there last Wednesday for dedicatory ceremonies.
other families from Tent City were being considered as occupants
portion of the land, and it is generally assumed that the deed area near Somerville will soon yield all the evictees to one
e farm projects the Baptists are providing for them at great
nse.

is of course is all for the better. "Tent City" did serve its purpose
inting up to this nation the urgency for immediate removal of
acial barriers. For how can a country purporting to assume world
rship of great proportions be unmindful of flagrant violation of
rights of its own citizens such as has been perpetrated in Hay-
and Fayette Counties against the Negro over a period of years?

was encouraging to note that the Civil Rights Commission under-
steps to guarantee the right of Fayette and Haywood County
oes to register and vote. They had not exercised this constitutional
lege in almost a hundred years, not since the days of reconstruction.
of even greater significance has been the action by the National

Baptist Convention to initiate a farm-aid program whereby the Negro
can also help raise his economic levels. Therefore, Tent City residents,
who are signing up for Freedom Farm give clear indication that they
understand democracy is a two-way street. It will provide for them
the benefit of a full life in return for their honest labor, and the exercise of responsibility in keeping with good citizenship. Those who in-
sist upon remaining in the tents, with no future outlook, and are
satisfied to remain wards of charity as now being dispensed by persons who profess to have their interest at heart may soon find themselves without any measure of help.

There is certainly no further need for anyone connected with the
Tent City Project to make trips over the country for purpose of
soliciting funds on behalf of the evictees. Freedom Farm, just seven
miles away from these people, beckons them to come and partake
of the new life. They have a choice between these two areas. One
represents the point of diminishing return. The other symbolizes an
everwidening scope of self-help, and economic freedom.

Dr. Joseph H. Jackson, president of the National Baptist Convention,
is to be commended for taking this far-reaching step. A study of his
plan, coupled with his dedicatory message last week, would bear testimony to the fact that the Baptist have come to Tennessee wih a program that calls for inter-racial good will rather than vindictiveness and
bitter rebuttals. For those of us who live in this state, special pride
can be taken in the fact that the development of the farm-aid program includes the active participation of such local and sectional leaders as Dr. A. E. Campbell, vice-president of the convention who also
serves as chairman of the farm commission; C. A. Rawls, of Brownsville, successful business man, who is coordinator for Freedom Farm;
Rev. Jasper W. Williams, pastor of Lane Avenue Baptist Church, and
a trustee of the farm, and Rev. W. Herbert Brewster, pastor of East
Trigg Avenue Baptist Church.

God does work in mysterious ways, his wonders to perform. For
the problems which created Tent City in West Tennessee, Providence
provided the solution in the National Baptist Freedom Farm.

—TIMES HERALD, MEMPHIS

THE TIMES-HERALD is applying for membership in the Associated
Negro Press, the National Newspaper Publishers Association, and the
United Press International. Second-Class Permit is pending.

"FREE AT LAST." This seems to be the expression registered on
the countenance of the Earl Anderson family, first to be signed up
as tenant occupants on Freedom Farm The Andersons were evictees
who had lived since the first of the year in "Tent City." His family
has already moved on Freedom Farm and will cultivate 202 acres,
half of the 404-acre tract of farm land. From left: Marshall Jones,
manager of the R. A. Rawls enterprise, Brownsville, Tenn.; Mr. Scott
Franklin, president of the Fayette County Civic and Welfare League,
Inc.; Mr. and Mrs. Anderson with their teen-aged daughter, O. D. Mac-
lin of Somerville, supervisor at the farm, and secretary of the Fayette
County Civic and Welfare League; A. L. Rawls, of Brownsville, coordinator of the farm, and prominent insurance executive; Melvin
Johnson, of District 5, Civic League; and Rev. B. F. Odeneal, chairman
of the board of directors of the league.

The following articles, pictures and philosophy can best describe Joseph Harrison Jackson's posture as a leader and the National Baptist Convention, U.S.A., Inc., whose membership is now six million and six hundred thousand.

The J.H. Jackson Memorial Library is located at 765 East Oakwood Boulevard, Chicago, Illinois. This was formerly a bank building of which the Convention was led to purchase and convert into a Library by its leader.

These 1977 statistics will give an idea of the Convention's growth under Dr. Jackson's leadership.

STATE	CON-VEN-TIONS	ASSO-CIA-TIONS	CHURCHES	PER-SONALS	MONEY
Alabama	2	23	459	10	$20,455.50
Arizona	1	1	10	3	625.00
Arkansas	2	23	260	9	14,250.75
California	3	6	152	8	29,850.50
Colorado	1	0	12	3	1,750.60
Connecticut	1	0	9	2	1,250.00
Delaware	1	1	12	2	1,910.00
District of Columbia	2	2	70	5	37,550.00
Florida	1	14	257	14	25,250.00
Georgia	1	12	348	12	16,350.50
Illinois	2	11	280	13	49,835.00
Indiana	2	3	96	9	12,620.00
Iowa	1	1	12	3	1,855.30
Kansas	1	4	56	6	12,355.84
Kentucky	2	2	71	7	9,450.00
Louisiana	2	12	284	10	19,650.00
Maryland	1	2	76	6	11,350.00
Massachusetts	1	0	8	2	1,920.00
Michigan	2	12	248	14	45,680.50
Minnesota	1	0	11	2	945.00
Mississippi	5	25	396	10	19,350.00
Missouri	1	8	130	9	17,450.00
Nebraska	1	0	16	5	1,930.00
Nevada	1	0	9	6	575.00
New Jersey	2	5	165	9	22,450.00
New Mexico	1	1	10	4	560.00
New York	1	5	220	12	32,650.35
North Carolina	1	1	80	9	5,850.00
Ohio	2	7	152	10	26,350.00
Oklahoma	1	9	82	9	5,455.00
Pennsylvania	1	3	160	14	73,455.30
South Carolina	1	5	159	9	14,225.00
Tennessee	2	16	262	14	18,456.22
Texas	2	19	196	17	17,450.50
Virginia	2	2	85	8	14,650.30
Washington	1	0	10	4	1,975.00
West Virginia	1	1	17	5	950.00
Wisconsin	1	2	38	4	3,350.00
	59	260	6,233	293	$602,136.86

Total Conventions	59
Total Associations	260
Total Churches	6,233
Total Personal Enrollment	293
Total Contributed	$602,136.86

September 10-14, 1980, the Centennial will be observed in Birmingham, Alabama. It has been a long trek from Montgomery on that beautiful November day in 1880, to the week of jubilance in Birmingham, "the all American City".

MEETING PLACES OF NATIONAL BAPTIST CONVENTION

YEAR	CITY	PRESIDENT	SECRETARY
1880	Montgomery, Ala.	Rev. W.H. McAlpine	Rev. J.M. Armstead
1881	Knoxville, Tenn.	Rev. W.H. McAlpine	Rev. J.M. Armsted
1882	Macon, Ga.	Rev. W.H. McAlpine	Rev. W.R. Pettiford
1883	Manchester, Va.	Rev. J.Q.A. Wilhite	Prof. J.E. Jones
1884	Meridian, Miss.	Rev. J.A. Foster	Rev. H.M. Mitchell
1885	New Orleans, La.	Rev. W.A. Brinkley	Rev. S.T. Clanton, B.D.
1886	St. Louis, Mo.	Rev. W.J. Simmons, D.D.	Rev. S.T. Clanton, B.D.
1887	Mobile, Ala.	Rev. W.J. Simmons, D.D.	Rev. S.T. Clanton, B.D.
1888	Nashville, Tenn.	Rev. W.J. Simmons, D.D.	Rev. J.L. Cochran
1889	Indianapolis, Ind.	Rev. W.J. Simmons, D.D.	Rev. J.L. Cochran
1890	Louisville, Ky.	Rev. W.J. Simmons, D.D.	Rev. J.L. Cochran
1891	Dallas, Texas	Rev. E.M. Brawley, D.D.	W.H. Steward
1892	Savannah, Ga.	Rev. M. Vann	W.H. Steward
1893	Washington, D.C.	Rev. M. Vann	W.H. Steward
1894	Montgomery, Ala.	Rev. E.C. Morris, D.D.	W.H. Steward
1895	Atlanta, Ga.	Rev. E.C. Morris, D.D.	W.H. Steward
1896	St. Louis, Mo.	Rev. E.C. Morris, D.D.	W.H. Steward
1897	Boston, Mass.	Rev. E.C. Morris, D.D.	W.H. Steward
1898	Kansas City, Mo.	Rev. E.C. Morris, D.D.	Prof. W.L. Cansler
1899	Nashville, Tenn.	Rev. E.C. Morris, D.D.	Prof. W.L. Cansler
1900	Richmond, Va.	Rev. E.C. Morris, D.D.	Prof. W.L. Cansler
1901	Cincinnati, Ohio	Rev. E.C. Morris, D.D.	Prof. W.L. Cansler
1902	Birmingham, Ala.	Rev. E.C. Morris, D.D.	Prof. W.L. Cansler
1903	Philadelphia, Pa.	Rev. E.C. Morris, D.D.	Prof. W.L. Cansler
1904	Austin, Texas	Rev. E.C. Morris, D.D.	Prof. W.L. Cansler
1905	Chicago, Ill.	Rev. E.C. Morris, D.D.	Prof. W.L. Cansler
1906	Memphis, Tenn.	Rev. E.C. Morris, D.D.	Prof. W.L. Cansler
1907	Washington, D.C.	Rev. E.C. Morris, D.D.	Prof. W.L. Cansler
1908	Lexington, Ky.	Rev. E.C. Morris, D.D.	Prof. R.B. Hudson
1909	Columbus, Ohio	Rev. E.C. Morris, D.D.	Prof. R.B. Hudson
1910	New Orleans, La.	Rev. E.C. Morris, D.D.	Prof. R.B. Hudson
1911	Pittsburgh, Pa.	Rev. E.C. Morris, D.D.	Prof. R.B. Hudson
1912	Houston, Texas	Rev. E.C. Morris, D.D.	Prof. R.B. Hudson
1913	Nashville, Tenn.	Rev. E.C. Morris, D.D.	Prof. R.B. Hudson
1914	Philadelphia, Pa.	Rev. E.C. Morris, D.D.	Prof. R.B. Hudson
1915	Chicago, Ill.	Rev. E.C. Morris, D.D.	Prof. R.B. Hudson
1916	Savannah, Ga.	Rev. E.C. Morris, D.D.	Prof. R.B. Hudson
1917	Muskogee, Okla.	Rev. E.C. Morris, D.D.	Prof. R.B. Hudson
1918	St. Louis, Mo.	Rev. E.C. Morris, D.D.	Prof. R.B. Hudson
1919	Newark, N.J.	Rev. E.C. Morris, D.D.	Prof. R.B. Hudson
1920	Indianapolis, Ind.	Rev. E.C. Morris, D.D.	Prof. R.B. Hudson
1921	Chicago, Ill.	Rev. E.C. Morris, D.D.	Prof. R.B. Hudson
1922	St. Louis, Mo.	Rev. E.C. Morris, D.D.	Prof. R.B. Hudson
1923	Los Angeles, Calif.	Rev. W.G. Parks, D.D.	Prof. R.B. Hudson
1924	Nashville, Tenn.	Rev. L.K. Williams, D.D.	Prof. R.B. Hudson
1925	Baltimore, Md.	Rev. L.K. Williams, D.D.	Prof. R.B. Hudson
1926	Ft. Worth, Texas	Rev. L.K. Williams, D.D.	Prof. R.B. Hudson
1927	Detroit, Mich.	Rev. L.K. Williams, D.D.	Prof. R.B. Hudson
1928	Louisville, Ky.	Rev. L.K. Williams, D.D.	Prof. R.B. Hudson
1929	Kansas City, Mo.	Rev. L.K. Williams, D.D.	Prof. R.B. Hudson
1930	Chicago, Ill.	Rev. L.K. Williams, D.D.	Prof. R.B. Hudson

1931	Atlanta, Ga.	Rev. L.K. Williams, D.D.	Prof. R.B. Hudson
1932	Cleveland, Ohio	Rev. L.K. Williams, D.D.	Rev. J.M. Nabrit
1933	Memphis, Tenn.	Rev. L.K. Williams, D.D.	Rev. J.M. Nabrit
1934	Oklahoma City, Okla.	Rev. L.K. Williams, D.D.	Rev. J.M. Nabrit
1935	New York, N.Y.	Rev. L.K. Williams, D.D.	Rev. J.M. Nabrit
1936	Jacksonville, Fla.	Rev. L.K. Williams, D.D.	Rev. J.M. Nabrit
1937	Los Angeles, Calif.	Rev. L.K. Williams, D.D.	Rev. J.M. Nabrit
1938	St. Louis, Mo.	Rev. L.K. Williams, D.D.	Rev. J.M. Nabrit
1939	Philadelphia, Pa.	Rev. L.K. Williams, D.D.	Rev. J.M. Nabrit
1940	Birmingham, Ala.	Rev. L.K. Williams, D.D.	Rev. J.M. Nabrit
1941	Cleveland, Ohio	Rev. D.V. Jemison, D.D.	Rev. J.M. Nabrit
1942	Memphis, Tenn.	Rev. D.V. Jemison, D.D.	Rev. J.M. Nabrit
1943	Chicago, Ill	Rev. D.V. Jemison, D.D.	Rev. J.M. Nabrit
1944	Dallas, Texas	Rev. D.V. Jemison, D.D.	Rev. J.M. Nabrit
1945	Detroit, Michigan	Rev. D.V. Jemison, D.D.	Rev. J.M. Nabrit
1946	Atlanta, Georgia	Rev. D.V. Jemison, D.D.	Rev. J.M. Nabrit
1947	Kansas City, Mo.	Rev. D.V. Jemison, D.D.	Rev. U.J. Robinson
1948	Houston, Texas	Rev. D.V. Jemison, D.D.	Rev. U.J. Robinson
1949	Los Angeles, Calif.	Rev. D.V. Jemison, D.D.	Rev. U.J. Robinson
1950	Philadelphia, Pa.	Rev. D.V. Jemison, D.D.	Rev. U.J. Robinson
1951	Oklahoma City, Okla.	Rev. D.V. Jemison, D.D.	Rev. U.J. Robison
1952	Chicago, Ill.	Rev. D.V. Jemison, D.D.	Rev. U.J. Robinson
1953	Miami, Fla.	Rev. J.H. Jackson, D.D.	Rev. T.J. Jemison
1954	St. Louis, Mo.	Rev. J.H. Jackson, D.D.	Rev. T.J. Jemison
1955	Memphis, Tenn.	Rev. J.H. Jackson, D.D.	Rev. T.J. Jemison
1956	Denver, Colo.	Rev. J.H. Jackson, D.D.	Rev. T.J. Jemison
1957	Louisville, Ky.	Rev. J.H. Jackson, D.D.	Rev. T.J. Jemison
1958	Chicago, Ill.	Rev. J.H. Jackson, D.D.	Rev. T.J. Jemison
1959	San Francisco, Calif.	Rev. J.H. Jackson, D.D.	Rev. T.J. Jemison
1960	Philadelphia, Pa.	Rev. J.H. Jackson, D.D.	Rev. T.J. Jemison
1961	Kansas City, Mo.	Rev. J.H. Jackson, D.D.	Rev. T.J. Jemison
1962	Chicago, Ill.	Rev. J.H. Jackson, D.D.	Rev. T.J. Jemison
1963	Cleveland, Ohio	Rev. J.H. Jackson, D.D.	Rev. T.J. Jemison
1964	Detroit, Mich.	Rev. J.H. Jackson, D.D.	Rev. T.J. Jemison
1965	Jacksonville, Fla.	Rev. J.H. Jackson, D.D.	Rev. T.J. Jemison
1966	Dallas, Texas	Rev. J.H. Jackson, D.D.	Rev. T.J. Jemison
1967	Denver, Colo.	Rev. J.H. Jackson, D.D.	Rev. T.J. Jemison
1968	Atlanta, Ga.	Rev. J.H. Jackson, D.D.	Rev. T.J. Jemison
1969	Kansas City, Mo.	Rev. J.H. Jackson, D.D.	Rev. T.J. Jemison
1970	New Orleans, La.	Rev. J.H. Jackson, D.D.	Rev. T.J. Jemison
1971	Cleveland, Ohio	Rev. J.H. Jackson, D.D.	Rev. T.J. Jemison
1972	Fort Worth, Texas	Rev. J.H. Jackson, D.D.	Rev. T.J. Jemison
1973	Los Angeles, Calif.	Rev. J.H. Jackson, D.D.	Rev. T.J. Jemison
1974	Buffalo, N.Y.	Rev. J.H. Jackson, D.D.	Rev. T.J. Jemison
1975	St. Louis, Mo.	Rev. J.H. Jackson, D.D.	Rev. T.J. Jemison
1976	Dallas, Texas	Rev. J.H. Jackson, D.D.	Rev. T.J. Jemison
1977	Miami, Fla.	Rev. J.H. Jackson, D.D.	Rev. T.J. Jemison
1978	New Orleans, La.	Rev. J.H. Jackson, D.D.	Rev. T.J. Jemison
1979	Cleveland, Ohio	Rev. J.H. Jackson, D.D.	Rev. T.J. Jemison
1980	Birmingham, Ala.	Rev. J.H. Jackson, D.D.	Rev. T.J. Jemison

MEETING PLACES OF THE NATIONAL BAPTIST CONGRESS OF CHRISTIAN EDUCATION

YEAR	LOCATION	PRESIDENT
1916	Memphis, Tennessee	Dr. D.W. Cannon
1917	Atlanta, Georgia	Dr. D.W. Cannon
1918	Galveston, Texas	Dr. D.W. Cannon
1919	Jackson, Mississippi	Dr. D.W. Cannon
1920	Washington, D.C.	Dr. D.W. Cannon
1921	Kansas City, Missouri	Dr. D.W. Cannon
1922	New Orleans, Louisiana	Dr. D.W. Cannon
1923	Hot Springs, Arkansas	Dr. D.W. Cannon
1924	Cleveland, Ohio	Dr. D.W. Cannon
1925	Wichita, Kansas	Dr. D.W. Cannon
1926	Brooklyn, New York	Dr. W.H. Jernagin
1927	Nashville, Tennessee	Dr. W.H. Jernagin
1928	Milwaukee, Wisconsin	Dr. W.H. Jernagin
1929	Charleston, South Carolina	Dr. W.H. Jernagin
1930	Chicago, Illinois	Dr. W.H. Jernagin
1931	Huntington, West Virginia	Dr. W.H. Jernagin
1932	Chattanooga, Tennessee	Dr. W.H. Jernagin
1933	Memphis, Tennessee	Dr. W.H. Jernagin
1934	Washington, D.C.	Dr. W.H. Jernagin
1935	Dayton, Ohio	Dr. W.H. Jernagin
1936	Kansas City, Kansas	Dr. W.H. Jernagin
1937	Raleigh, North Carolina	Dr. W.H. Jernagin
1938	Tuskegee, Alabama	Dr. W.H. Jernagin
1939	Tulsa, Oklahoma	Dr. W.H. Jernagin
1940	Columbus, Ohio	Dr. W.H. Jernagin
1941	Houston, Texas	Dr. W.H. Jernagin
1942	Atlanta, Georgia	Dr. W.H. Jernagin
1943	Cincinnati, Ohio	Dr. W.H. Jernagin
1944	Birmingham, Alabama	Dr. W.H. Jernagin
1945	St. Louis, Missouri	Dr. W.H. Jernagin
1946	Chicago, Illinois	Dr. W.H. Jernagin
1947	Oakland, California	Dr. W.H. Jernagin
1948	Cleveland, Ohio	Dr. W.H. Jernagin
1949	Memphis, Tennessee	Dr. W.H. Jernagin
1950	Louisville, Kentucky	Dr. W.H. Jernagin
1951	Shreveport, Louisiana	Dr. W.H. Jernagin
1952	Milwaukee, Wisconsin	Dr. W.H. Jernagin
1953	Brooklyn, New York	Dr. W.H. Jernagin
1954	Birmingham, Alabama	Dr. W.H. Jernagin
1955	Atlantic City, New Jersey	Dr. W.H. Jernagin
1956	Los Angeles, California	Dr. W.H. Jernagin
1957	Dallas, Texas	Dr. W.H. Jernagin
1958	Omaha, Nebraska	Dr. O. Clay Maxwell
1959	Memphis, Tennessee	Dr. O. Clay Maxwell
1960	Buffalo, New York	Dr. O. Clay Maxwell
1961	St. Louis, Missouri	Dr. O. Clay Maxwell

1962	Denver, Colorado	Dr. O. Clay Maxwell
1963	Birmingham, Alabama	Dr. O. Clay Maxwell
1964	Pittsburgh, Pennsylvania	Dr. O. Clay Maxwell
1965	Tulsa, Oklahoma	Dr. O. Clay Maxwell
1966	Charlotte, North Carolina	Dr. O. Clay Maxwell
1967	Milwaukee, Wisconsin	Dr. O. Clay Maxwell
1968	Chattanooga, Tennessee	Dr. O. Clay Maxwell
1969	Miami, Florida	Dr. E.A. Freeman
1970	Omaha, Nebraska	Dr. E.A. Freeman
1971	Little Rock, Arkansas	Dr. E.A. Freeman
1972	Wichita, Kansas	Dr. E.A. Freeman
1973	Dallas, Texas	Dr. E.A. Freeman
1974	Detroit, Michigan	Dr. E.A. Freeman
1975	Birmingham, Alabama	Dr. E.A. Freeman
1976	San Francisco, California	Dr. E.A. Freeman
1977	Houston, Texas	Dr. E.A. Freeman
1978	Memphis, Tennessee	Dr. E.A. Freeman
1979	Pittsburgh, Pennsylvania	Dr. E.A. Freeman
1980	St. Louis, Missouri	Dr. E.A. Freeman

Bibliography: National Baptist Journals, **Baptist Advance,** 1964, E.A. Freeman, **The National Baptist Bulletin,** Roland Smith.

Chapter 14
PERSONALITIES

Churches, associations and conventions are people movements. For Blacks in America, it is a very important industry. It has been through the Christian church, our trails were blazed and our destiny forged.

The very strong personalities of this text, that contributed toward our race's ascendency and flight over the airways of success; as well as the mighty ground crew unlisted that have worked unrelentlessly in the shadows of unrecognition; but their labors were no less assiduous than those in the forefront. Because of all their untiring efforts, the shackles of bondage were removed from our person and our minds.

When the Holy writer penned a message to the Hebrew Christians, included in that Spiritual document were a long list of the Patriarchs of their race who kept the faith. Any people that wades through the marshes of bewilderment or treads the waters of perplexities, or attempts to conquer the mountains of opposition, will have a long list of Patriarchs.

Any complete history of the one hundred and ninety-two year trek of Black Baptist in Georgia, from Tybee's Light in Savannah, through the marshes of Glenn, along the banks of the Savannah, Flint, Oconee, Chattahoochee Rivers, across the rolling north, east, and west Georgia mountain ranges and the Chattahoochee valley, will produce a lot of regional, state, national and international Patriarchs.

All facets of our society have been touched by products of the soils of Georgia. Whose training ground was on the premises of Black Baptist churches, whose first audience away from home was one of the associations and arena was the General Missionary Baptist Convention of Georgia.

Martin Luther King, Jr., the "dreamer" who led the "non violent army" that revolutionized the twentieth century world is a product of the soils of Georgia, the black Baptist church, the General Missionary Baptist Convention of Georgia, Inc. Two of the auxiliaries of the National Baptist Convention, U.S.A., Inc. are headed by products of this state, black Baptist churches, associations and convention, namely, Dr. E.A. Freeman, Superintendent of the National Baptist Congress of Christian Education, and Dr. Mary O. Ross, President of the Women's Convention. Mrs. C.N. Adkins, Executive Director of the National Baptist Publishing House must be included in the number. Many others whose names may not flash upon the marques of prominence, but they have been equally as committed and their labors as profound.

With such a trained, equipped and brave comraderie of soldiers that have walked under the Christian Baptist banner since the first church was organized in 1788, there is little wonder of the great accomplishments and contributions made in Jesus' name during this period.

251

Regretfully all who have done so much for so long, for so many in His name could not be included with those listed. Their exclusion does not lessen or minimize their importance. These listed portray a graphic panorama of our Christian Baptist communion since its inception to present. We are all benefactors of their sacrifices, toils and contributions.

REV. H.M. ALEXANDER

God has such strange ways of developing lives and making of those lives far reaching productive characters. To be black and born in Hart County Georgia at the turn of the century was rather unpretentious. His expected travels were not to go much beyond the county line. He was not expected to climb the educational ladder much higher than it would take to till the soil, plant the seed and harvest the crops.

That was not the case of Homer M. Alexander, who was born in Hart County around this era, to Harkness and Cressie Alexander. He attended the public schools of Hart County and the Savannah River Baptist Association School. He was destined to do more than the norm. His parents, although tillers of the soil, looked farther than the boundaries of the farm land. They filled their children with hope and dreams that could not be realized in Hart County.

This son who was enshrouded with God's providence accepted Christ at twelve years of age. He expressed his new found belief by joining the Sardis Baptist Church. He was baptized by Rev. W.M. Pulliam. It was under Rev. Pulliam's pastorate in 1921 that he accepted the Divine Call to the Gospel Ministry, and was licensed and ordained by his pastor.

Rev. Alexander realized he had reached his plateau in his native surroundings. In 1921, he moved to Atlanta where he enrolled in the Sylvia Bryant Baptist Institute, and remained until completing all academic requirements. The next four years he was a student at Morehouse School of Theology where he earned a Bachelor of Theology Degree.

His pastoral Ministry began in 1924 while he was a student at Morehouse College He pastored as many as five churches at one time, thus acquiring the name "Bishop of the Woods".

For fifty-three uninterrupted years, Rev. H.M. Alexander was in the pastoral ministry. The list of churches he pastored are as follows: Early Hope Baptist Church, Newton, Georgia, Philadelphia Baptist Church, Hampton, Georgia, Mount Olive Baptist Church, Henry County, Georgia, twenty-seven years, Neria Baptist Church, Senoia, Georgia, Flint Ridge Baptist Church, Kenwood, Georgia, Macedonia Baptist Church, Thomaston, Georgia, fourteen years, Good Hope Baptist Church, Zebulon, Georgia, two times, each time three years, Fellowship Baptist Church, Upson County, Georgia, twenty years, Eighth Street Baptist Church, Griffin, Georgia, six years. He pastored Atlanta's Linsey Street Baptist Church for twenty-seven years. During this time he built and completely furnished this modern church plant. It is air-conditioned, paved parking lot, and completely organized. When he retired it was debt free. This church did the unusual, when his health began to fail, they gave him without a squabble full retirement.

During these fifty-three years in the pastorate, he has licensed and ordained 29 ministers, one of whom is his son Cameron. He has performed approximately 2600 marriages, and baptized 10,685 candidates. His largest baptizing one time was 85, when he pastored the Macedonia Baptist Church in Thomaston, Georgia. He has preached 3062 funerals. He has conducted revivals throughout America. During his prime, he conducted revivals from January to January with very few vacant weeks.

His outreach and influence has not only been confined to the pastoral ministry but has extended into the connectional affairs of the denomination. He pastored in the General Missionary Baptist Convention of Georgia for fifty-four years. Twenty-six of those years he served as President of the Fifth District Convention. When he began pastoring in the convention, Dr. J.M. Nabrit was President. He was extremely instrumental in Doctors L.A. Pinkston, L.M. Terrill, E.J. Grant, and C.M. Alexander, becoming presidents and was supportive and cooperative of their total programs.

For fifty-two years, Rev. Alexander has been a member of the Cabin Creek Baptist Association. Half of this time, twenty-six years, he has served as their Moderator.

In 1932, he entered in Holy Wedlock with Miss Augusta Hutchins. To this union one son was born, Cameron Madison Alexander. He has had the distinct honor of baptizing Cameron, and performing the ceremony that united he and his wife in Holy Matrimony, Inspiring his son to follow into the same pathway to "go preach My Gospel saith the Lord", he licensed and ordained him. He preached and participated in each of the four churches his son has been installed as pastor and participated in the Inaugural Services and Inauguration Banquet when Cameron was Inaugurated as President of the General Missionary Baptist Convention of Georgia, Inc.

Rev. and Mrs. Alexander have four grandchildren, and one great grandchild. Their grandchildren are: Cameron Eric, Gregory Madison, Kenneth Lamont and Barbara Maria. Mrs. Alexander was by his side and close behind him in all of his endeavors until her death in January of 1980.

Both the prophet Isaiah and Ezekiel have words that can adequately describe the philosophy and personality of Rev. H.M. Alexander, Isaiah 46:8, 9 says, "Remember...and show yourselves men...for I am God and there is none else". Ezekiel 23:30 says, "I sought for a man among them that should build up the wall, and stand in the gap for me". All of these years he has stood in the gap for God.

REV. R.L. BOYD

Nearly ninety-three years ago in Burke County, Georgia, near Girard, on August 30th a son was born to Ed Felix and Kitty Boyd. They named him Robert. He was their oldest. Two others were to be born to them, before the matriarch's death, when Robert was seven years old. Father Boyd would remarry and father another eleven children.

Bob, as called by family and friends, grew up on his father's Burke County plantation. His early education was attained in the county school system at the Beech Branch Baptist Church.

Rev. Green Jackson Campbell was reported to have been one of the most successful pastors and farmers in Burke County at this time. He was highly respected by his social, business and religious peers, black and white. Although born a slave, he was unmatched in his endeavors and accomplishments. Six years after the signing of the Emancipation Proclamation he was a one horse cropper. In 1908 he owned eight hundred and thirty acres of Burke County land and operated a twenty horse farm.

While pastoring Beech Branch Baptist Church in Sardis, Georgia, Robert L. Boyd was converted at eighteen years of age. Four years later under this pioneer preacher's influence he accepted the call to preach the Gospel of Jesus Christ. He was licensed and ordained by his pastor. Over sixty years later Pastor Campbell's influence in his life is alive, never having been altered and remains one of the most influential persons in this senior pastor's life.

Hungry for more knowledge and to widen his horizens of exposure, Robert left Burke County and moved to Richmond County. His mind being young and fertile, he enrolled in Walker Baptist Institute in Augusta. Completing his studies there, but his academic cup was not filled to the brim, further studies were taken at Morehouse College in Atlanta, Georgia.

School now behind him, for the next four years, he taught school in Burke and Screven Counties. This profession was relinquished to give full time to the Christian ministry. The remainder of his life has been fully committed to His service.

R.L. Boyd's first church was Second McCoy Baptist Church in Sardis, Georgia. Soon thereafter he was called to Williams Grove Branch Baptist Church, Waynesboro, Georgia. Beech Branch Baptist Church, of which he was a member, extended him a call. For a brief period he served Palmer Grove Baptist Church, McBean, Georgia as pastor.

For sixty years he has been the shepherd of the Springfield Baptist Church, Alexander, Georgia. Fifty-two years, Hart Grove Baptist Church, Stapleton, Georgia and fifty years, Elim Baptist Church, Augusta, Georgia. This church was organized in 1886. Dr. E.K. Love, a well known missionary at that time, author and pastor of First African Baptist Church in Savannah, who later became president of the Missionary Baptist State Convention of Georgia, preached the organization sermon. Dr. W.G. Johnson was the second pastor. Serving eleven years, until called to the pastorate of

First Baptist Church of Macon, Georgia, later to become president of the General Baptist Convention of Georgia. This church has had the direct influence of two state presidents, two vice presidents of the National Baptist Convention U.S.A., Inc., and has been influential in the lives of two state presidents and two vice presidents of the National Baptist Convention U.S.A., Inc.

Rev. Boyd laughs in telling about his call to Elim. "The ladies didn't want me. They thought I was too small and my size would prohibit me from preaching and couldn't bear the pastoral load. I was the deacons choice. Everyone said I wouldn't stay there anytime". Their prediction was false. Fifty years later and at ninety-three years old, he is still there.

Can you imagine one person having a total of one hundred and sixty-two years as a continuous pastor? If you know Rev. R.L. Boyd or could meet him, you would find such a person and wouldn't have to imagine.

More than twenty-five years he served as moderator of the historic Walker Baptist Association. Within the last three years he yielded the helm of responsibility, for moderator emeritus, in recognition for his long tenure of trustworthy and faithful leadership.

He and Marie Schumake exchanged vows of Holy Matrimony. This union produced three children, two girls and one boy. The son, George F. Boyd, Ph.D., is an educator at South Carolina State College, Orangeburg, South Carolina. Ms. Robbie Boyd, public school teacher, Atlanta Board of Education. Mrs. Anna Mozell Byas, housewife, residing in New York City.

Rev. R.L. Boyd of the twentieth century is reminiscent of Joshua of old. He too took a stand for God...."as for me and my house, we will serve the Lord". Joshua 24:15.

Dr. D.D. CRAWFORD
1865 - 1942

In the one hundred and nine years of the existence of the General Missionary Baptist Convention of Georgia, no other man has held an administrative position as long as D.D. Crawford. He served as Executive Secretary from 1915 to 1941, twenty-six years.

He was born in Tallapoosa County, Alabama, March, 1865. He was of Scotch, Negro and Indian ancestry. From his paternal side, he was able to date back to 1600 A.D. to John, Earl of Scotland, and Captain David Crawford.

Two Crawford brothers came to America in the seventeenth century. One settled in Pennsylvania with his posterity migrating west. The other in Virginia with his posterity migrating south.

His grandfather Dr. Nathan Crawford, came to Columbia County, Georgia, from South Carolina, and married Martha Marshall, the oldest daughter of Dr. Daniel Marshall. The oldest daughter of this union, Mary Ann married Dr. Jubal Kimbrough, overseer for Dr. Crawford. Mary Ann's oldest son was his father.

Dr. Crawford's mother was the second child of John Dunn or Blair and Patience Crawford. His grandmother was the mother of nineteen children, and her father was two-thirds Indian and her mother was one-third. Her father was what was known as a "run-a-way Negro", spending most of his time in the woods, where he died.

This child of destiny was born in Alabama, because his mother's owner bought a large tract of land near Loachapoka, Alabama and moved to it, carrying his mother with him. As soon as he reached adulthood, he returned to Georgia.

After being called to preach the gospel of Jesus Christ, he joined the ranks of revered missionaries of that day. They traveled throughout the state preaching, organizing churches, visiting associations and carrying the message of the convention.

He ranked with E.K. Love and was highly respected by his ecclesiastical peers. The minutes of the Walker Baptist Association reflect the presence of Dr. D.D. Crawford in the 1890's.

Letters from files, and reports from minutes can best describe this venerable administrator, who served his race and denomination through their struggling formative years. He used the vantage point of his office and the numbers of the organization he represented to the fullest, for every opportunity.

D.D. Crawford served Black Georgia Baptist approximately fifty years. He was to them, what Ezra was to Israel and retains that captivating position, historically. "Ezra the scribe stood at a wooden podium which they had made for the purpose. And Ezra opened the book in the sight of the people for he was standing above all the people; and when he opened it, all the people stood up:" Nehemiah 8:4, 5.

DR. EDWARD A. FREEMAN

A son of Christian parents James H. and Ollie Watts Freeman, both members of the Mount Pleasant Baptist Church, Atlanta, Georgia. His father was a deacon in his church. When quite young his mother passed, leaving the father to rear his seven sons without a mother.

With youthful determination to succeed, Edward's first step in that direction was accepting Christ, under the pastorate of Rev. R.H. Milner of Mount Pleasant Baptist Church. Rev. Milner baptized him. Under this shepherd's ministry, he accepted the call of Jesus Christ to preach his gospel. Was licensed in 1935 and ordained in 1936, all by his pastor.

His elementary education was received from Fulton County Public School. He graduated from Booker T. Washington High School, Atlanta, Georgia. The A.B. degree was earned from Atlanta's Clark College. Chaplaincy training for the United States

Army was received from Harvard University. The B.D., Th.M., Th.D degrees were all earned from Central Baptist Theological Seminary in Kansas City, Kansas.

Edward Freeman was first called to pastor Liberty Baptist Church, Cornelia, Georgia in 1936; First Baptist Church, Clarkston, Georgia, 1939; Bethesda Baptist Church, Austell, Georgia, 1942. He was Chaplain in the United States Army from 1942 to 1946, attaining the rank of Major. In 1946, the historic First Baptist Church of Kansas City, Kansas called him as pastor.

During his forty-five year ministry, he has baptized approximately twenty-five hundred candidates, performed approximately seven hundred marital ceremonies, and conducted between fourteen- to fifteen hundred funerals. Renovated the First Baptist Church in Clarkston, Georgia, the Bethesda Baptist Church in Austell, Georgia, built and educational center and extensive renovation of the First Baptist Church in Kansas City, Kansas.

Since 1957, he has been President of the Missionary Baptist State Convention of Kansas. From 1968, he has been Superintendent of the National Baptist Congress of Christian Education. Current President of Black Cooperative Bus Ministry of Kansas City, Kansas; President of Washington Development Company; Chairman of Board of Directors, Gateway Plaza Homes, Inc.; Chairman of Board of Directors, Chelsea Plaza Homes, Inc.; Chairman of Kansas City, Kansas Planning Commission; Vice-President of Kansas City Operation PUSH; Board, Member, American Baptist Theological Seminary, Nashville, Tennessee; Western Baptist Bible College, Kansas City, Missouri; National Baptist Convention, U.S.A., Inc.; Member of General Council,

Baptist World Alliance; and Study Commission on Cooperative Christianity.

Dr. Freeman's travels have been quite extensive, serving during World War II in Europe; 1955 touring Europe and the Holy Land; 1960 South America; 1968 Switzerland and West Africa; 1970 traveled around the world; 1972 visited Europe, including Austria; 1975 Finland, Sweden, and Russia; 1976 Hawaii and Australia; and 1978 Alaska.

Travels, educational attainment, nor ecclesiastical recognition have not crowded out his memory and gratitude for those people that played important roles in his life during the formative and developing years. He gives much credit to the women of the community for their motherliness after his mother passed. Doctors W.L. Greene and S.H. Davage of Clark College, contributed so much toward his college education.

He and Mrs. Ruth Anthony Freeman are the parents of three children, Edward, Jr., Constance, and William Norman, and grandparents of two grandsons.

This scholar, administrator, theologian and pastor, whose native background was rather unpretentious, but his seed took roots in the fertile soil of Georgia and was properly cultivated. The roots of that tree went deep, producing a strong trunk, branches, foilage and seeds that Georgia could not contain, but was compelled to share with the world. His influence has been wide spread and many lives touched. This writer is among the many, having ordained me to the gospel ministry, performing the first pastoral installation and marital ceremonies.

"The fruit of the righteous is a tree of life; and he that winneth souls is wise." Proverbs 11:30.

REV. CALVIN BOYD JOHNSON

Born in Mitchell County, Georgia in 1892, to Noah and Ammy Johnson, who were tillers of the soil. Both were Christians and Father Johnson was a deacon.

Quite early in Life, C.B. accepted Christ and united with the Mount Calvary Baptist Church on East Force Street in Valdosta, Georgia.

He attributed much to Rev. J.J. Davis. His personal statement was, "If I owe anybody anything other than the Lord, I owe it to Rev. J.J. Davis".

It was under the pastorate of Rev. J.T. Sanders, he was converted, baptized, called to preach, 1914, licensed, 1914, and ordained, 1919 at the Mount Calvary Baptist Church.

The first church to call him to pastor was the family membership church, in Mitchell County, Mount Zion Baptist, serving from 1920 to 1922; followed by Concord Baptist Church, Lake Park, Georgia, 1922 - 1974; Mount Moriah Baptist Church, Boston, Georgia, 1922 - 1924; Providence Baptist Church, Hahira, Georgia, 1923 - 1924; Greater Morning Star Baptist Church, Valdosta, Georgia, 1924 until death, 1979; Mount Olive Baptist Church, Fort Pierce, Florida,

1925 - 1935; Mount Zion Baptist Church, Cordele, Georgia, 1936 - 1958; New Emanuel Baptist Church, Nashville, Georgia, 1963 to death.

During his sixty-five year ministry and fifty-nine year pastorate, he was Moderator of the South Georgia Missionary Baptist Association from 1946 to death; President of the Eleventh District Convention of the General Missionary Baptist Convention of Georgia, Inc. from 1937 until death; Chairman of the Finance Committee of the Convention from 1941 to 1975. He attended forty-one sessions of the National Baptist Convention, U.S.A., Inc. His first was in Nashville, Tennessee in 1924. The last was 1967, in Denver, Colorado. Missing only three because of illness. The first State Convention attended was in 1923 in Thomasville, Georgia. His last in 1976 in Tifton, Georgia. His declining health forced him to discontinue attending.

His ministry was fruitful in many ways, baptizing more than three thousand candidates, performing more than eight hundred marriages, conducting more than nine hundred funerals. The Morning Star Baptist Church was constructed under his leadership, valued at three hundred and seventy-five thousand dollars. A four thousand dollar improvement on New Emanuel Baptist Church was made just before his death.

Had he lived until November 24, 1979, he and Mrs. Maude Judge Johnson would have been married for sixty-seven years. To this union two children were born, Marion and Catherine. Marion followed in his father's footsteps and accepted the call to the gospel ministry and now pastors the First Baptist Church of West Tampa, Florida.

Deprived of the opportunity for formal academic exposure, because of the era and location of which he was born, reared and served. He did not allow that to lessen his love for his Savior or his commitment to His cause. He accepted the illustration of Jesus, "Well done, good and faithful slave; you were faithful with a few things, I will put you in charge of many things, enter into the joy of your master". Matthew 25:21.

MRS. MARY OLIVIA ROSS

Born in Dawson, Terrell County, Georgia, Mary Olivia Brookins, into a Christian family. Accepting Christ early in life, attending the Americus Baptist Institute, Americus, Georgia, the educational objective of the Southwestern Georgia Baptist Association, and graduating from the Baptist oriented Spelman College, Atlanta, Georgia.

For nearly four decades she was married to Rev. S.D. Ross, who

was a professor at the Americus Baptist Institute, Americus, Georgia, and at time of death, Pastor of Shiloh Baptist Church, Detroit, Michigan. Was an ardent worker in her church giving untiring support to her husband and continues in the same vein.

She began denominational service in the National Baptist arena as an enrollment clerk in the Women's Auxiliary. During the annual meeting of the National Baptist Convention in Atlanta in 1946, the women chose her as the Second Vice-President. After rendering faithful service in this capacity, in Houston, Texas in 1948, she was elected First Vice-President. Dr. Nannie Helen Burroughs died in 1961 and she succeeded her as President of the world's largest body of Black women, the Women's Convention Auxiliary of the National Baptist Convention, U.S.A., Inc.

Many significant literary contributions have been made by this phenomenal leader. In 1953 a contributing writer to the **Detroit Free Press Lenten Series,** "What My Religion Means to Me"; **Ministers Wife,** published by J.L. Hudson Company, **What's and Why's of Minister's Wife,** by Methodist Publishing House. In recognition for these, an honorary Doctor of Literature degree was received. Other appreciable honors have been a listing in **Who's Who Among American Women,** invitations to the White House on numerous occasions, and meaningful appointments by President Jimmy Carter.

Georgia born, bred, exposed indoctrinated, a product of the General Missionary Baptist Convention of Georgia. Her effects have reached to the far points of the world, either in travels, literary documents, or oral messages. She must be listed among the, "number of leading women". Acts 17:4.

MRS. JEWEL E. TERRILL

Names are far more than identity. They are usually given out of respect for the name sake, which gives the bearer a responsibility to live up to. In the case of Jewel Middlebrooks Terrill, she has been true to her name. She is a jewel. Many struggling young people, including myself who came to Atlanta during the years of her late husband's lifetime, were fed in her home, given wise counsel and tender loving care. To us she has been a jewel.

Her parents, James M. and Victoria Middlebrooks, probably saw a jewel when she was born. They hoped, prayed and set the right example in order for her to fulfill their expectancy. They provided the influence of a Christian home. Mr. Middlebrooks was a successful brick mason in their native home of Griffin, Georgia. This jewel received the needed polish of a Christian mother's love and the strong protection of a Christian father's love.

Early in life she accepted Christ as her personal Savior and was baptized by Rev. William Bivins, pastor of Mount Zion Baptist Church in Griffin. During her developing years the Sunday School and Baptist Young People's Union utilized her services as pianist. By being faithful with her talent and growth spiritually, the Senior Choir sought her for their pianist, a position she held from 1919 to 1929.

Mr. and Mrs. Middlebrooks were also sensitive to their daughter's educational needs. They enrolled her in Griffin's Broad Street Elementary School from the first through the third grade. Desirous of her receiving Christian education simultaneous with secular education they placed her in the Cabin Creek Missionary Baptist Association School where she completed all her required work and finished with honors.

From 1927 to 1929 she was a normal student at Atlanta University where she graduated with a certificate, and for one year attended Savannah State College, Savannah, Georgia. Further studies in Christian Education have been attained from the National Baptist Sunday School and B.T.U. Congress. Marriage, rearing of children, and encouraging her husband to higher academic study prohibited further formal preparation. Living and life have been transformed into a classroom.

On January 12, 1929, while a student at Atlanta University, Dr. J.M. Nabrit united she and Levi Maurice Terrill into Holy Wedlock. The groom was pastor of Macon's Tremount Temple Baptist Church. This union produced three children, Jewell, Levi, Jr., and Victoria. There are six grandchildren.

For forty-two years and nineteen days she was a faithful and effective pastor's wife. She was the first lady of Macon's Tremount Temple Baptist Church, Savannah's First Bryan Baptist Church, and Atlanta's Zion Hill Baptist Church, and for twelve years the first lady of the 500,000 member General Missionary Baptist Convention of Georgia, Inc. Most people who have known her in any of these circles call her affectionately, "Momma Terrill".

She made no attempt to overshadow her husband who was a profound, prolific preacher, astute scholar, able administrator, wise counselor and gifted singer. But in addition to being a good homemaker, loving mother and alert first lady, she established a record of service. For eleven years she was president of the women's Department of the Atlanta Baptist Association, eleven years as president of the Women's Department of the Original Metropolitan Baptist Association, and eight years on the faculty of the National

261

Baptist Sunday School and B.T.U. Congress. She presently serves as lecturer in the Young People's Department of the General Missionary Baptist Sunday School and B.T.U. Congress, and currently the Assistant Corresponding Secretary of the Women's Auxiliary of the National Baptist Convention, U.S.A., Inc. Mrs. Terrill is the prevailing Secretary of Fraternal Council of Church Women, and immediate President of Georgia State Association of Ministers' Wives, Interdenominational. Her services began in the State Sunday School and Baptist Young People's Convention in Macon, Georgia as Instructor in the Junior Department during Rev. J.H. Evans' tenure as president. Later her service was needed in the music department and she was elected chairlady of the department.

Travel is another vehicle of training. She and her late husband took advantage of this greatly, and traveled widely in the United States, Canada, Mexico and in 1955 attended the Baptist World Alliance in London, England.

A few years ago she transferred her church membership from the Zion Hill Baptist Church where her husband pastored for twenty-eight years and she held membership for thirty-three years, uniting with the Antioch Baptist Church-North, pastored by Rev. Cameron M. Alexander.

Death broke the Terrill family chain first in January, 1971, when Dr. Levi Maurice Terrill, Sr. exchanged this world's sunsets for heaven's sunrise; and in October of 1978 when her youngest daughter Victoria caught the wings of the morning exchanged mortality for immortality. Through both of their lengthy illnesses, Jewell remained a jewel.

Webster's new student dictionary defines a jewel as one that is highly esteemed; a precious stone. That is an exact description of Mrs. Jewell Evelyn Middlebrooks Terrill. To all who have taken the time to know her have found she possesses and displays high esteem. Her gained friendship is precious and valuable. Her heart and the doors of her home are always open to those whose integrity has proven to be above reproach. Her total contributions and life's impact will never be properly appraised because she has done so much for so many through so many.

Her life has been spent in giving all she had toward glorifying God's earthly kingdom. Her all has not been this world's riches, for she has not been endowed with such. Her all has not been high academic acclaim, gained from the halls of higher learning, she has not been so exposed. Her all has not been through capturing life's scenes and arresting them in oil upon canvas, nature did not provide her with such abilities. Her all has not been through the captivating melodies of music, this was not God's intent for her return to others. Her all has been through Christian service. Whenever and wherever called upon she gave the very best quality. For that is what her Savior had given her, His all! His best!

Solomon spoke of wisdom and compared it with a jewel. His description of wisdom also describes "Momma Terrill", "she is more precious than jewels; and nothing you desire compares with her". Proverbs 3:15

DR. C.T. WALKER

On February 5, 1858 a son was born to the late Deacon Charles Thomas Walker, deceased two days earlier, and Hannah. He was named after his father, Charles Thomas. The birthplace was Hephzibah, Richmond County, Georgia.

Although disadvantaged by his father's death, he was greatly advantaged by being the property of the Walker family, who were known to give humane treatment to their slaves.

His uncles, Rev. Joe Walker, for whom the Walker Baptist Association would later be named, and Rev. Nathan Walker, founder of

the said association, would share in rearing him. His brother, Rev. Peter Walker would become first moderator of the association.

Under Rev. Nathan Walker's pastorate of the Franklin Covenant Baptist Church, Charlie accepted Christ and was baptized the first Sunday in July 1873. The following year he entered Augusta Baptist Institute, (later to become Atlanta Baptist College and Morehouse College). His educational venture began with barely enough money to pay one month's board.

After two years of study, he was licensed to preach and ordained to the gospel ministry, the following year in 1877. His pastorate began in the rural with a circuit of churches, Franklin Covenant Baptist Church, Hephzibah, Thankful Baptist Church, Waynesboro, and McKinnie Branch Baptist Church, McBean, Georgia. Sometime later he was called to the Mount Olive Baptist Church in Augusta, only to remain a brief time.

Simultaneous with his early pastorate, he pursued a brief educational career, teaching school in Richmond and Jefferson counties. His deepest commitment was to the Christian ministry, and his early realization of that gave him clear directives as to where he was going and how he was to get there.

First Baptist Church of LaGrange, Georgia, a very flourishing church on the extreme western side of the state, extended him a call to pastor their church in 1880. For three years his labors there were crammed with fruitfulness. He was instrumental in establishing a school for Baptists in that city, later to become LaGrange Academy. Time was found to read law under Judge Walker, a very able practitioner of the day, although he was never known to practice before the human bar of justice. His work was only before the throne of God for His mercy on behalf of the souls of men and his oppressed people.

Returning to Augusta in 1883 in answer to a call to pastor Central Baptist Church, the return to his native Richmond County was longed for. Central had been engaged in a long vicious internal battle for more than a year, this did not daunt him, although it did not subside after his arrival. The two factions continued to fight, without any evidence of an agreement in sight. They were forced into a legal fight that caught the attention of the entire city. The only agreement reached was to sell the property valued at $4,000.00 and both sides equally divide the amount. This they did.

More than four hundred members organized the Beulah Baptist Church in the Union Baptist Church, August 21, 1885. Immediately after organizing, they called C.T. Walker as their pastor. In the next church meeting, he requested to rename the church, Tabernacle. Overwhelmingly they accepted his request. Amazingly, within four months after their organization, they entered their new house of worship. Its construction cost around $15,000.00. This new church experienced great numerical growth as well.

Tabernacle from inception, met her Christian responsibilities in missions, education and benevolence, but also showed revered love for their pastor. They gave him a three month trip to the Holy Land, that caught the nation's attention. This national and international attention did not phase the Walker Baptist Association however. When Tabernacle first extended an invitation for the association to convene with them in 1889, they refused, by saying they preferred to meet in the rural. An invitation was not accepted by them from C.T. Walker and Tabernacle until 1896.

In the spring of 1891, Dr. C.T. Walker and Dr. E.R. Carter, pastor of Friendship Baptist Church in Atlanta, departed from New York harbor for the Holy Land. This tour would take them to Liverpool, England where they landed, to London, Paris, Turin, Genoa, Pisa, Rome, Pompeii, Alexandria, Cairo, Joppa, Jerusalem, Bethlehem, Hebron, Jericho, Bethany, Mount of Olives, Gethsemane, and many other places. Upon returning to America, a domestic tour, lecturing on "The Holy Land and What I Saw", was conducted.

America entered into the Spanish American War in 1898. Dr. Walker was appointed chaplain in the army and assigned to the Ninth Immunes at St. Louis, Cuba, where a few months service was rendered, and an honorable discharge was received. This was another means of broadening his horizons of service, experience and knowledge.

New York City's Mount Olive Baptist Church called him as their pastor in 1899. Tabernacle protested this greatly, but he accepted the call. Immediately upon arrival in New York, he took the reins of leadership as he had done in Augusta. Probably also because he realized his stay away from the south would be limited. He provided leadership in establishing a permanent location and equipping a Y.M.C.A. for blacks and whites. His activities through preaching, lecturing and publications attracted the attention of the press, thus giving the race a better image through him. An image that countless non-blacks had been unable to see, and inspired hope in many of his own people.

Being away from the south in New York did not anesthetize his memory of his own past suffering and the plight of his people in the southland. He opened economic doors in the north for the operation of his beloved Walker Baptist Institute, now located in Augusta.

His immediate successor resigned from Tabernacle after only staying about a year. In 1901, they recalled C.T. Walker. Whatever attracted him to New York two years earlier, was unable to keep him any longer from his beloved Tabernacle, Walker Baptist Association and Walker Baptist Institute. He rejoined them all immediately, rolled up his sleeves and pitched in working.

Long before the Federal Government initiated care for the aged, Tabernacle Baptist Church, under Dr. Walker's leadership operated one in Augusta, Georgia.

Early in his ministry, wedding vows were exchanged with Miss Violet Franklin of Hephzibah, on June 19, 1879. Three children were born to this union, of which two died very early, leaving one son.

Regardless of race, denomination or era, Charles Thomas Walker, D.D.; L.L.D. was a reknown preacher, pastor, organizer, educator, founder, traveler, evangelist, possessor of social concern, and was a "Prince of Israel".

"Do you not know that a prince and a great man has fallen this day in Israel?" II Samuel 3:38.

REV. W.W. WEATHERSPOOL

Swainsboro is the county seat of Emanuel County, Georgia. Most Georgians would need directions to arrive there. Its location is generally unknown. Promise Land is even more remote.

William Wright Weatherspool, a native of Swainsboro, a product of the soil of Promise Land, was born to Christian parents, Zenephone and Nancy Green Weatherspool. Was destined to go far beyond the scope of his native bailiwick into the far reaches of a Land of Promise.

His father was a native North Carolinian. Who supported his family as a turpentine farmer. His mother was Georgia born and bred. During the school year she taught in the rural schools of her area.

To get the proper start in life, young Weatherspool's first positive step toward his destiny, was to accept Christ as his Lord and Savior. He joined the Saint Galilee Baptist Church, located one mile west of Summertown, Georgia. Rev. Cooper was pastor at the time of his conversion. During his formative years, he taught Sunday School. Later, he accepted the call to enter the Christian Ministry, preached his trial sermon, licensed and ordained in this same church.

Among his first organizational positions, were President of the Second Union Baptist Association Sunday School Convention; Chairman of the Ministers and deacons meeting.

From the first through the eighth grade, he attended the Public Schools of Emanuel County. After these years of education, he attended the following institutions, Walker Baptist Institute, Augusta, Georgia; Forsyth Norman and Industrial School, Statesboro, Georgia; Central City College, Macon, Georgia. He

reached the deep wells and broad rivers of study at Princetown University Princetown, Indiana; Moody Bible Institute, Chicago, Illinois; Florida A&M (College) University, Tallahassee, Florida; the University of Indiana, Bloomington, Indiana; University of Pittsburgh, Pennsylvania; Columbia Theological Seminary, Decatur, Georgia.

Dr. W.W. Weatherspool, holds degrees from these schools, Florida A&M University, A.B. Degree; Chicago Bible School, M. Th. Degree; Honorary Doctor of Divinity from Natchez College, Natchez, Mississippi; Doctor of Sacred Theology from Princetown University, Princetown, Indiana.

Only God can direct us where He wants us to be and to mold us into the vessel to fit the job. He did no less in Weatherspool's life to get him to Mount Olive Baptist Church in Atlanta in time for the job at hand. According to our geography it may appear a roundabout way. But with God's geography His plan was a direct route for His servant, "From Promise Land to a Land of Promise".

To get His children to the Promise Land, God marched Israel around the foot of Mount Horeb for thirty-nine and one half years. A circumference of about eleven miles. He marched His servant Weatherspool by the Salem Baptist Church, Abbeville, South Carolina. All of the following are in Georgia: Eureka Baptist Church, Higgston; Gethsemane Baptist Church, Lexsy; New Hope Baptist Church, Register; Green Grove Baptist Church, Modoc; Bethel Baptist Church, Vienna; First African Baptist Church, Bainbridge; Metropolitan Baptist Church, Columbus; for more than forty years Mount Olive Baptist Church, Atlanta.

After pastoring this church for this period of time, his momentum has not lessened from the beginning of his pastorate. If presented the question of his success, he would answer, unequivocally, "Putting God first". This same philosophy has infiltrated into this church family. An avid reader whose mind has been exposed to the works of the world's literary geniuses. He contends the Holy Bible remains supreme in his library and the main source of reading material.

Mount Olive Baptist Church has an enviable record of denominational support, contributor to educational causes, community activities and other worthy causes. This church through the leadership of this ecclesiastical cyclopic is the force that has brought her into the marching ranks beside this nation's great churches. On November 21, 1979, for the third time during this pastoral administration this Christian Church family burned a mortgage on the church. Pastor and church labor together in their attempt to be a blessing through Christ to all humanity.

Throughout his pastorate, there has been numerous denominational responsibilities. Namely, Executive Secretary-Treasurer, General Missionary Baptist Convention of Georgia, Inc. While holding this position a large indebtedness was liquidated. He is a past President of the Atlanta Baptist Ministers Union, current historian of the convention and ministers union, presently a member of the National Baptist Convention, U.S.A., Inc.

Weatherspool's travels have carried him throughout the United States of America, many European Countries, Africa, Asia, Australia, South America, China, Japan, Alaska, Canada, Hawaiian Islands, Jamaica, Cuba, Russia, Haiti, Dominican Republic, Leeward Islands, Windward Islands, Philippine Islands, Barbados and the Port of Spain.

Preaching and lecturing carried him on many trips. The opportunity to write and research took him to the Holy Land on occasions. On other travels he supervised group travel.

Significant contributions have been made by his hand and mind for the current generations and others to come in the area of writing. He has authored a number of books and tracts. The latest book was released in April, 1980, "The Secret of a Long Pastorate". This promises to be a help for any preacher or pastor who desires effectiveness in his role.

The Foreign Mission Board of the National Baptist Convention, U.S.A., Inc. has solicited his services on Preaching Missions, in such places as Bahama Islands, east and west coast to Florida, West Africa and evangelistic services in Liberia and other areas.

His life has been committed to help develop stalwart leaders for Christ service. This interest allowed him another opportunity to participate on other Preaching Missions. In such places as Hjorring, Denmark, Europe and Alice Springs, Australia. While in the later place he was invited by the public school masters to speak in their schools.

This man's impact, has been felt in education and business. He served as teacher-principal to Common Schools of Georgia and principal of Metter High School, Metter, Georgia. His display of business ability, encouraged members of the Board of Directors of Mutual Federal Savings and Loan Association of Atlanta, Georgia to invite him to become one of their peers.

With God's help this lad from Emanuel County's dust, who survived by engaging in hard work from kin to can't. Twelve or more hours daily hacking pinetrees, splitting rails, getting out post, dipping turpentine boxes during winter, with feet wrapped in burlap, because he didn't own shoes, was determined that none of these handicaps would keep him from reaching his life's goals.

Despite the adversity of his background, he graduated from Florida A&M, valedictorian of his class after living off of forty-five cents per week and serving as a student-teacher to his fellow collegiates. His weekly budget while attending the University of Indiana at Bloomington, Indiana and the University of Pittsburgh, Pittsburgh, Pennsylvania, was three dollars per week. While a student at the later he served as Director of Seminars.

The momentum of his climb upward was intensified after marrying, Lillie Mae Sirmans, the charming Spelmanite, from Dixie Brooks County, Georgia. A product of good stock, the daughter of Elihue and Mahalia Spencer Sirmans. Their labors together these many years has proven success beyond measure.

The motto that has brought him from "Promise Land to a Land of Promise", has been, "Put God first; Seek His guidance; Commit thyself to Him; Trust Him implicitly and Humbly walk by Faith". This motto is far more than words. It has been put to practice. The results have been the colorful productive career of William Wright Weatherspool - Preacher-Pastor, writer, historian, newspaper correspondent, editor, public school teacher, educational administrator, church builder, world traveler. Self acclaimed, "poor humble, hard working Baptist Preacher - from the country".

Solomon adds these proverbs, "Better is a poor man who walks in his integrity, Than he who is perverse in speech and is a fool. Also it is not good for a person to be without knowledge, and he who makes haste with his feet errs. The foolishness of man subverts his way, and his heart rages against the Lord. Wealth adds many friends, But a poor man is separated from his friend". Proverbs 19:1-4.

Bibliography: History of Walker Baptist Association, biographical interviews.